IMAGES
of America

WHEATLAND

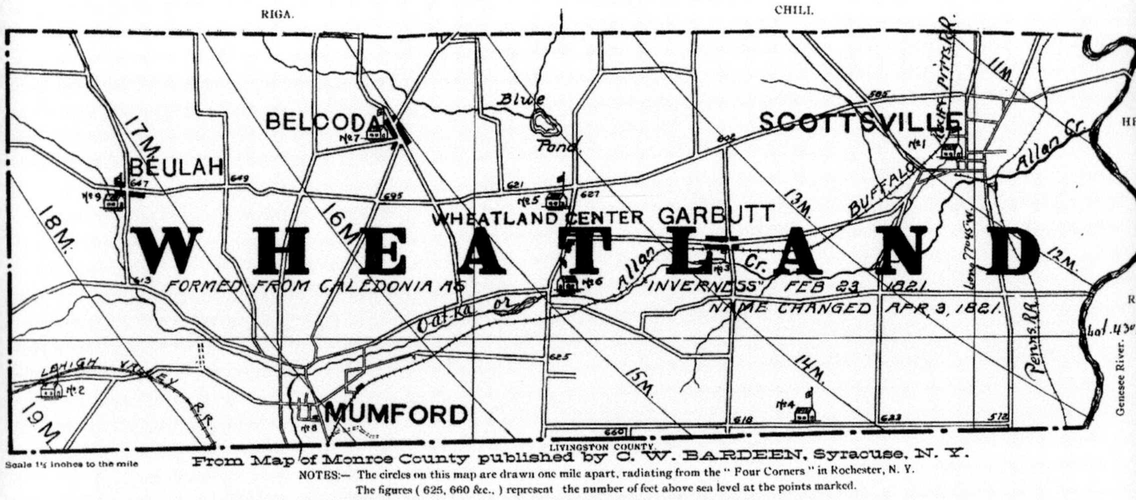

This map of Wheatland was part of a map of Monroe County published by C. W. Bardeen in 1900. It was included as a 15-inch fold-out page inside the back cover of George Slocum's *Wheatland: Monroe County, New York*, published in 1908. It shows the village of Scottsville and the hamlets of the town. The locations of the nine district schools are indicated by drawings of schoolhouses.

On the cover: See page 82. (Courtesy of the Wheatland Historical Association.)

IMAGES
of America

WHEATLAND

Catherine Gilbert and Barbara Chapman

ARCADIA
PUBLISHING

ISBN 978-0-7385-6321-3

Published by Arcadia Publishing
Charleston, South Carolina

Printed in the United States of America

Library of Congress Catalog Card Number: 2008926849

For all general information contact Arcadia Publishing at:
Telephone 843-853-2070
Fax 843-853-0044
E-mail sales@arcadiapublishing.com
For customer service and orders:
Toll-Free 1-888-313-2665

Visit us on the Internet at www.arcadiapublishing.com

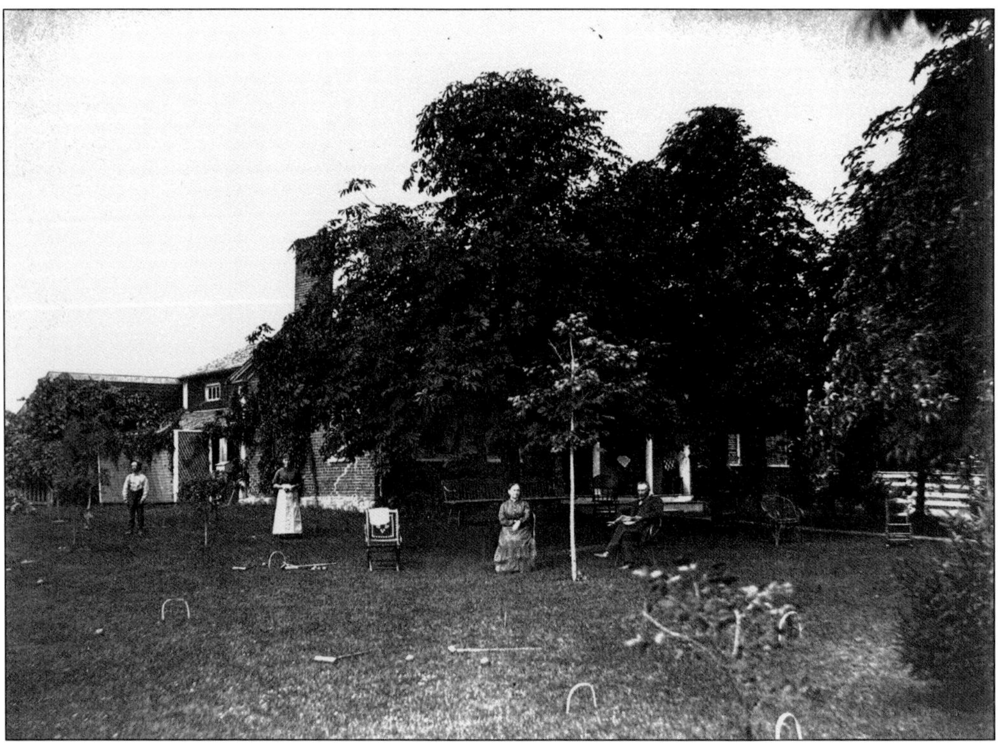

T. R. and Annis Mary Sibley are shown relaxing in the yard of their home at 9 Chili Avenue in Scottsville about 1875. Their hired help, Amasa P. Maltby and Lizzie Farley on the left, are posing with them. Adm. Franklin Hanford purchased the Sibley farm in 1895. (Courtesy of Richard LeRoy.)

Contents

ACKNOWLEDGMENTS

The town of Wheatland is fortunate to have three sources of historical information available to the public. Records in the Town of Wheatland Historian's Office include cemetery lists, photographs, census records, and newspaper clippings. The Scottsville Free Library Cox Local History Room holds a reserve collection of maps, photographs, burial information, and the Schmidt family history file. The Wheatland Historical Association has a unique assortment of 19th- and 20th-century books and boxed papers featuring western New York and Wheatland history. Except for those credited to individuals or institutions, the photographs in this book came from these three collections.

The references consulted during the preparation of this book were Carl F. Schmidt's *History of the Town of Wheatland*; George E. Slocum's *Wheatland, Monroe County, New York*; Ella McGinnis's *Pictorial Wheatland*; F. W. Beers's *Atlas of Monroe County, N.Y.*; Landmark Society of Western New York's *Historic Preservation Report, Wheatland, Scottsville, Mumford*; and W. H. McIntosh's *History of Monroe County, New York*.

We wish to acknowledge those people and groups that assisted us. Rebekah Collinsworth, our editor, clarified Arcadia Publishing procedures and has been our guide. Our special thanks go to Richard LeRoy and James Lesch for their generous assistance in proofreading the manuscript and to Ann Mathias for her technical assistance. Town historian Florence Field provided historical information.

We are grateful to all those in the community who graciously shared their old pictures with us. We extend our thanks to our families and friends for their support and help with this project. Hundreds of images of local scenes were considered; we hope you enjoy those used in the final selection.

INTRODUCTION

The town of Wheatland is located in the southwest corner of Monroe County, about 11 miles from Rochester. The township is three and a half miles wide and nine miles east and west in length. The land, at an elevation of 605 feet, is varied in some places with rolling hills sculpted by glaciers. Oatka Creek flows east across the entire town from the Genesee County line to empty into the Genesee River.

When the first permanent settlers, the Sheffers, came to the area in 1789, all of western New York was included in Ontario County. During the 1790s, there was a trickle of new settlers, including Isaac Scott, for whom the village of Scottsville is named, and immigrants from Scotland, who settled the hamlet of Mumford. In 1797, the town of Northampton was formed, extending from the Genesee River to Lake Erie.

After 1800, the flow of newcomers increased to a steady stream, and the hamlets of Garbutt, Wheatland Center, Beulah, and Belcoda were founded. In 1821, the town of Inverness, renamed Wheatland after six weeks, was formed as part of the new Monroe County.

In spite of the hardships of life on the frontier, the settlements flourished. The fertile land yielded abundant wheat crops, and gypsum was discovered under its surface. The 1830s and 1840s were years of great prosperity in Wheatland. The successful farmers, millers, and businessmen became wealthy. Improved transportation made it possible to ship wheat and other products to Rochester and beyond. The citizens of Wheatland established schools, churches, and civic organizations, and built many of the area's renowned Greek Revival houses.

After enjoying half a century of prosperity the tide turned in the 1850s when the wheat crops failed, and then the Civil War took its grim toll. Through the next 100 years, the population of Wheatland remained stable at about 2,000. The 1950s and 1960s brought new growth to the town, as Rochester workers sought houses in outlying rural areas.

Today over 5,000 people live in Wheatland, but most of them work and shop elsewhere. Because of its tranquil setting, Wheatland has become a popular destination for recreation. Visitors come from all over to fish in Oatka Creek, hike the trails, drive along the country roads, picnic in the parks, or stroll through Genesee Country Village and Museum. As the pictures in this book clearly illustrate, Wheatland has a rich heritage, cherished by its citizens. An understanding and appreciation of the past will guide future generations in maintaining the quality of life that is enjoyed in the town of Wheatland.

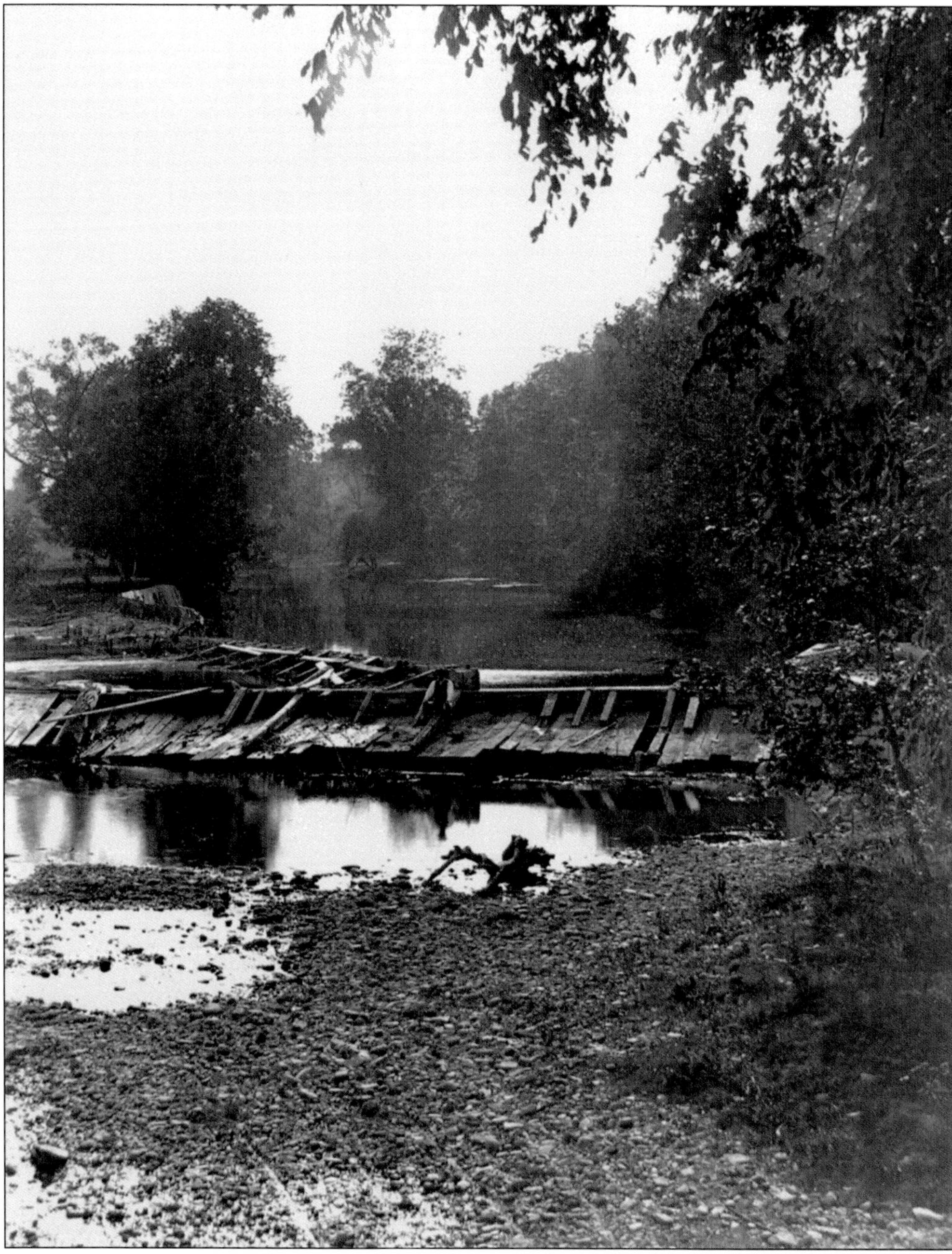

Oatka Creek has been the centerpiece of the town of Wheatland throughout its history. This picture shows the remains of the wooden dam near Bowerman Road where water was diverted to the millrace that powered mills in the village of Scottsville. In the early days, mills were built and communities grew up along the creek banks. The Oatka remains important today, as people now come to fish, canoe, swim, or to be refreshed by the beautiful scenery.

One

The Pioneers

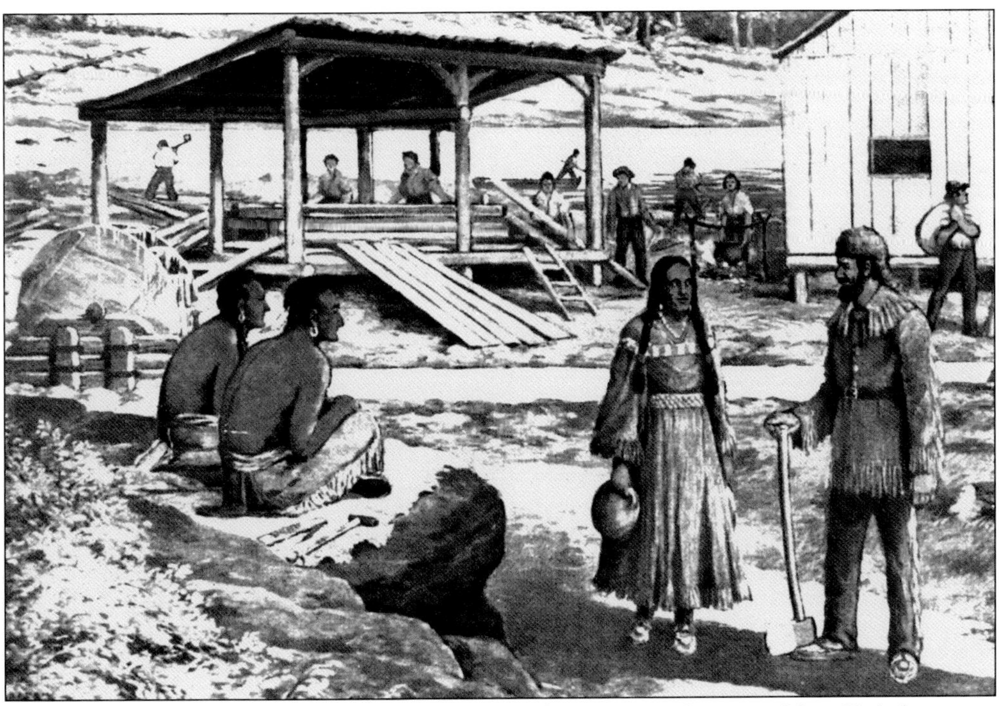

Pioneer settlement of the entire region west of the Genesee River in New York began in Wheatland. The first settler was Ebenezer "Indian" Allan, who came in 1786 and built a cabin near the confluence of Oatka Creek with the Genesee River. In 1790, Allan and his family left for the waterfalls of the Genesee River, where he built a sawmill and a gristmill, the first structures in what is now the city of Rochester.

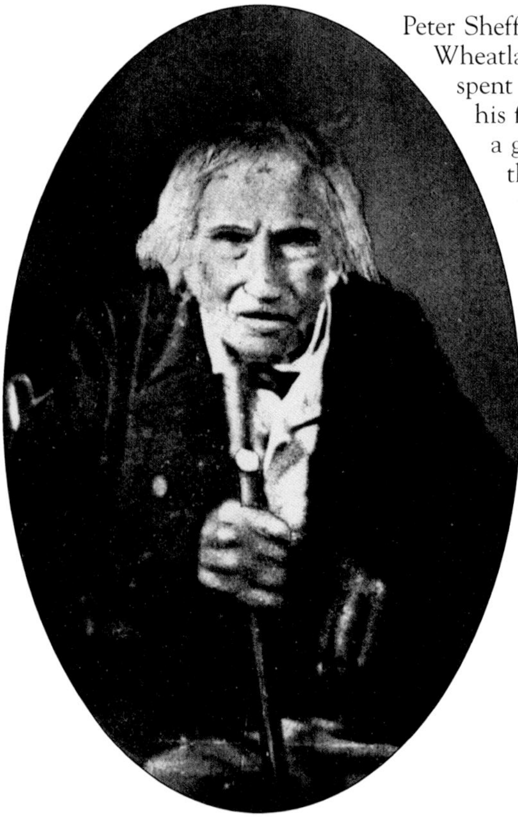

Peter Sheffer and his sons, Peter Jr. and Jacob, came to Wheatland from Pennsylvania in the fall of 1789 and spent the winter with Ebenezer "Indian" Allan and his family. In the spring, the Sheffers gave Allan a good price for his land and cabin. They were the first permanent settlers in the town. This is a picture of Peter Jr., who married Elizabeth Schoonover and lived to be 89 years old.

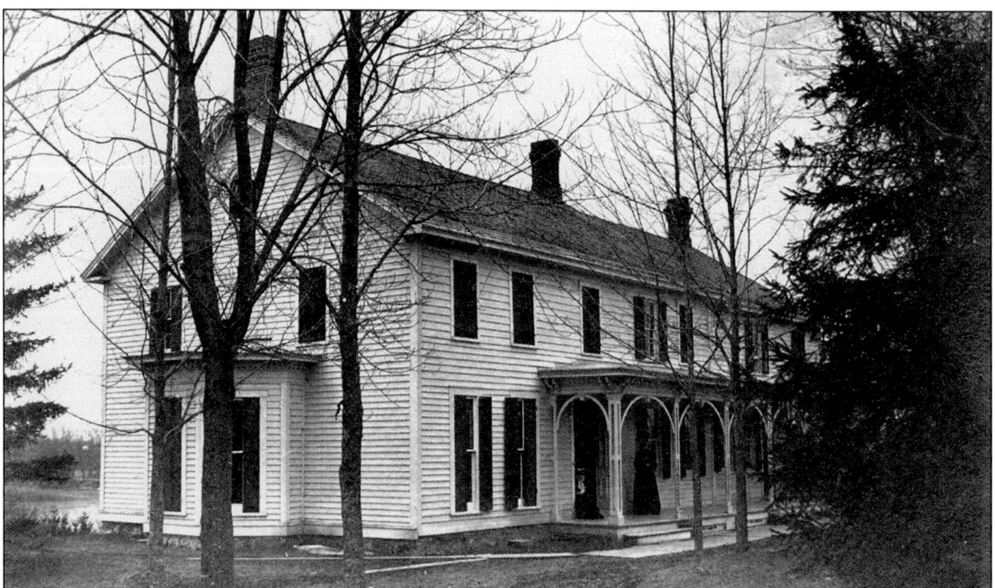

This house, built by Peter Sheffer Jr. in 1799, was the first frame house west of the Genesee River. It was here that the Sheffers raised their 11 children. Later it became the home of the Thomas Brown family, large landowners in Scottsville. Although completely changed by many renovations, the house is still standing at 88 Scottsville-Henrietta Road.

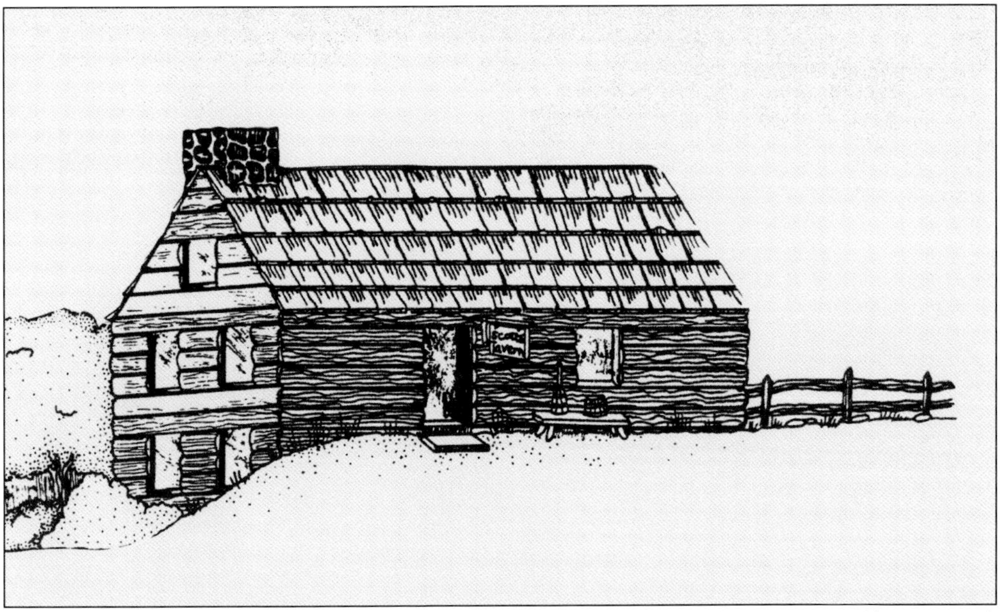

The tavern of Isaac Scott is represented in this sketch. Scott, for whom Scottsville is named, arrived in 1790 and bought about 150 acres of land that now comprise the village. His log house was built on the north bank of Oatka Creek at the present corner of Main Street and River Road. He opened it as a hotel and place of entertainment.

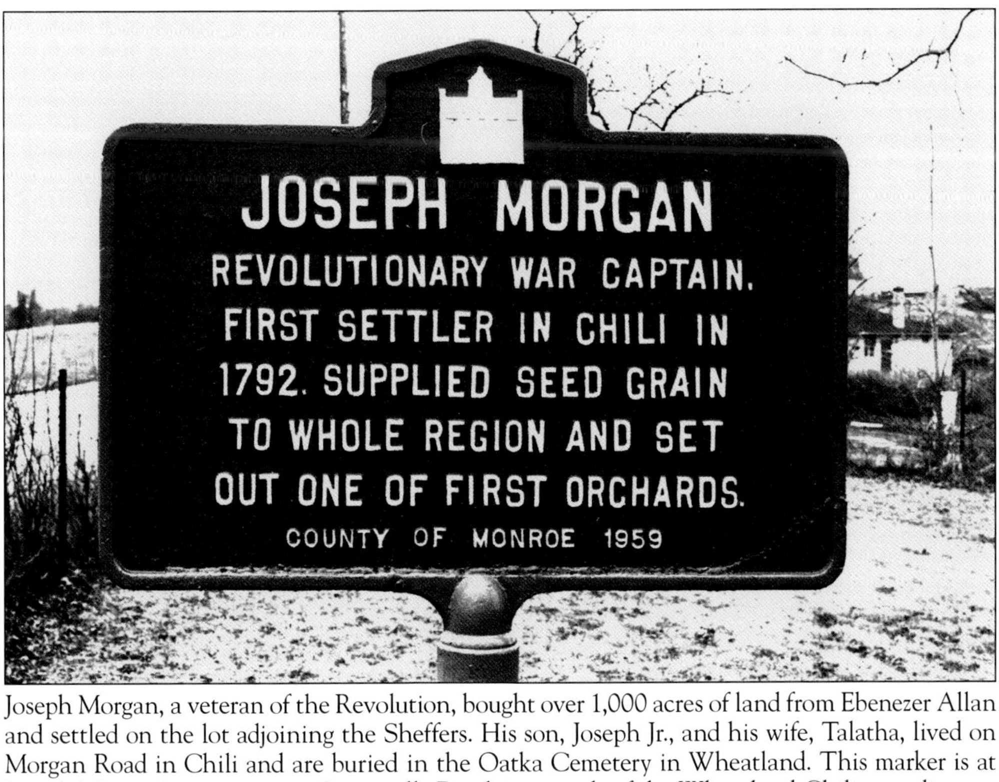

Joseph Morgan, a veteran of the Revolution, bought over 1,000 acres of land from Ebenezer Allan and settled on the lot adjoining the Sheffers. His son, Joseph Jr., and his wife, Talatha, lived on Morgan Road in Chili and are buried in the Oatka Cemetery in Wheatland. This marker is at Joseph Morgan's grave next to Scottsville Road, just north of the Wheatland-Chili town line.

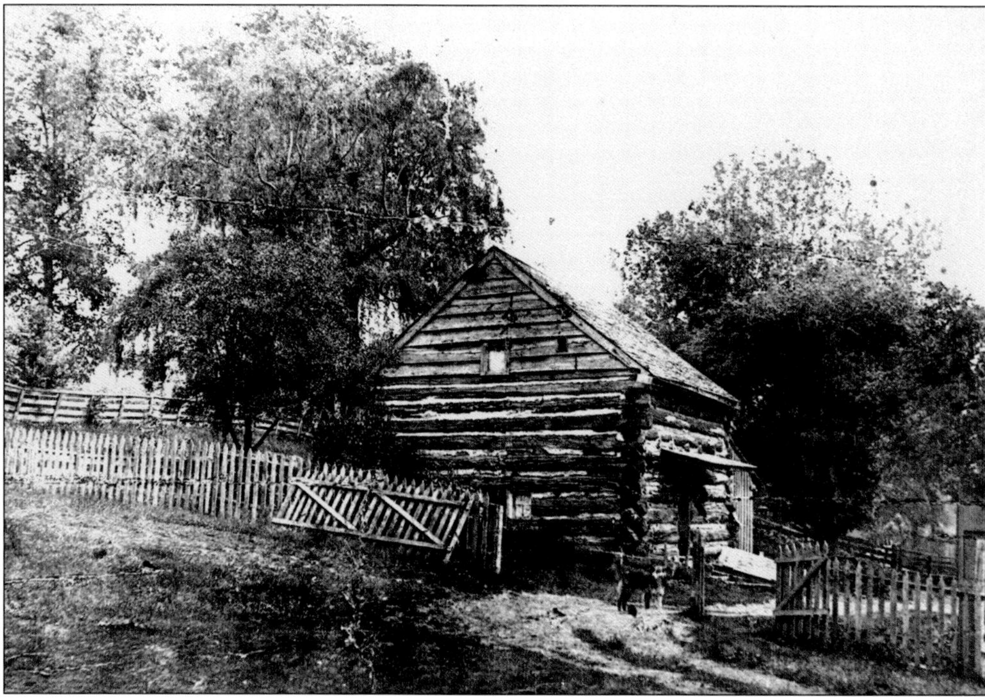

Settlers from Scotland bought large plots of land for farming along Oatka Creek and in the Big Springs area near what is now Mumford and Caledonia. This cabin was built by Findley McArthur, who came about 1803. It is still standing as part of a residence at 2389 Scottsville-Mumford Road.

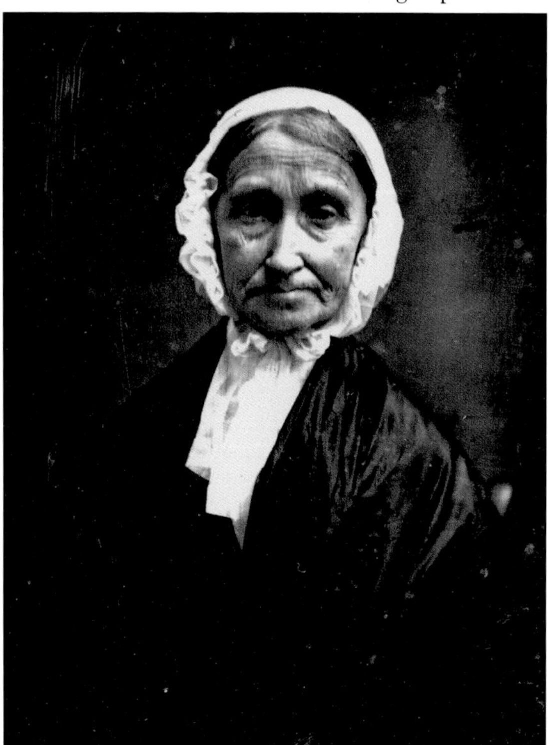

This daguerreotype is of Nancy Sheffer Garbutt, the daughter of Elizabeth and Peter Sheffer Jr. She was the first white child born west of the Genesee River. Nancy married Philip Garbutt, who emigrated with his family from England. The Garbutts came to Wheatland about 1805 and established the hamlet then called Garbuttsville along Oatka Creek and Braddocks Bay Road, now Union Street.

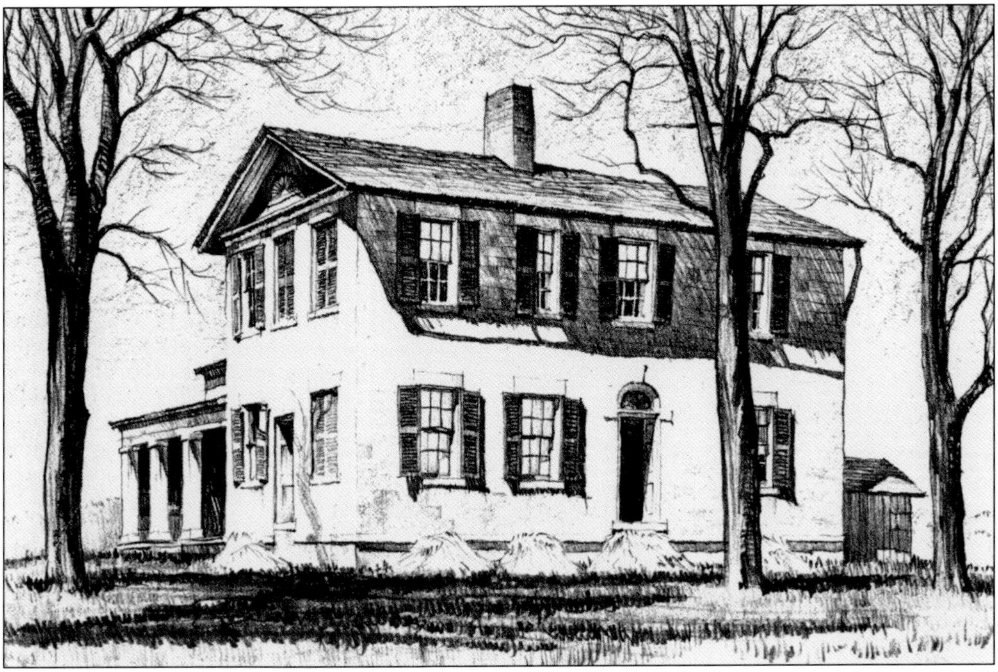

The three Garbutt brothers first lived in log cabins, but they soon built permanent homes, which have all survived to the present. This sketch shows the ledge stone house built by Philip Garbutt in 1825 on the northwest corner of Union Street and Route 383.

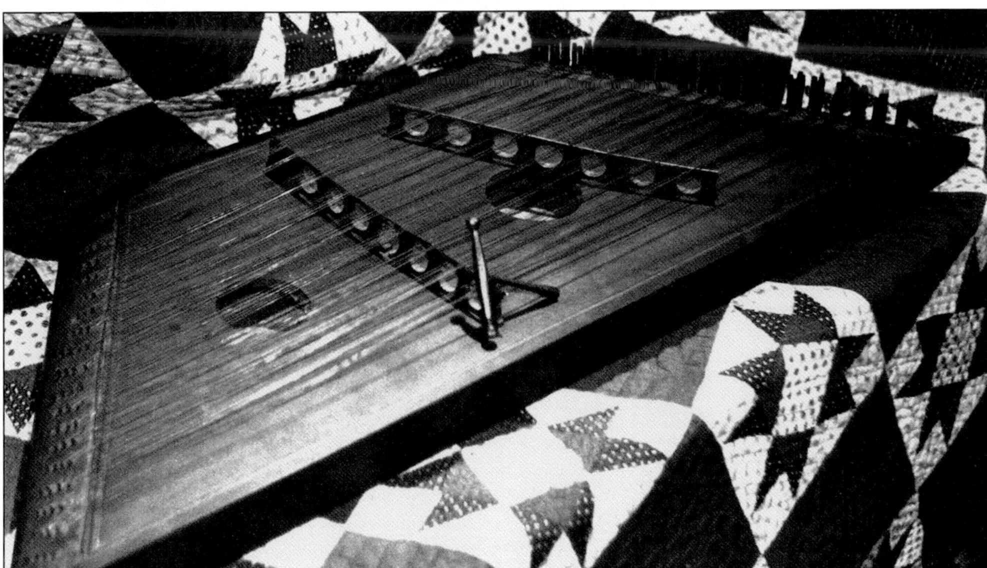

This dulcimer was made for Elizabeth Garbutt, Philip's sister, about 1800 and is now on display at the Scottsville Free Library. According to a family story, she received a surprise visit by Native Americans one day as she worked alone in the family's cabin. Elizabeth "went to her dulcimer and played a few lively airs," which fascinated her visitors and possibly saved her from danger.

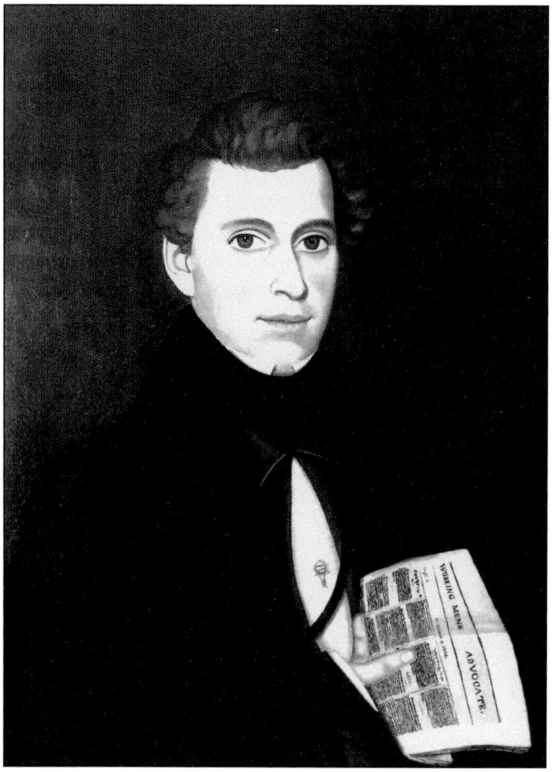

Joseph Cox and his brother, Isaac, came from Saratoga County in 1804 in a long sleigh. At night they turned it on its side as a shelter from the cold and the wolves. This 1836 portrait of Joseph Cox is now in the collection of the Wheatland Historical Association. Although it is unsigned, it is likely the work of Noah North, an important local portrait painter.

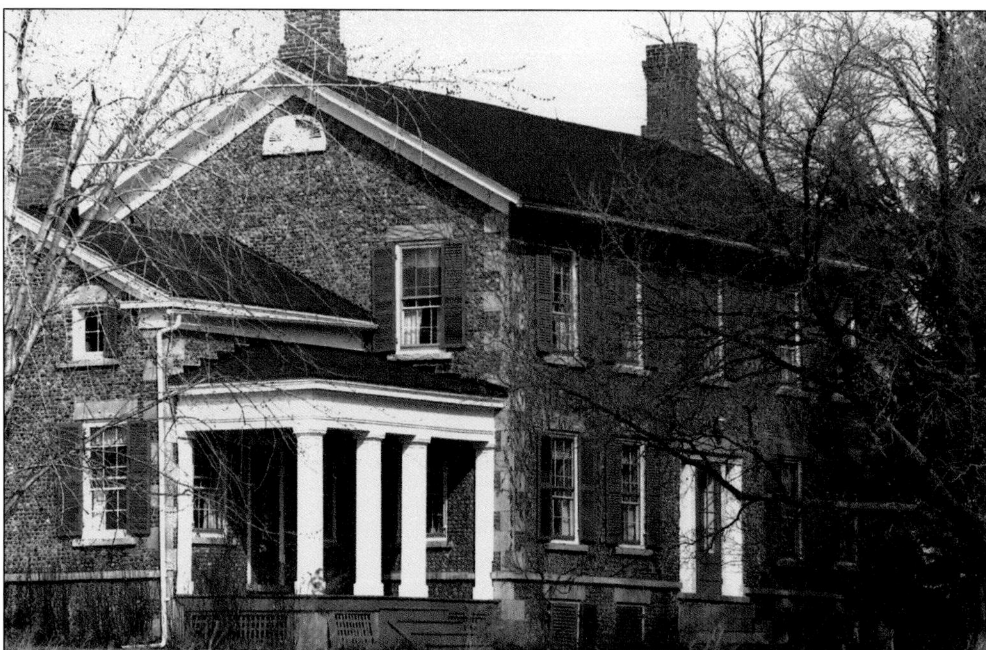

The Coxes settled on River Road, formerly called Canawaugus Road, south of Scottsville. In 1838, Isaac Cox began work on this two-story, two-family cobblestone house at 5015 River Road. It is an excellent example of cobblestone masonry and of early Greek Revival architecture.

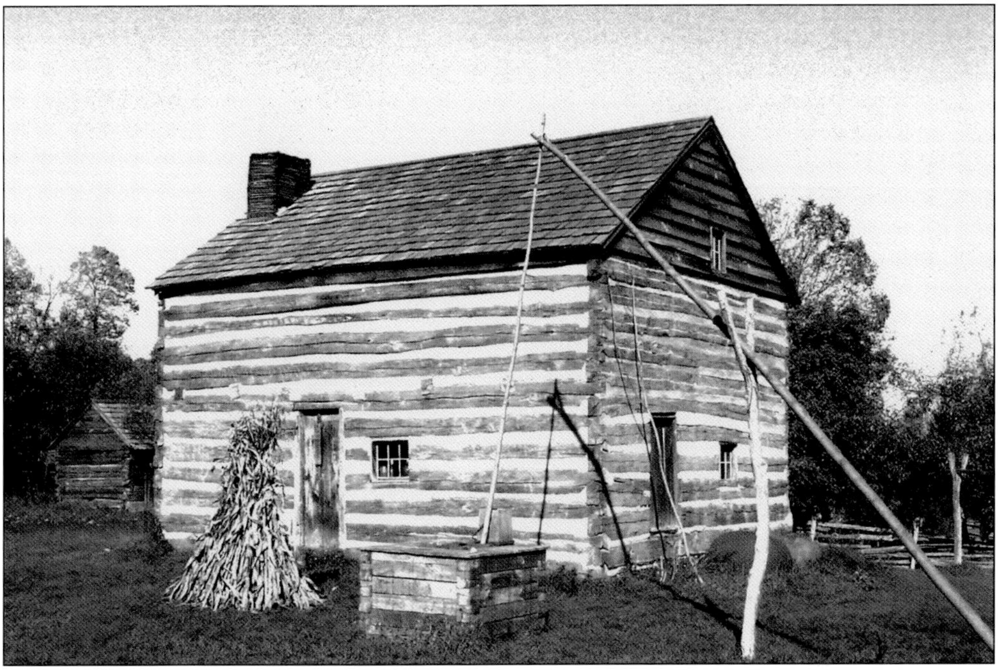

Nicholas Hetchler and his brother, Frederick, came from Pennsylvania about 1795. They settled near the corner of North Road and Chili Avenue, where this cabin was built about 1806. Later owners, the Burns family, donated the cabin to the Genesee Country Museum, where it now serves as the Pioneer Settlement exhibit pictured here.

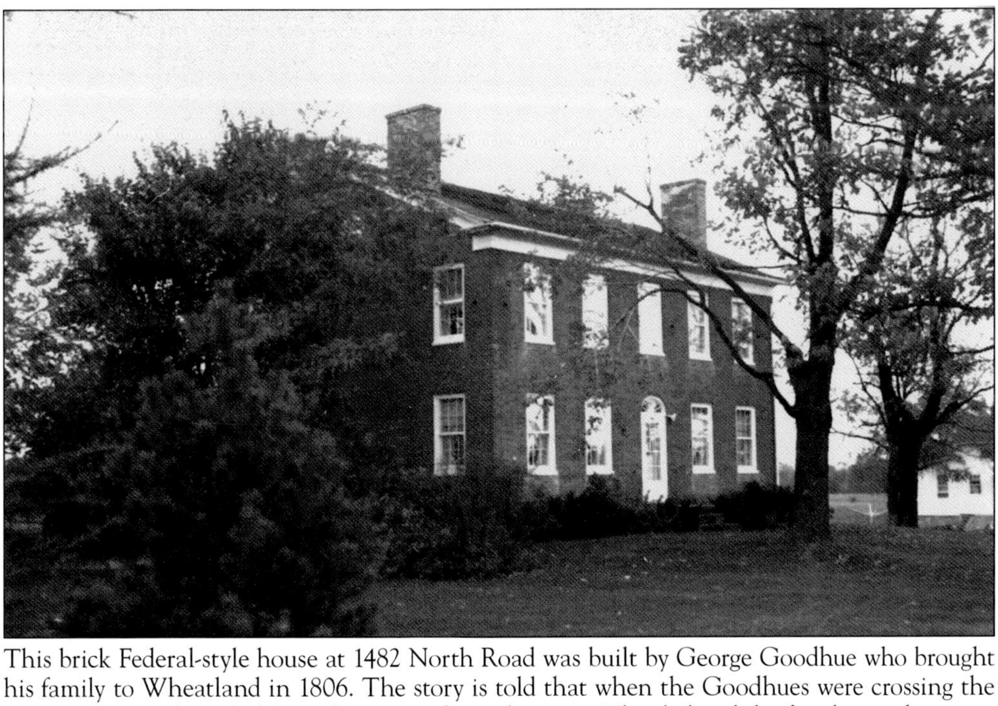

This brick Federal-style house at 1482 North Road was built by George Goodhue who brought his family to Wheatland in 1806. The story is told that when the Goodhues were crossing the Genesee River, their sled floated away on the melting ice. The sled and the family members in it were rescued from a large chunk of ice just before it went over the falls.

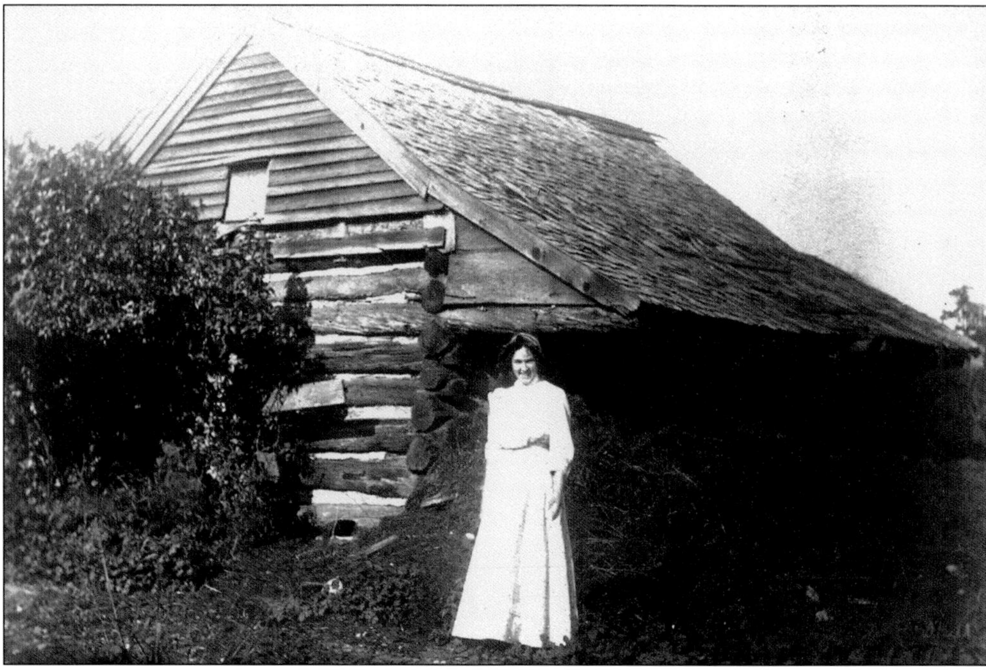

William Fraser came from Scotland about 1804 and first settled near Caledonia before moving to Wheatland. This picture, taken in the early 1900s, shows his great-granddaughter Ruth Miller standing in front of the Fraser cabin long after it had been abandoned. Today a stone monument on South Road near Bowerman Road marks the spot where the cabin once stood.

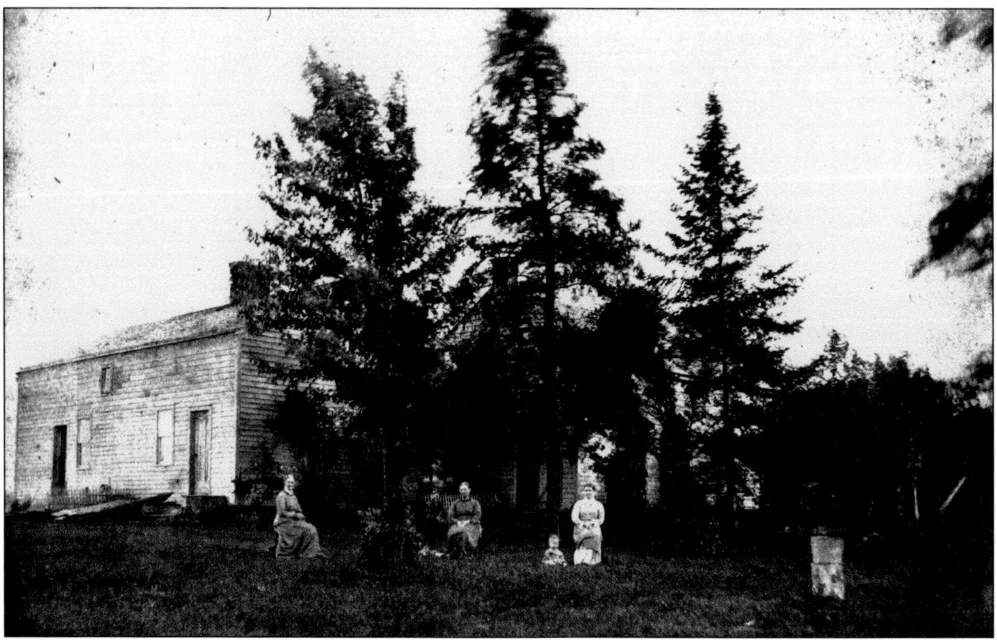

This photograph of the original Stokoe homestead, near what is now Bowerman Road, was taken in 1879. Pictured from left to right are Elizabeth Stokoe, Susan Stokoe, Susie Cox, and her mother, Alice Stokoe Cox. Thomas Stokoe began farming here in 1812, making Stokoe Farms the longest continuous farming operation in Wheatland. (Courtesy of Larry Stokoe.)

Two

Early Farming and Milling

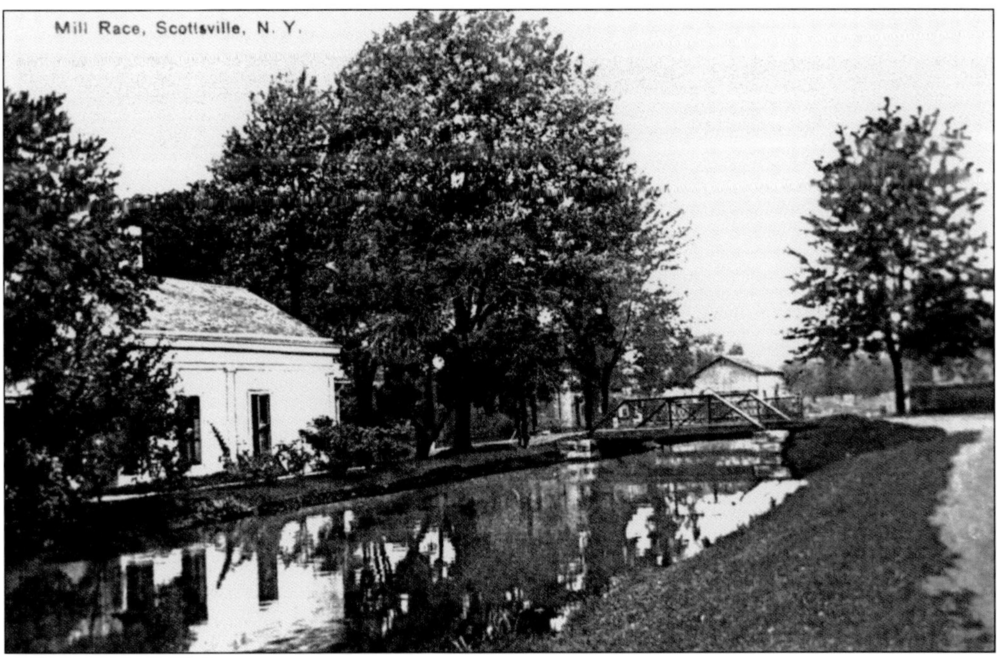

Early settlers were drawn to Wheatland because of the rich, fertile soil and the promise of waterpower for mills along Oatka Creek and Spring Creek. This 1909 photograph shows the millrace that was built in 1826 from a dam near Bowerman Road to the mills in the village of Scottsville. Remaining portions of the race are a reminder of its importance to the area's history.

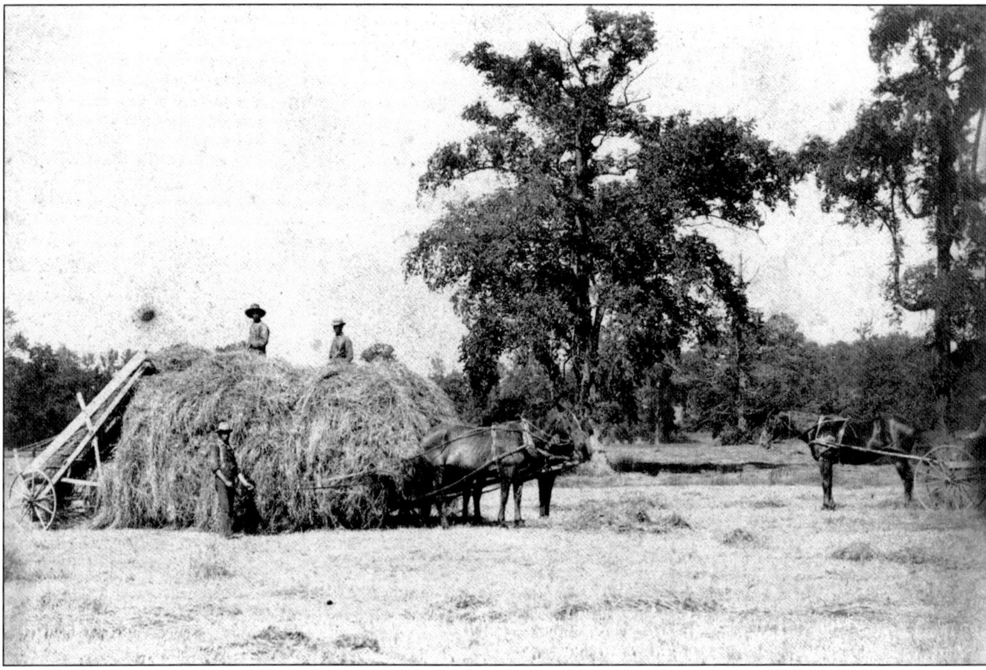

All of the Wheatland pioneers were farmers. Even those with other trades, such as blacksmiths or doctors, ran farms in addition to their other work. Farm work was laborious with only oxen or horses to help with the heavy manual labor. This photograph shows men haying on Isaac Budlong's farm before power equipment was used. (Courtesy of Elizabeth Boutwell Marlowe.)

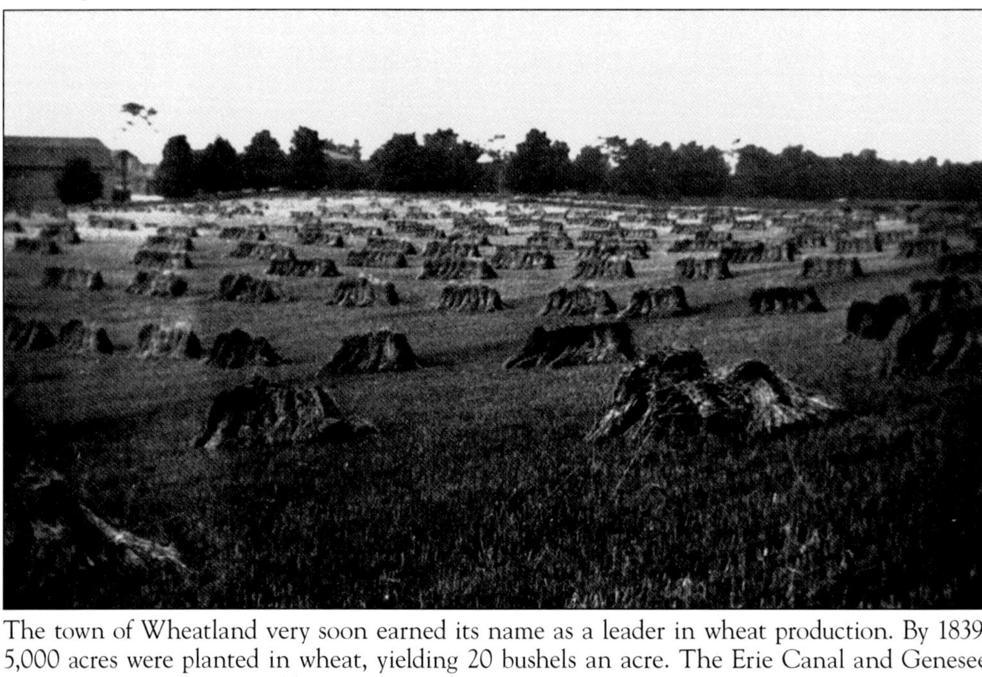

The town of Wheatland very soon earned its name as a leader in wheat production. By 1839, 5,000 acres were planted in wheat, yielding 20 bushels an acre. The Erie Canal and Genesee Valley Canal made it possible to ship flour all over the east. The photograph above shows the wheat crop of 1927 on Harmon's farm, cut and gathered into shocks, waiting to be threshed. (Courtesy of John Harmon.)

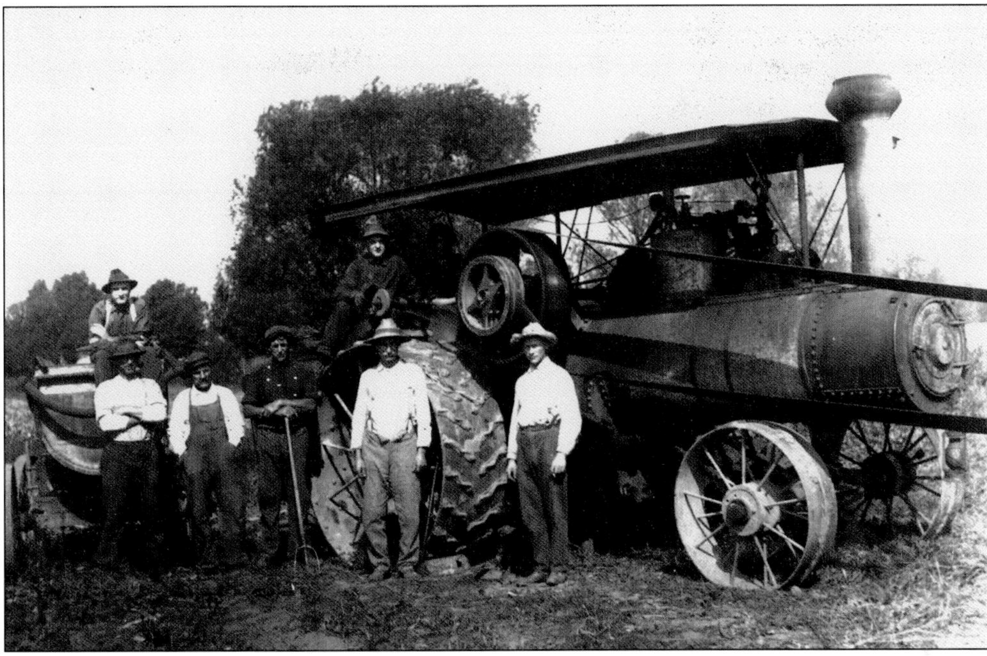

Later the work of the farmer was eased a great deal by the invention of the steam engine. Here Spencer Stamm and his crew stand before his steam engine on the Giles farm around 1915. Stamm lived on East Genesee Street in Scottsville and traveled from farm to farm doing custom threshing.

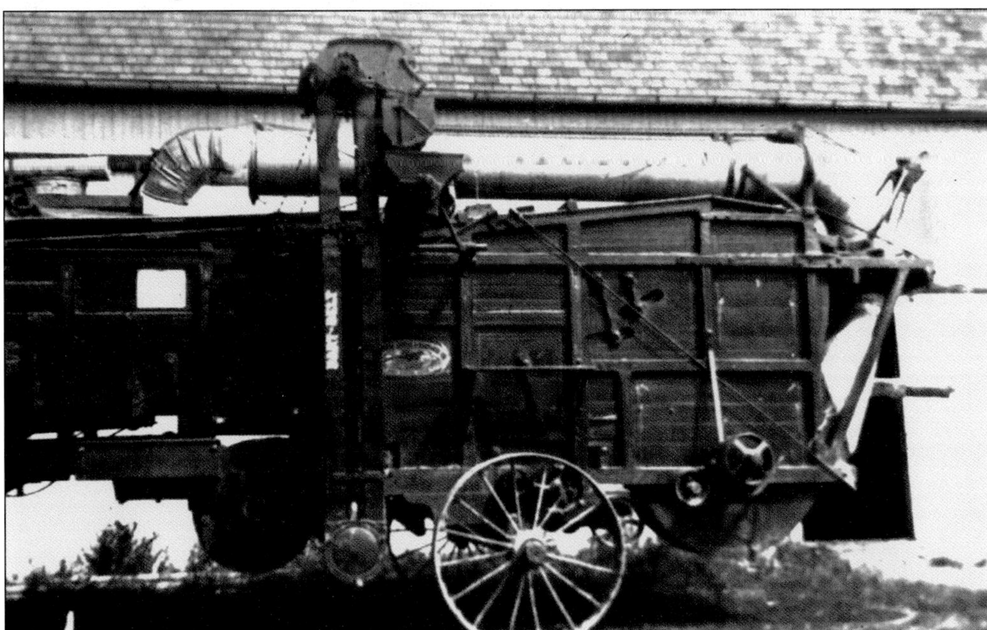

During the early years, area farmers had used grain cradles to cut their wheat and simple flails to beat the grain from the stalks. By the mid-19th century, threshing machines such as this one were available. The belt seen on Stamm's steam engine above was attached to his threshing machine, powering its operation.

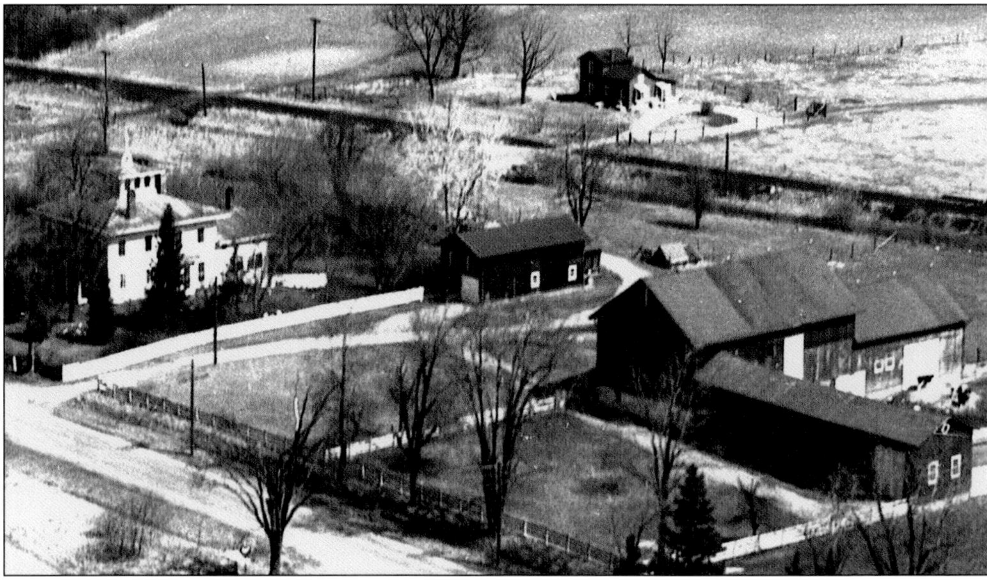

One of the large, successful farming operations in Wheatland during the late 1800s was that of Isaac Budlong. As seen here, the farm buildings were located between River Road, in the foreground, and the Genesee Valley Canal. Delos Boutwell bought the beautiful Italianate-style house in 1943. (Courtesy of Elizabeth Boutwell Marlowe.)

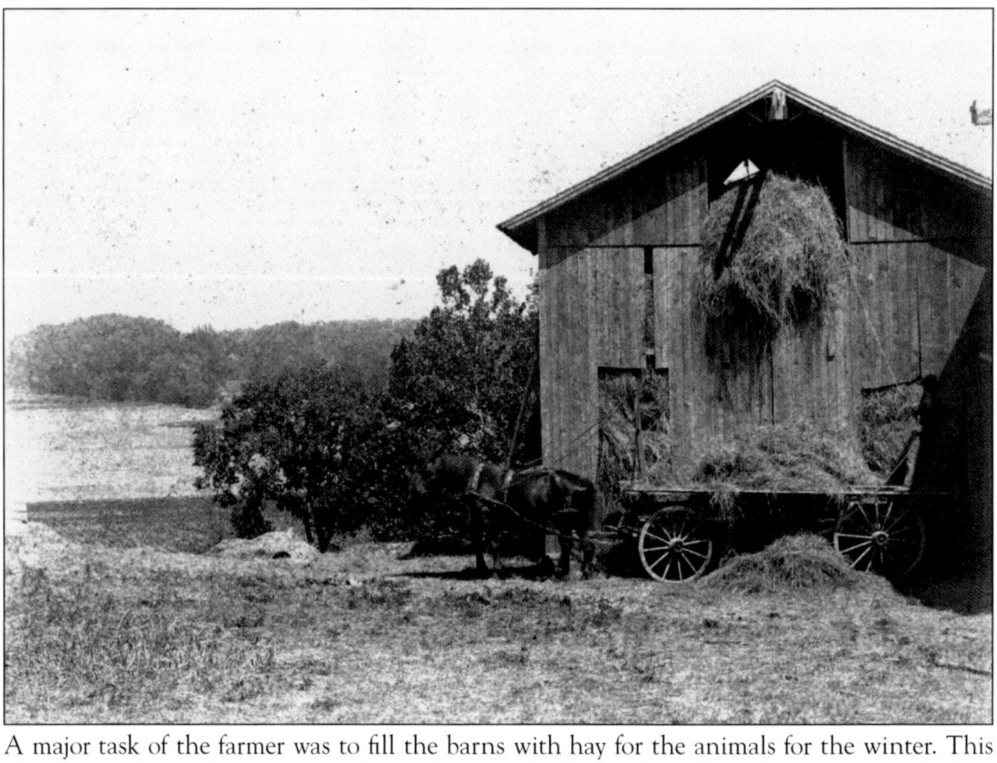

A major task of the farmer was to fill the barns with hay for the animals for the winter. This photograph shows that operation being done on Budlong's farm. Here hay is being lifted by a fork and pulley that carried it along the ridge of the barn and dropped it into the haymow. (Courtesy of Elizabeth Boutwell Marlowe.)

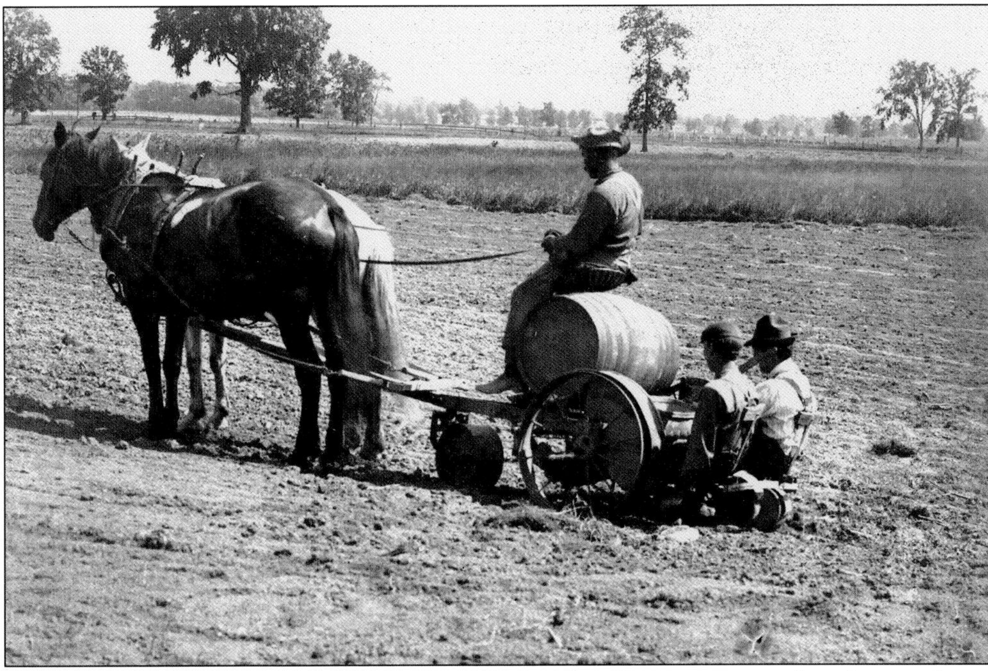

Another crop on Isaac Budlong's farm was cabbage. The plants were started in the greenhouse and then transplanted by hand. This photograph shows a cabbage planter with a barrel for watering. The planter cut a groove for the plants and then closed the soil over the transplants that had been placed by the workers. (Courtesy of Elizabeth Boutwell Marlowe.)

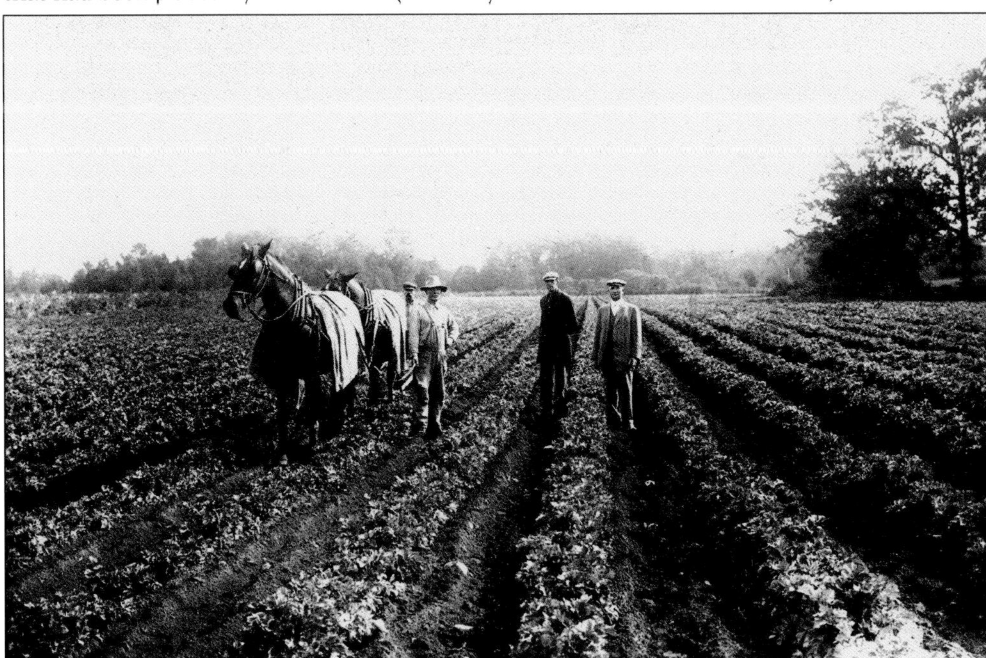

In the 1890s, the Guthries were farming the muck flats in Mumford, the only land of this type in Wheatland. Pictured here from left to right are brothers Robert, Andrew, James J., and William Guthrie tending to their crop. (Courtesy of Jean Guthrie.)

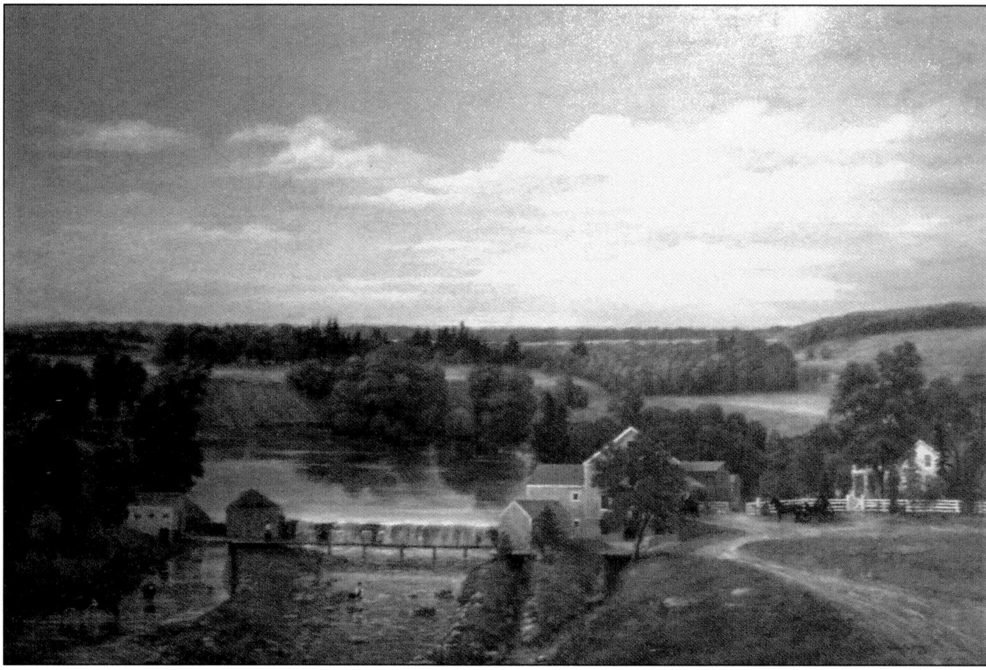

The first mill on Oatka Creek was built by Francis Albright in 1804 in what is now Wheatland Center. Clark Hall purchased the mill in 1832 and then sold it to Hiram Smith in 1844. This 1866 painting by Emily Smith, which hangs in the Scottsville Free Library, shows Smith's mill with the house at the extreme right and the mill and dam in the center.

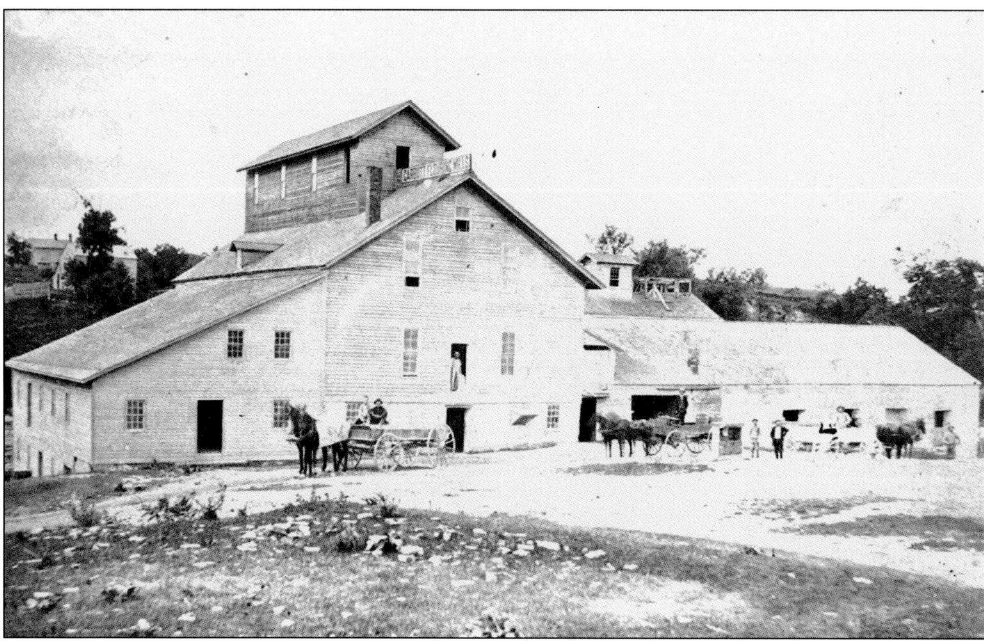

In 1811, Peter Sheffer built a gristmill on Oatka Creek in Garbutt. The mill prospered and expanded until, by 1840, it was one of the largest on the creek. This photograph was taken around 1880 when the gristmill was run by Isaac Salyerds and then by George Page. After it closed, the building remained vacant for some years before it was converted to a gypsum mill.

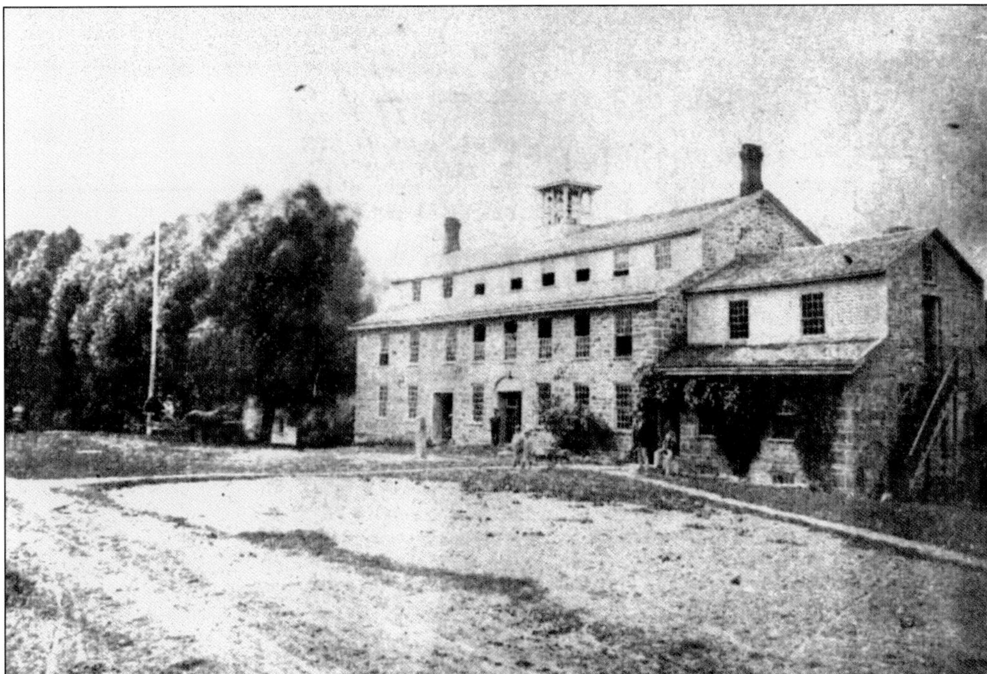

OATKA WOOLEN MILL AT MUMFORD, AS IT LOOKED IN 1860

Donald McKenzie started a clothier works and woolen factory on Oatka Creek in Mumford about 1810. Oliver Allen and William Remington took over the business and built this large stone mill building about 1830. They began to manufacture woolen goods on a large scale. The business grew and prospered for three generations of the Allen family, closing about 1902. The photograph below shows the bog limestone Allen mill office at 622 Armstrong Road. Oliver Allen II is on the right holding a satchel.

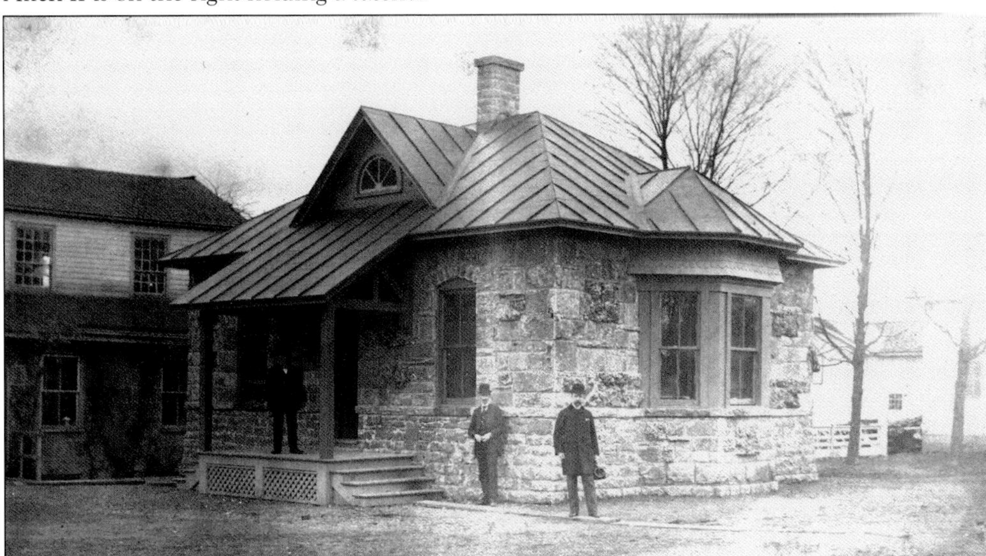

WHEATLAND PLASTER.

DISCOVERED IN 1812.

THE FIRST GYPSUM USED IN WESTERN NEW YORK.

It has proved far superior to any other for farming purposes and makes a stronger cement than Nova Scotia.

This Gypsum has 85 per cent, pure Sulphuric Acid, and is recommended by the Massachusetts Farmer's Association in preference to all others for Agriculture.

For Grass-Land it is known to produce one-half more yield per acre.

For Wheat, it causes a greater growth of straw and an increase in the number of heads, often amounting to twenty or twenty-five bushels per acre.

In Barley and Oats the effect of Gypsum is still more wonderful, increasing the yield from 40 to 50 per cent.

But probably the most wonderful effect of Plaster on any crop is upon Indian corn, producing double the amount of stalks and corn.

For sale by

J. W. GARBUTT,
SCOTTSVILLE,
Monroe Co., N. Y.

Keeler's Job Print.

Only a few years after the settlement of the area, it was discovered that ground gypsum could be spread on fields to enhance crop growth. It is not a fertilizer, but it contains a high percentage of sulfate of lime, which aids in moisture retention. Philip Garbutt was the first to take advantage of the vast deposits of gypsum that lay underground on his property and elsewhere in the area. His son, John W. Garbutt, continued his business into the early 20th century.

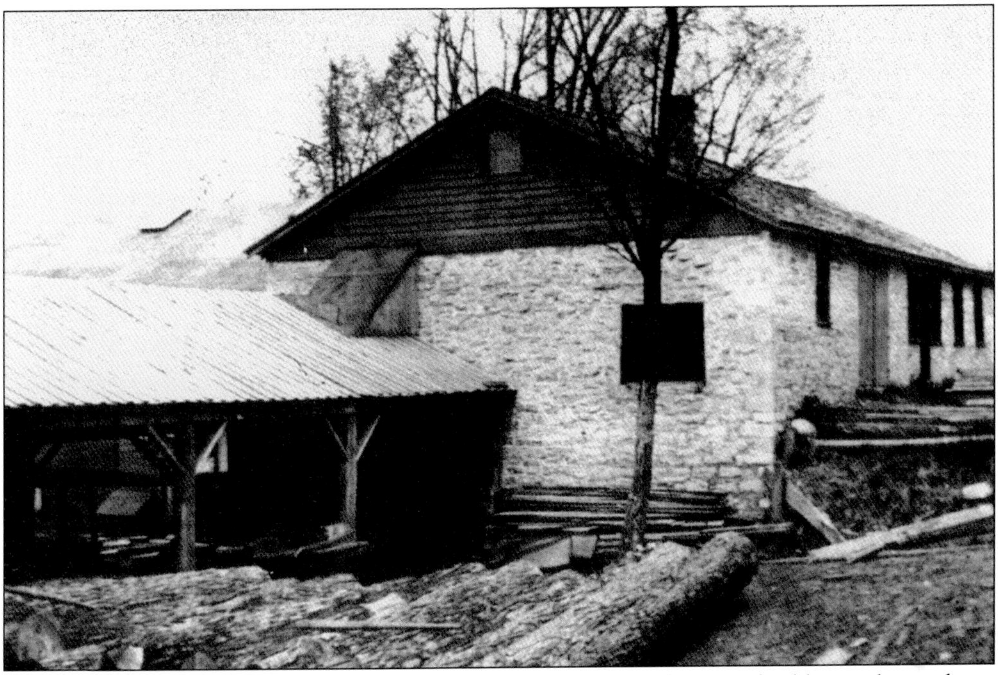

Philip Garbutt bought land in Mumford in 1833 and constructed a stone building to be used as a plaster mill. The business thrived until the 1880s when it was converted to the sawmill and shop shown here. In the early 1900s, it was remodeled into a residence and is now a bed-and-breakfast at 948 George Street.

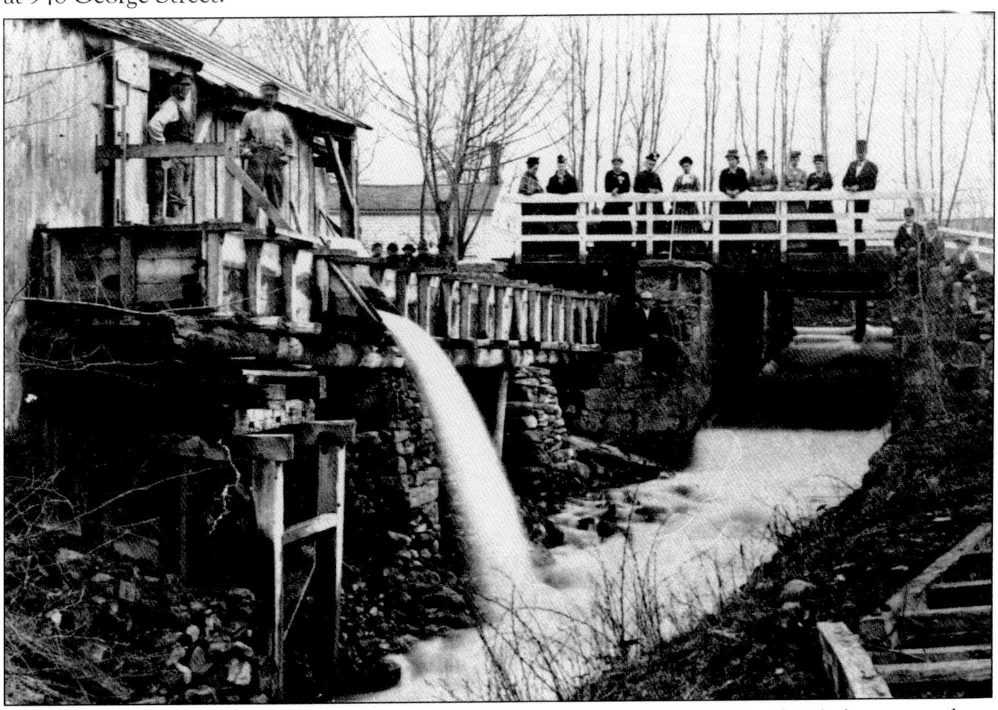

During the 1850s and 1860s, Ira Harmon, and later Dugald McQueen, hauled gypsum from Belcoda and ground it at this mill on Spring Creek.

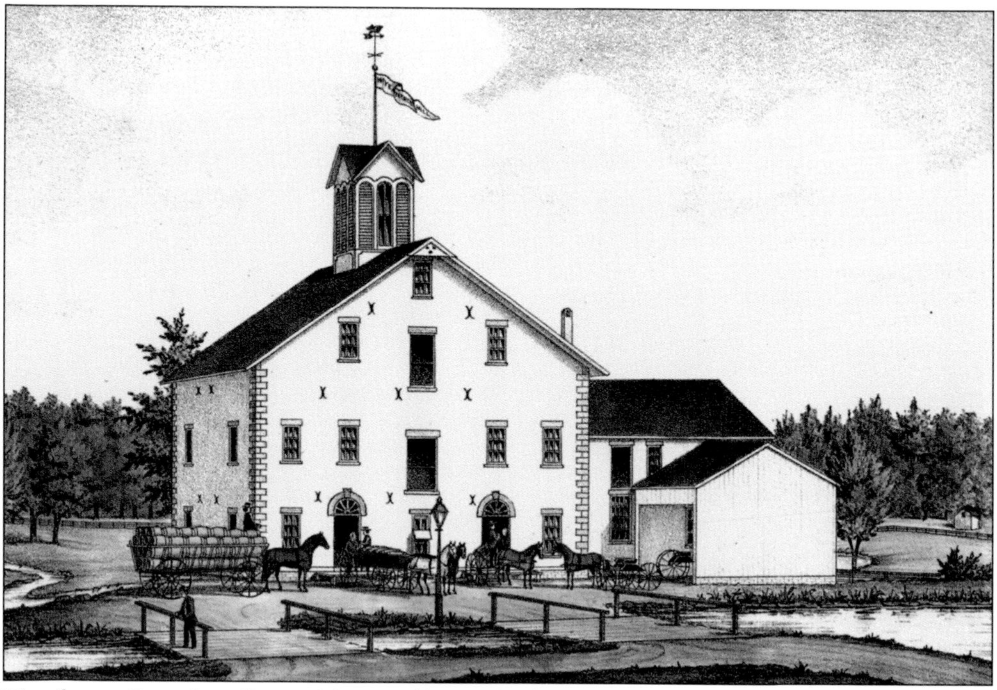

The first mill in the village of Scottsville was built in 1816 by Donald McVean. A later mill, depicted above, was near the first mill on the north bank of the Oatka. It was built by Powell Carpenter in 1830 and run by his son, Ira, and others. It was owned and operated by Malcolm McVean as a flour mill when it burned to the ground in 1878. (Courtesy of Timothy Hallock.)

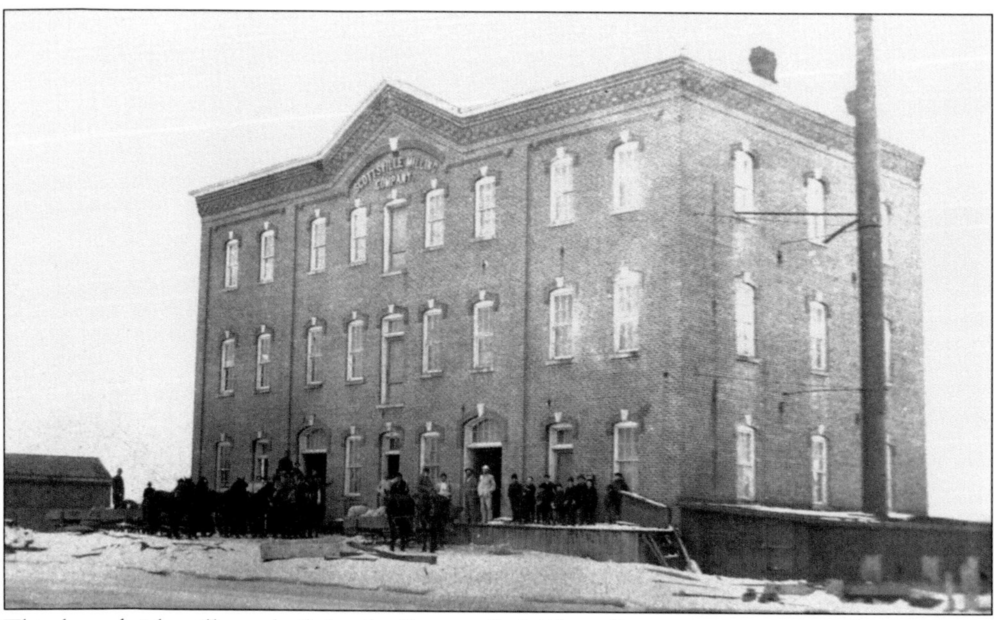

This large brick mill was built by the Scottsville Milling Company in 1880 on the site of the Carpenter-McVean mill. M. C. Mordoff conducted a fruit evaporator and cider mill here until the building was outfitted as a flour mill in 1886 by L. M. Godley and Company.

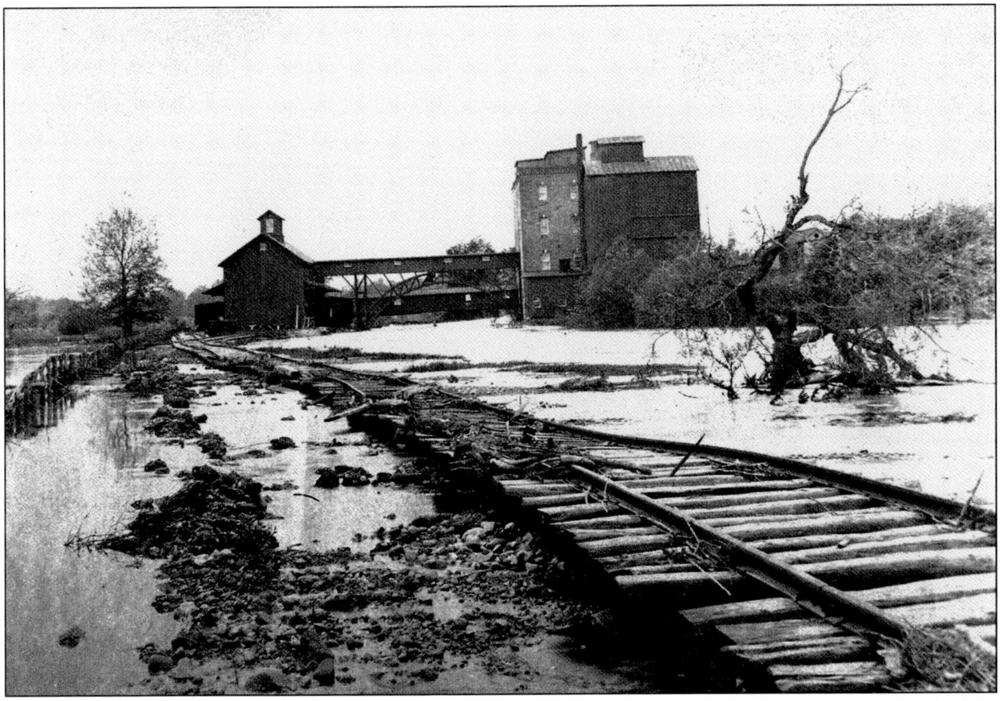

This photograph shows the Godley Mill on the right and the warehouse, with the track that connected it to the Western New York and Pennsylvania Railroad, later the Pennsylvania Railroad. The business was very successful for several years before being destroyed by fire in 1895. The invoice below is for two types of flour, one in paper sacks and the other in cotton, to be shipped on the Buffalo, Rochester and Pittsburg Railroad to D. P. Campbell in Mumford.

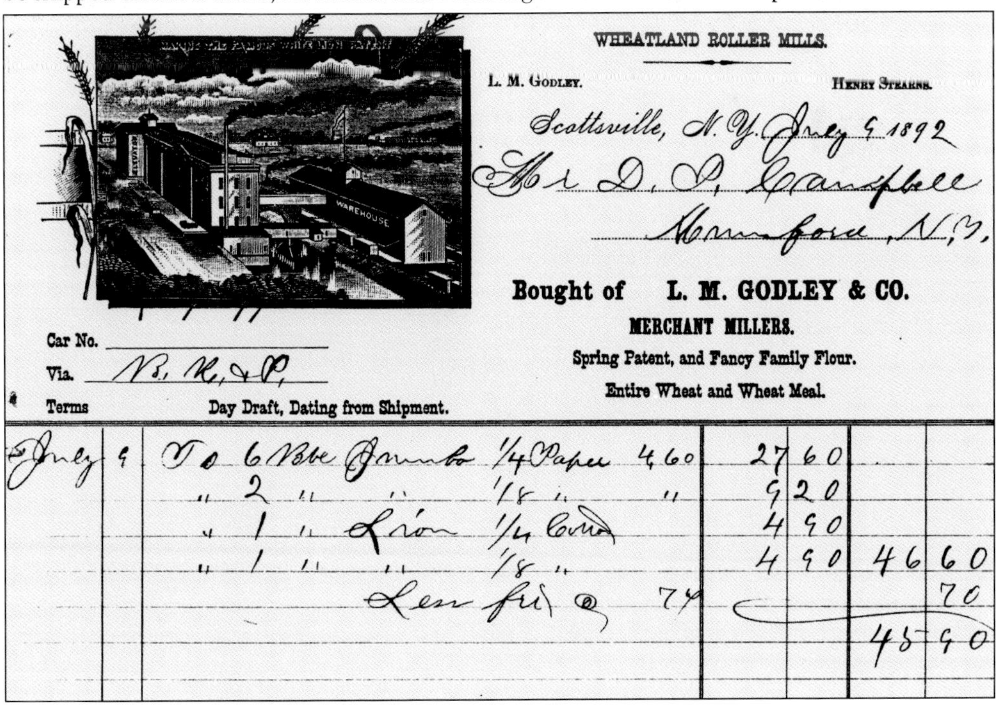

WHEATLAND ROLLER MILLS.

L. M. Godley. Henry Stearns.

Scottsville, N.Y. July 9 1892

Mr D. P. Campbell

Mumford, N.Y.

Bought of L. M. GODLEY & CO.

MERCHANT MILLERS.

Spring Patent, and Fancy Family Flour.

Entire Wheat and Wheat Meal.

Car No.

Via. B, R, & P,

Terms Day Draft, Dating from Shipment.

July	9	To 6 Bbl Jumbo 1/4 Paper	4.60	27 60	
		" 2 " " 1/8 "	"	9 20	
		" 1 " Lion 1/4 Cotton		4 90	
		" 1 " " 1/8 "		4 90	46 60
		Less frt @	7¢		70
					45 90

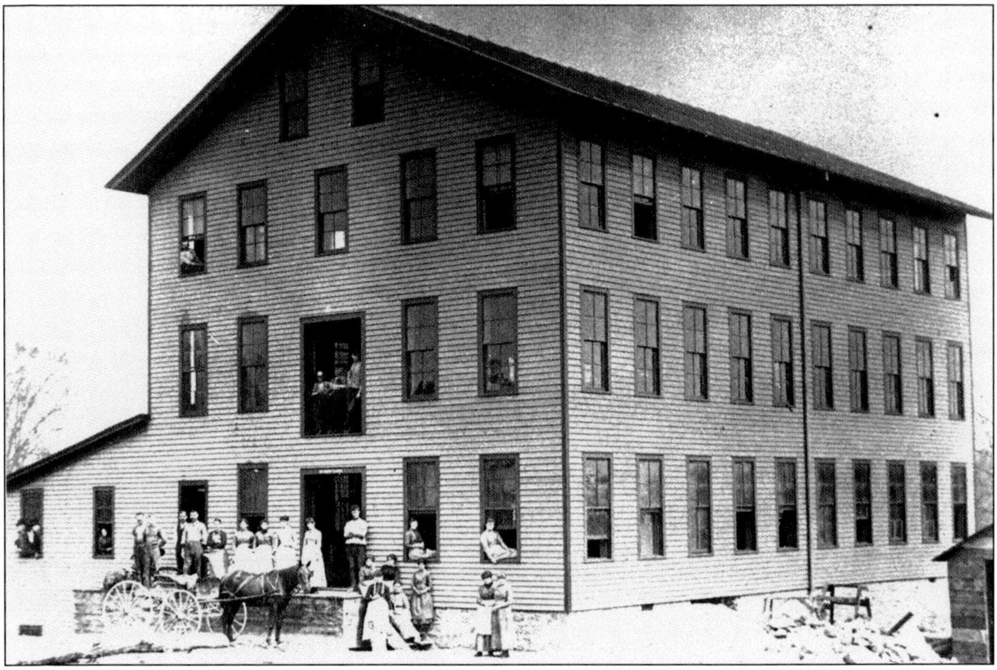

W. D. Strobel Jr. came from Long Island and built the Trout Brook Woolen Mill on Spring Creek in Mumford in 1882. He installed the latest equipment and employed as many as 50 people. The woolens produced there were in great demand in all the large eastern cities.

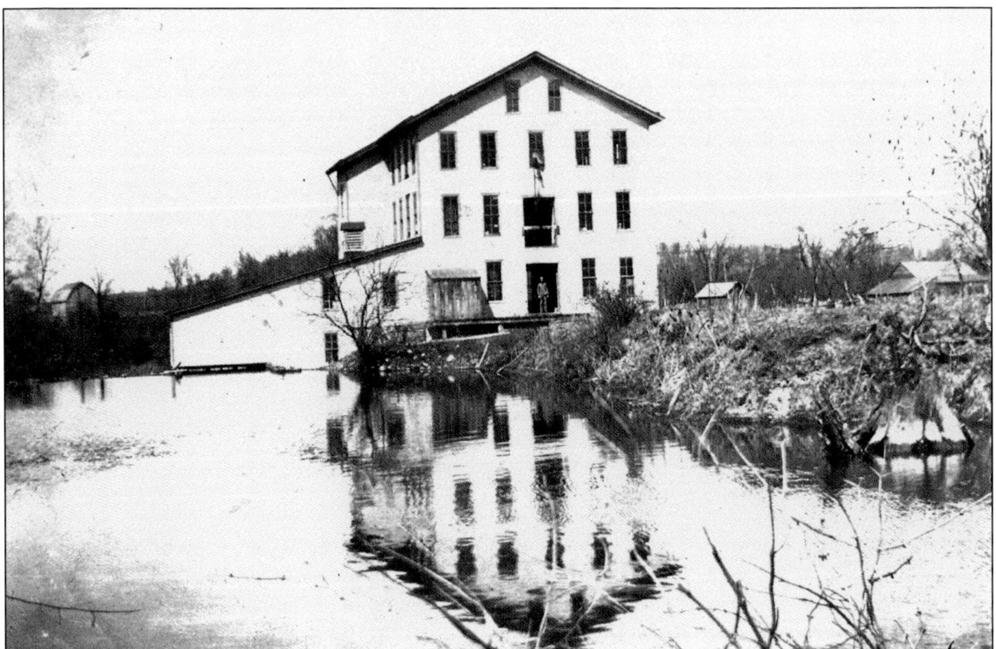

The business of the Trout Brook Woolen Mill declined because of competition from large mills in the east. In 1899, the building on Spring Creek was rented to E. Turner, who installed machinery for the manufacture of smoking pipes. The pipes were made from apple wood, grown in nearby orchards.

Three

MUMFORD

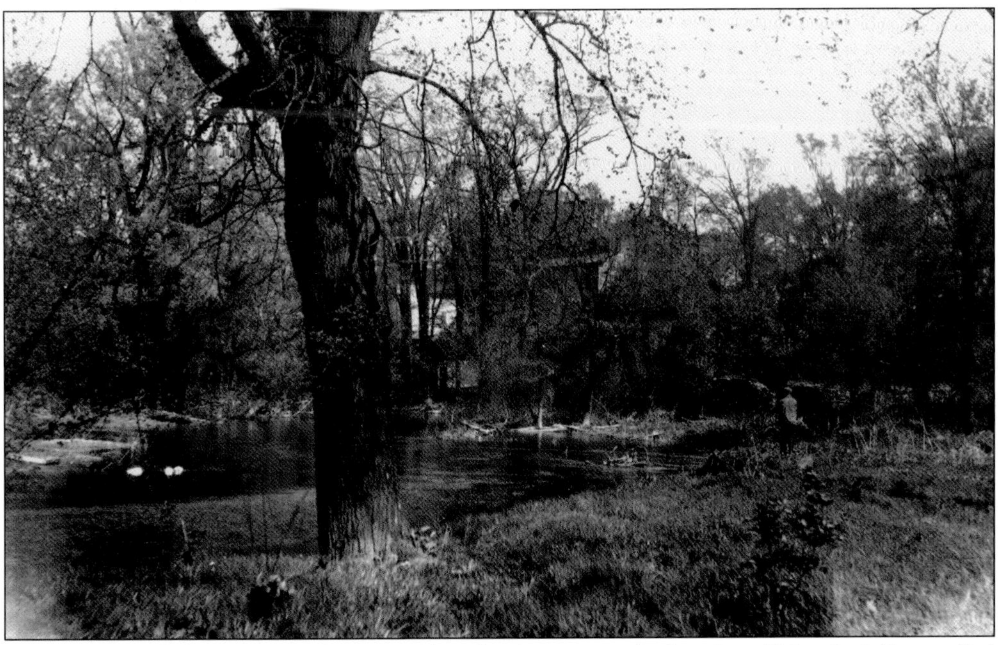

As Oatka Creek flows eastward across Wheatland, it passes the hamlet of Mumford. First called McKenzie's Corners, it was named Mumfordville about 1832 to honor a leading citizen. The determination and ingenuity of its first inhabitants, and the ones that followed them, made Mumford a prosperous community. Today thousands of tourists from all over the world come to Mumford each summer to visit the Genesee Country Village and Museum.

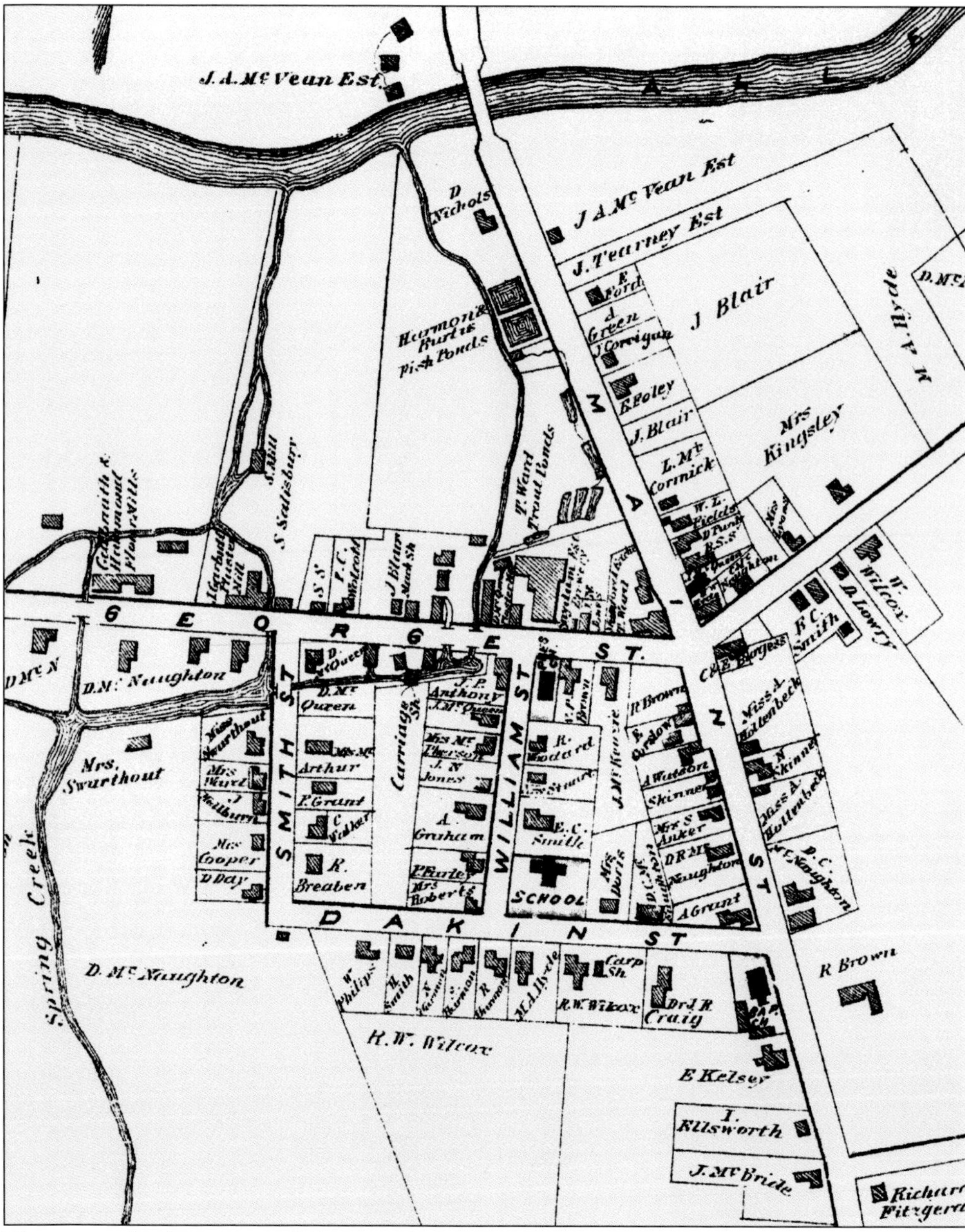

The reason for the success of the Mumford enterprises is evident from this map from the 1872 *Atlas of Monroe County, N.Y.*, published by F. W. Beers. Spring Creek, which originates at Big Springs in Caledonia, flows into Oatka Creek at Mumford. Mills and businesses lined the creeks and the millraces that were created from them. The four corners, at the intersection of Main Street, State Street, and George Street, provided an ideal location for shops and hotels.

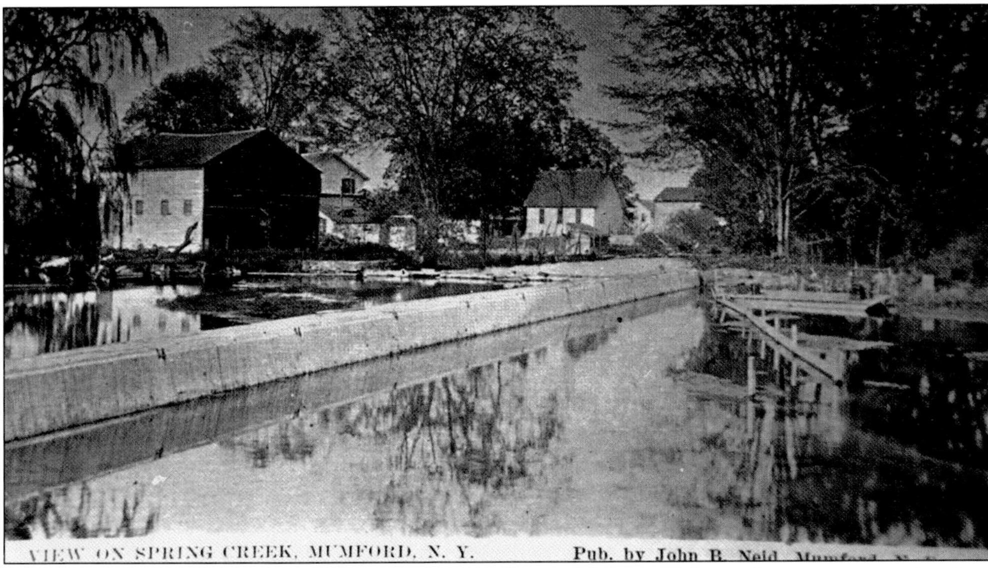

In the early days, when the settlers were seeking sites that would supply waterpower for their mills, they were able to channel the flow of Spring Creek. The first mills in Mumford were built on this creek.

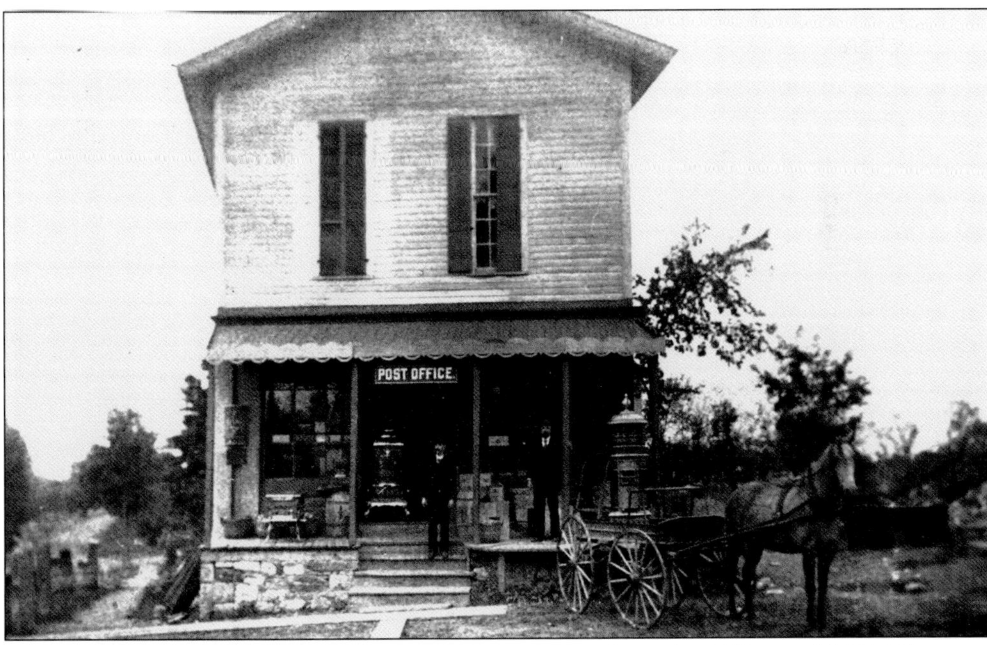

Phoenix Hall stood on the southeast of the four corners from the 1850s until 1943. There was a store on the first floor and an entertainment hall on the second. It served as a general store under several owners and then became an ice-cream parlor from 1923 until about 1931, when it was closed and then demolished. John E. Harvey, on the left, and Fred Paine are standing on the steps.

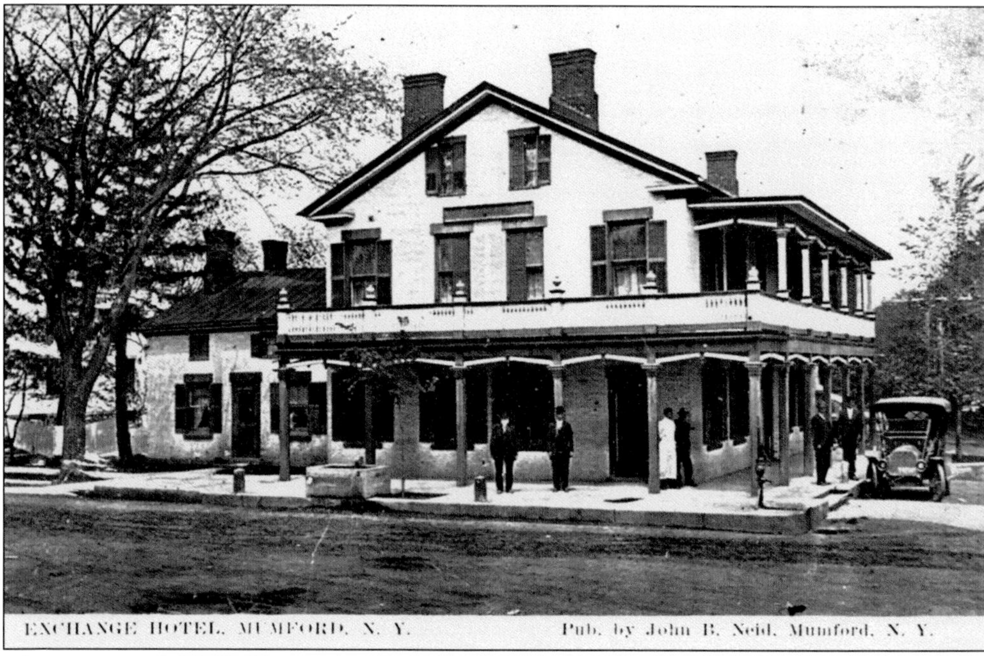

This two-story brick building, on the northwest of the four corners, was built by Libbens White in 1835. Duncan McNaughton became the host of the Exchange Hotel for the next 20 years. Thomas Ward bought the hotel in 1862 and, during his 20-year proprietorship, he built the porches on the front and south side.

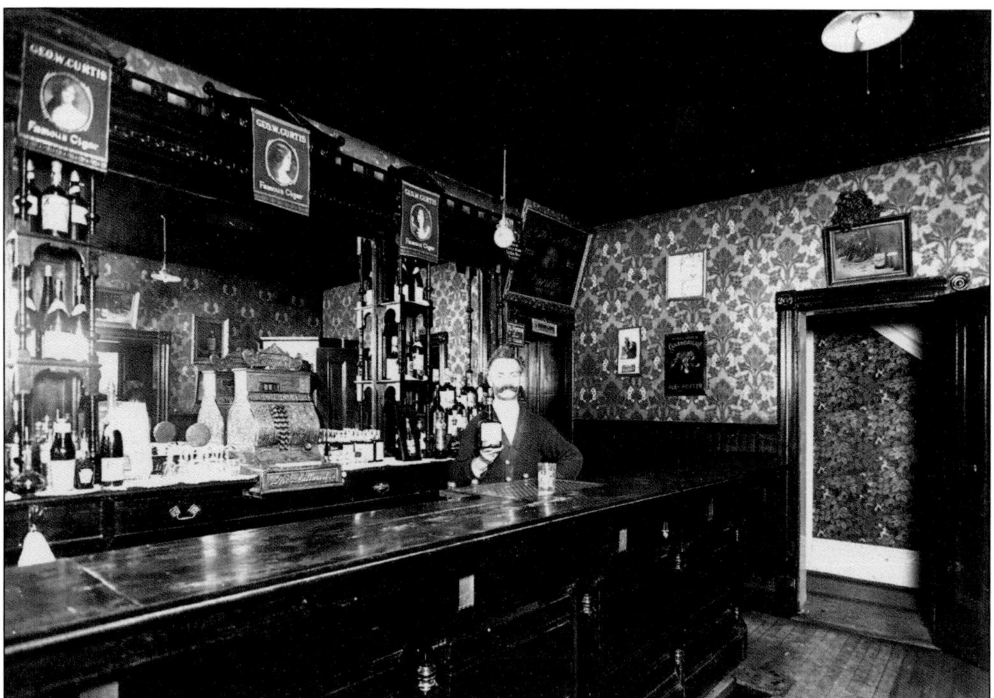

This is a picture of the bar in the Exchange Hotel in the early 1900s. Tom McGinnis was the bartender.

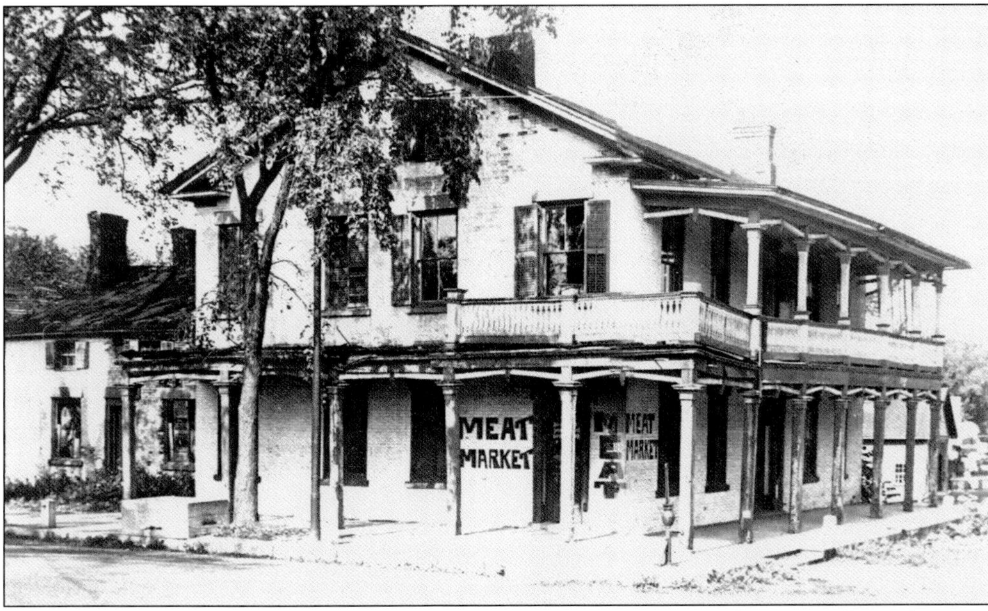

When the Exchange was no longer a busy hotel, it became a rooming house. In the early 1930s, Frank Ellington ran a meat market in the south end. He advertised sirloin steaks for 25¢ a pound and pork roast for 12¢. A men's club called the 101 Ranch occupied the north side.

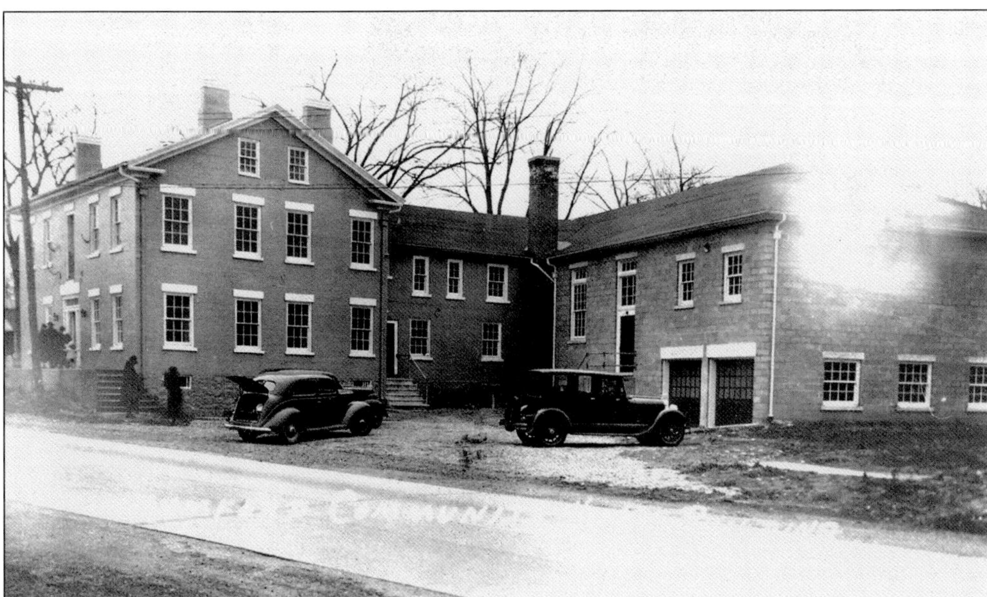

The old Exchange Hotel was extensively damaged by fire in 1934. A group of community members organized themselves to rebuild the historic landmark. The old sheds and barns were torn down, and a new addition was built on the north side. It became the Mumford Community Building, dedicated in 1937, which has housed village offices, the fire department, the library, and a meeting hall.

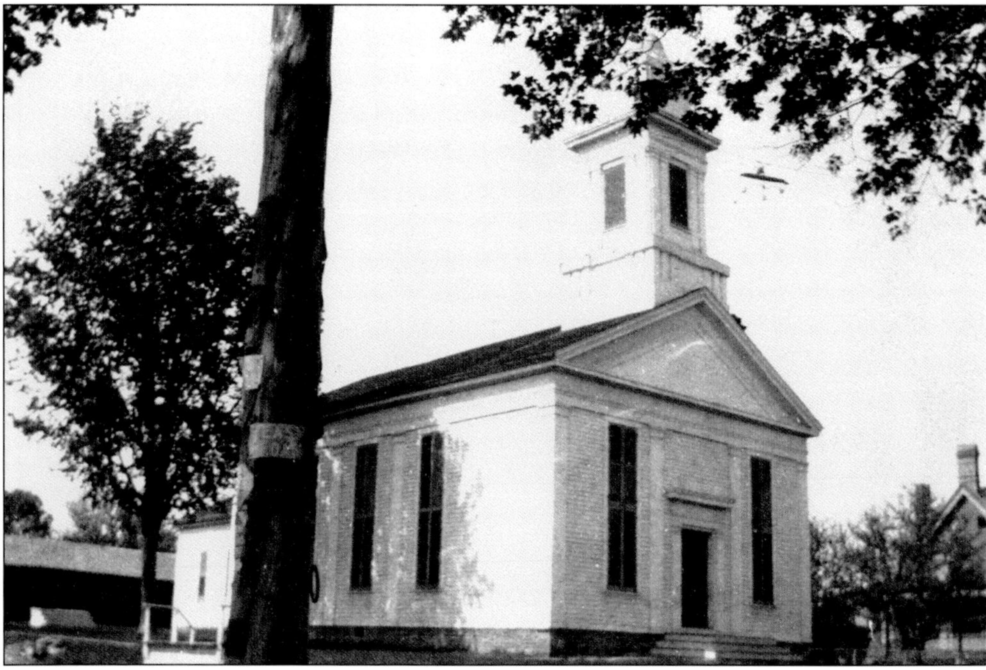

In the early 1850s, the First Baptist Church of Wheatland in Belcoda became the mother of a church in Mumford. The site on the corner of Main Street and Dakin Street was purchased, and Renssalaer Wilcox was engaged as the builder. The First Baptist Church of Mumford was dedicated in 1853, then electricity was installed in 1897, and stained-glass windows in 1903.

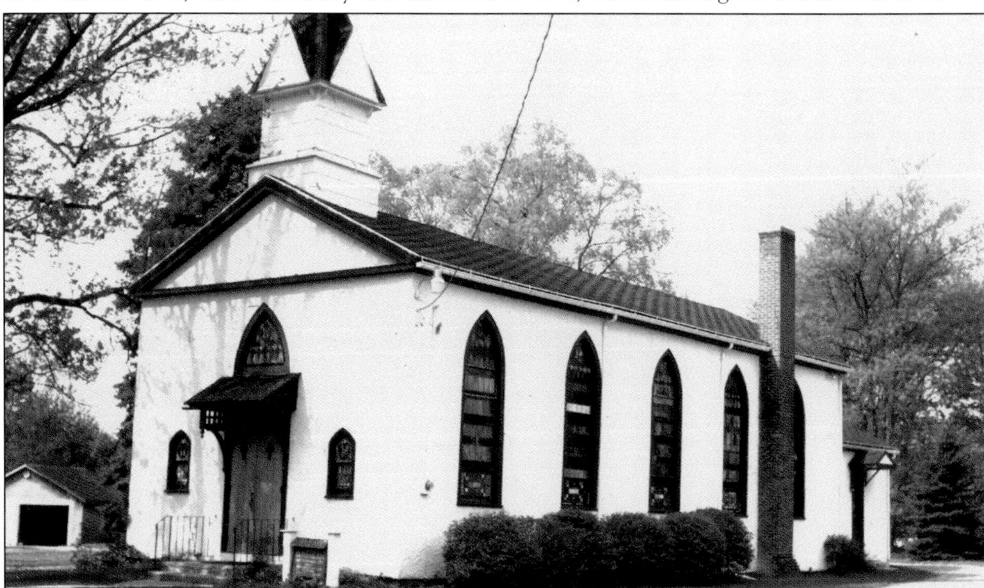

The Irish population of Wheatland had increased, and in 1848, a Catholic parish was established in Scottsville. For a time, mass was offered at Patrick Callan's house in Mumford, until funds were raised to build a church. After it was completed in 1854, St. Patrick's Roman Catholic Church served both the Caledonia and Mumford communities until Caledonia Catholics built St. Columba's Church in 1886. (Courtesy of Big Springs Historical Society and Museum.)

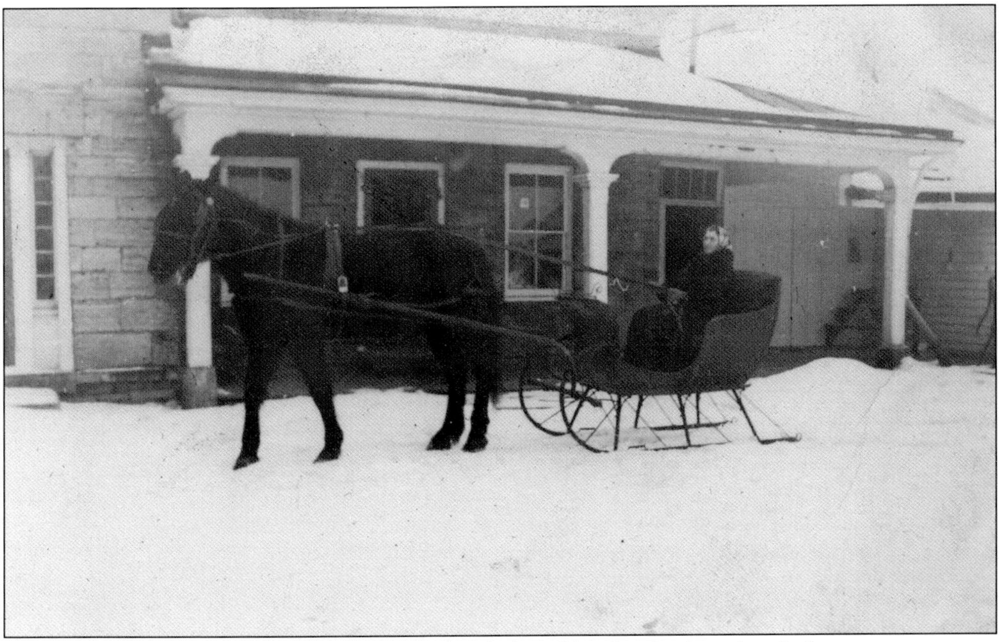

This is the homestead at 256 Guthrie Road, inhabited by the Guthrie family for six generations. It was constructed over a period of 10 years from tufa, a rare fossilized limestone, which is unique to the area. The house was built between 1830 and 1840 by Whiting Merry and purchased by the Guthrie family after the Civil War. The Guthries had come to western New York from Scotland with the early immigrants about 1800. Pictured below, seated in front of the homestead, are the Guthrie brothers, from left to right, Robert, William, and Andrew, with their hired men. Above, their sister, Jenny, was about to take a ride in the cutter. (Courtesy of Jean Guthrie.)

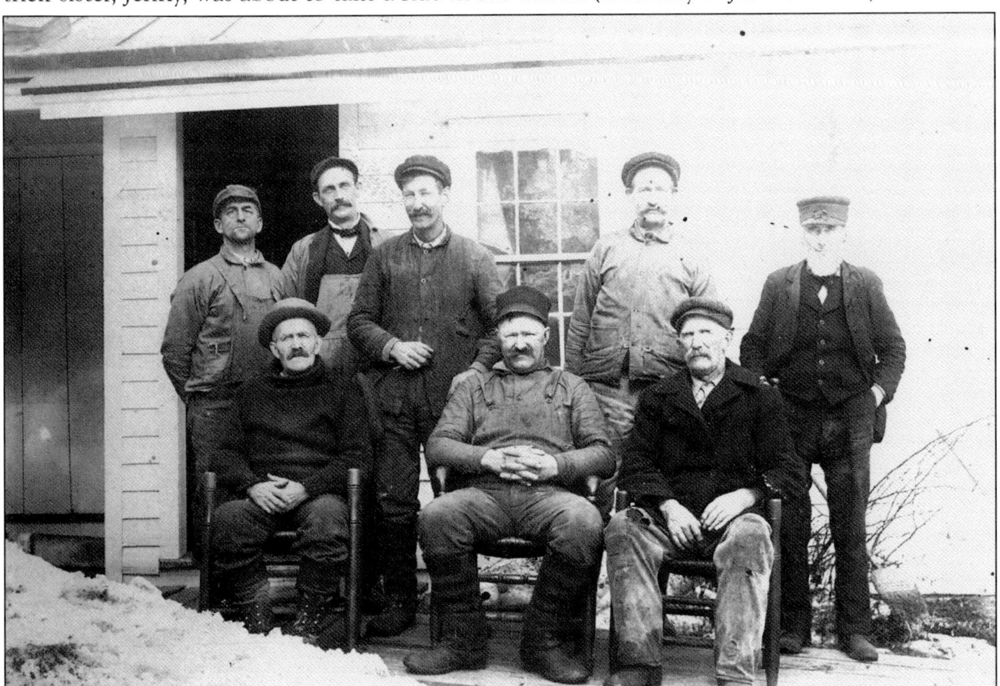

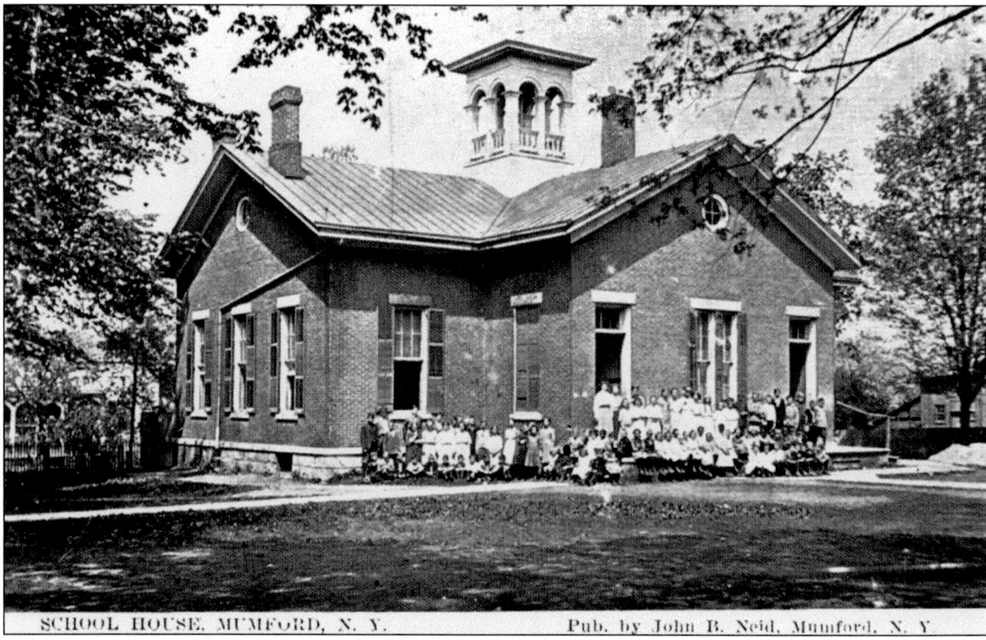

The first schoolhouse in Wheatland was a log cabin, built in 1803, east of Mumford on Oatka Creek. Later a schoolhouse for Wheatland District No. 8 in Mumford was located on William Street, and in 1832, that school was replaced with a building on Dakin Street. The fine brick schoolhouse above was built in 1860 on the corner of Dakin and William Streets. At that time, there were about 180 pupils enrolled in the school. Below, pupils of Ellen Guthrie pose in one of the classrooms of the Mumford School in 1906. Some of the familiar local names in the class were Skivington, Campbell, Baldeck, and Nichols.

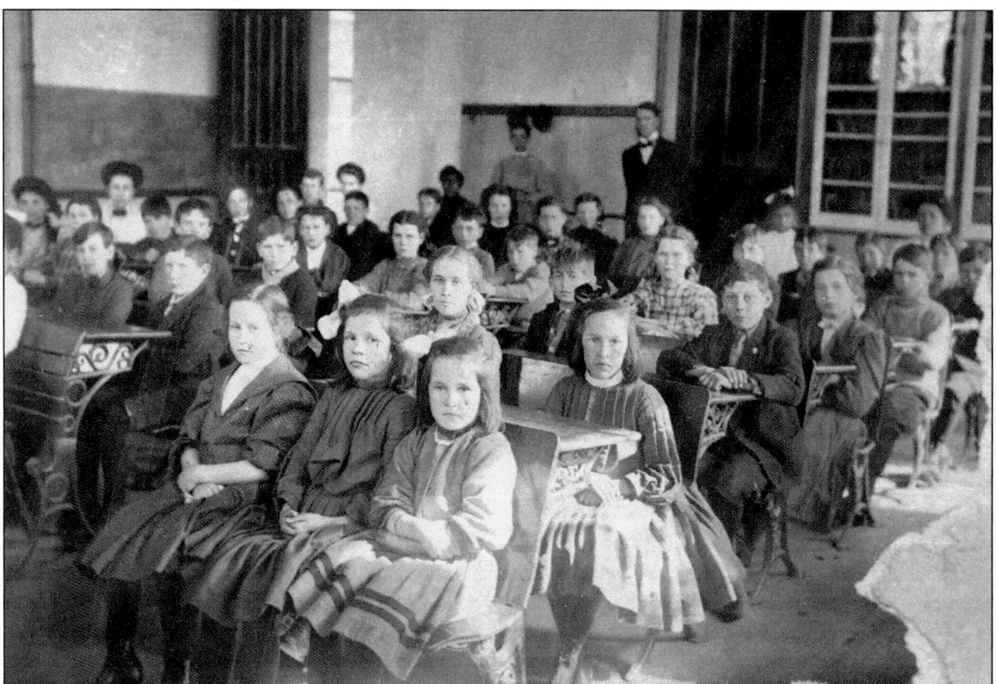

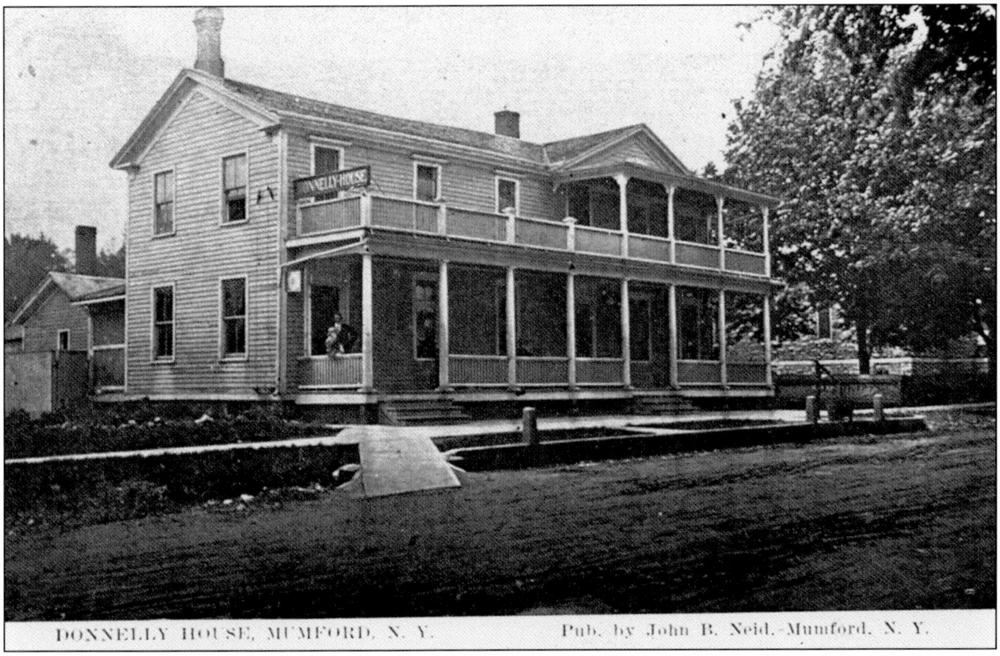

This was originally the home of the John McKenzie family. For a time in the 1870s, the Mumford village board refused to grant liquor licenses. McKenzie opened his house as a temperance hotel where he sold a drink called bitters that contained a small amount of whiskey. William Donnelly purchased the hotel and ran it as the Donnelly House from 1876 until 1904.

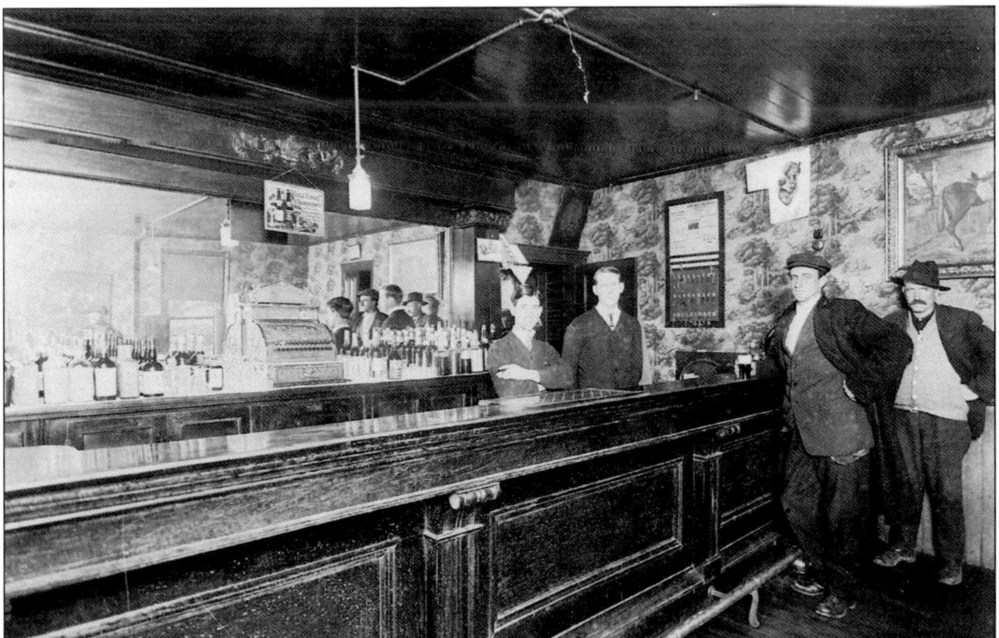

From the time Donnelly bought the hotel, the amount of whiskey in the bitters had increased, and the village board relented on granting liquor licenses. This taproom was located in the center room of the ground floor of the Donnelly House. The Town of Wheatland purchased the building in 1974 and renovated it into meeting rooms and offices. It now houses the Mumford Branch Library.

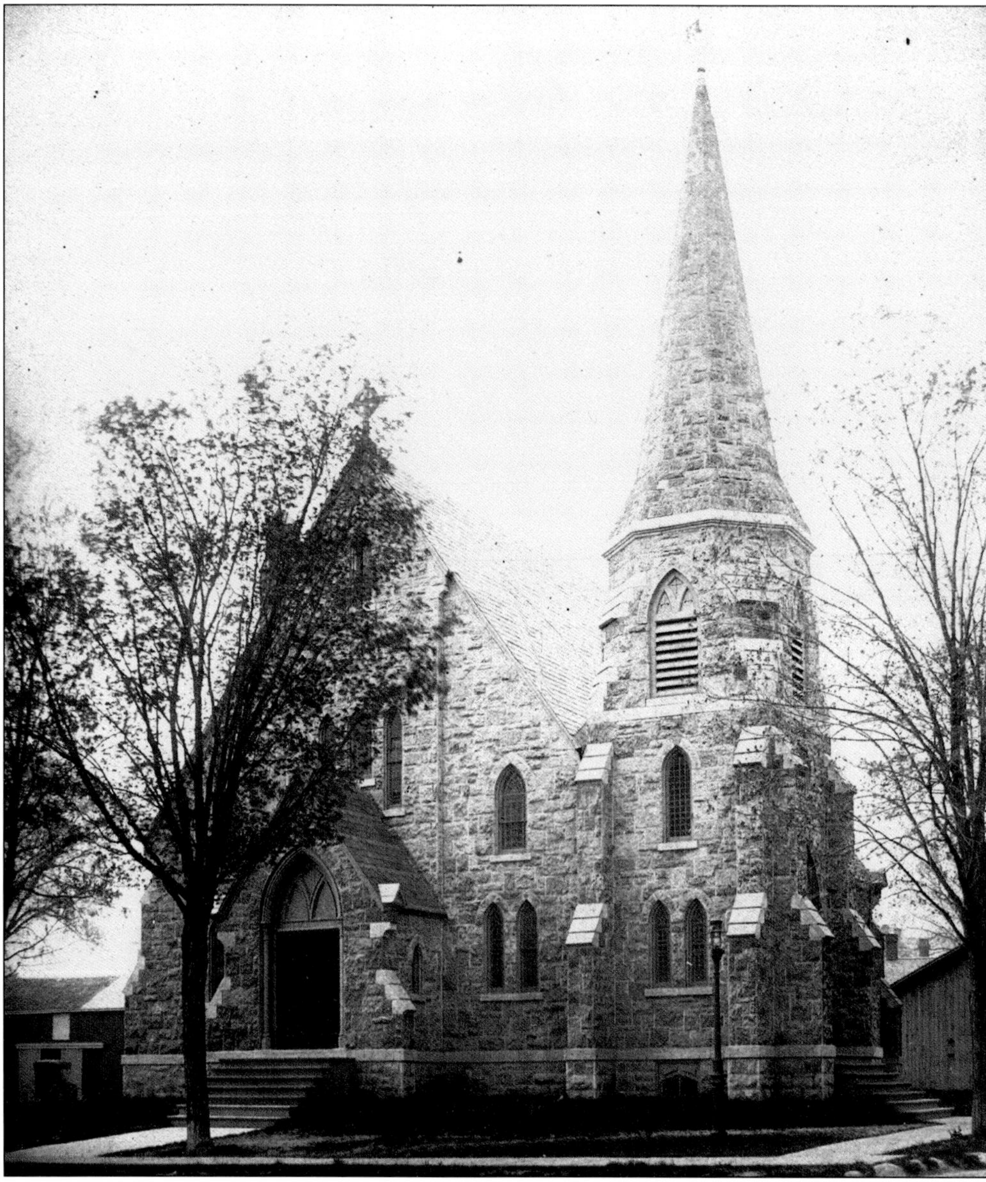

The United Presbyterian Church of Mumford was organized in 1869, and the next year construction began on the building on the corner of George Street and William Street. Architect A. J. Warner of Rochester designed the church to be built of bog limestone, or tufa, which was quarried on the farm of church member Oliver Allen. Bog limestone is a combination of petrified wood and vegetation that hardens as it is exposed to the atmosphere. The church's distinctive Gothic architecture and its unique construction have earned it a place on the National Register of Historic Places. (Courtesy of the First United Presbyterian Church of Mumford.)

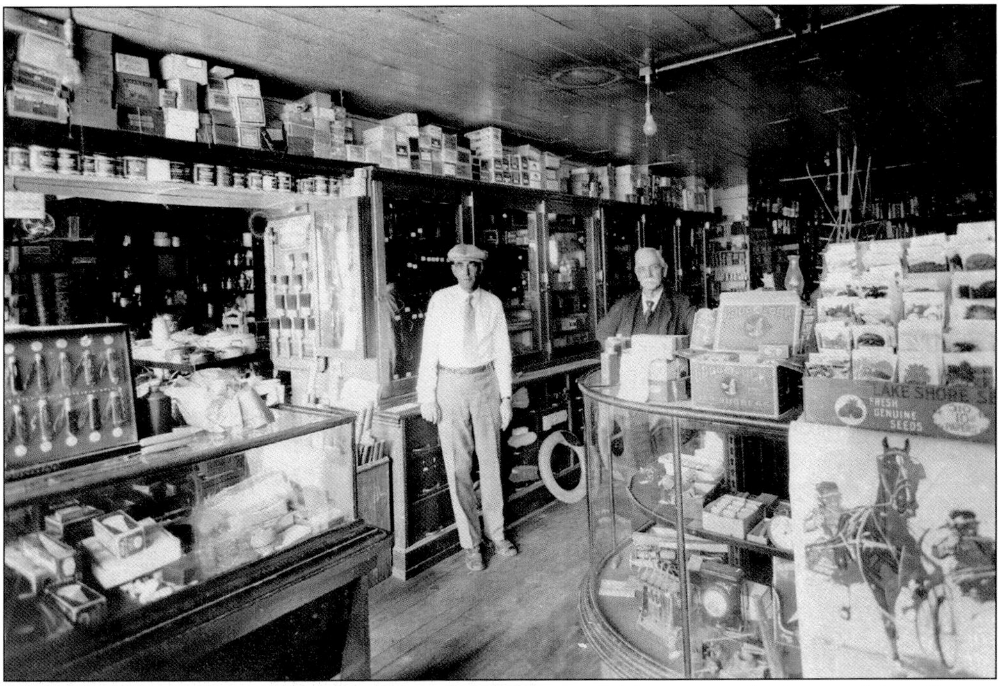

John E. Harvey came to Mumford about 1880 and opened his tinsmith shop on Main Street. Business was good, so he moved to larger quarters, built a new storefront, and then bought out a nearby hardware store in 1900. His son, Harry, joined him in the business, and they enlarged the store again in 1907. John E. (right) and Harry Harvey are pictured above. Below is a photograph of Harry and Daisy Ward Harvey in their carriage in front of their Queen Anne–style house at 18 Dakin Street.

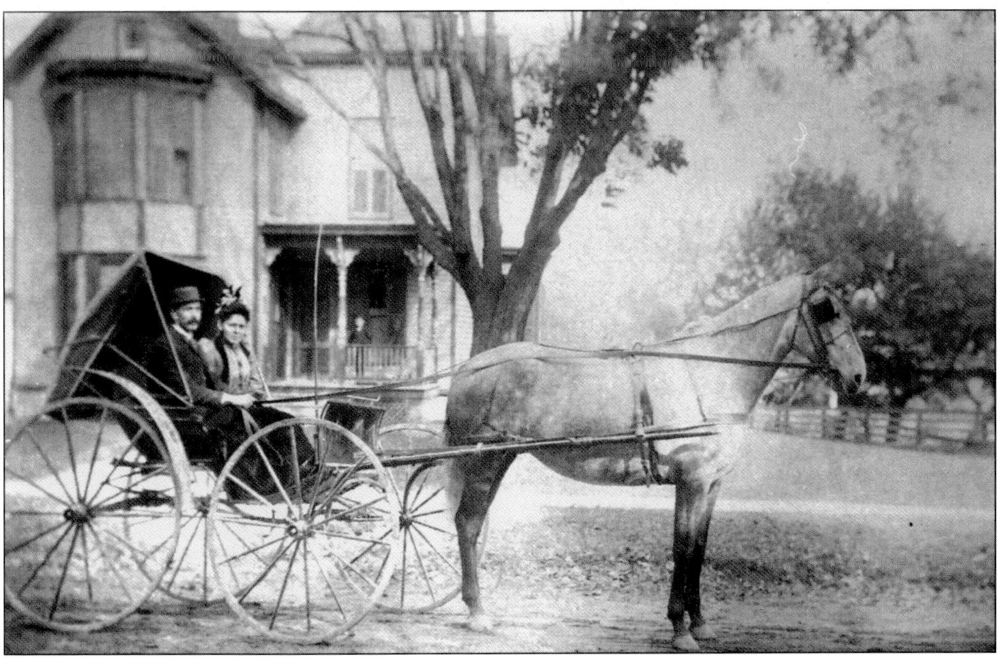

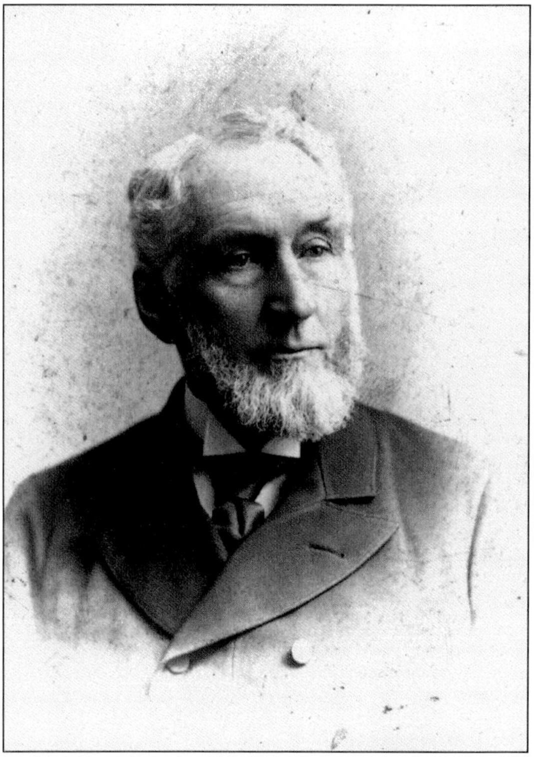

Donald McNaughton, the son of pioneer John C. McNaughton, attended the local schools, studied law, and was then admitted to the bar in 1865. He was one of the promoters of the Rochester and State Line Railroad. He served several terms as supervisor of Wheatland and in Albany as 29th District state senator from 1888 until 1892. He died in 1893.

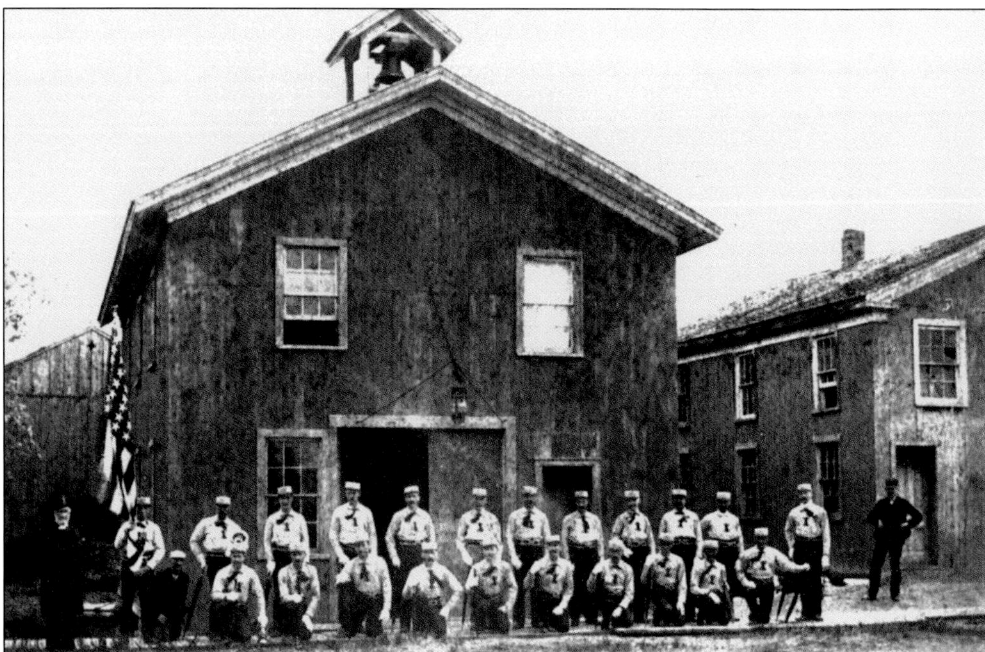

The Mumford Fire Hall, shown here about 1880, stood on the south side of George Street across from Brookside Drive. The man on the left in the stovepipe hat is Sen. Donald McNaughton. Pat Freeman is holding the flag. The building was razed, and the fire company moved to the Mumford Community Building in 1937.

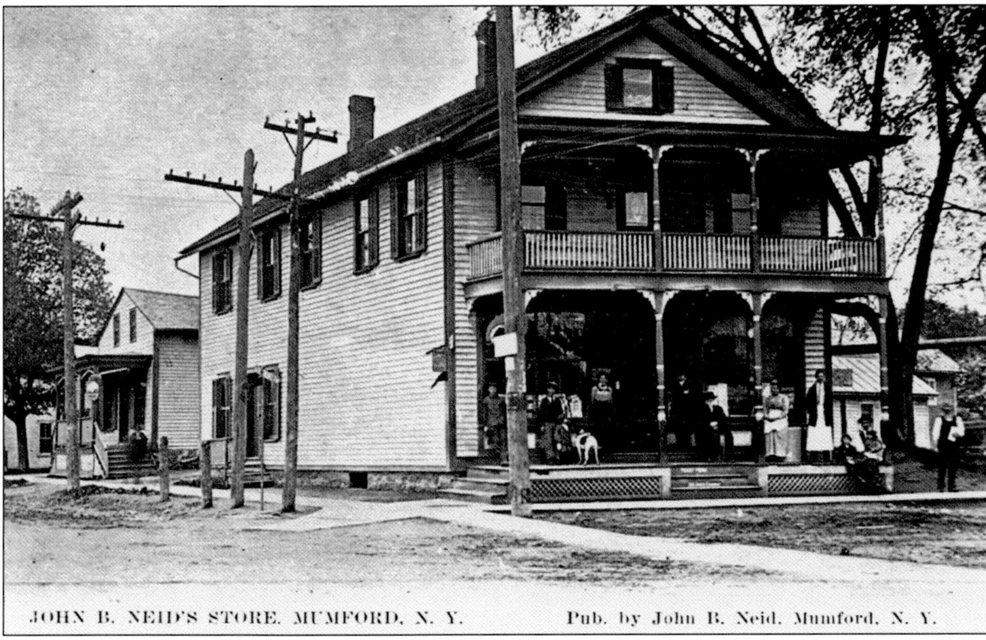

John Neid operated a general store in Mumford from about 1885 until his death in 1926. For a time, he drove a peddler's wagon around the countryside while his partner, Chester Woodward, clerked in their store. In 1902, he opened this new store on the southwest of the four corners at 875 George Street. Following him, John Lockard and John H. Sheehan ran the store.

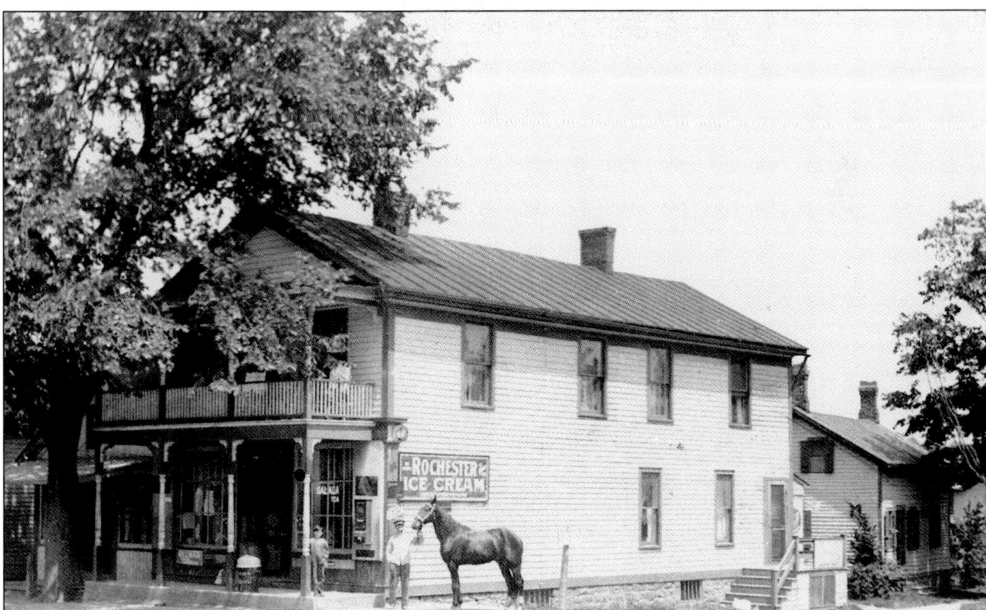

John Frey purchased the store on the northeast of the four corners at 1020 Main Street in 1907. It had been a general store since the 1850s run by Otis Comstock, Milton Hyde, and others. This 1913 photograph was taken during the time it was Frey's Store. He died in 1946, and the store was taken over by John H. Sheehan, who moved across the corner to this location.

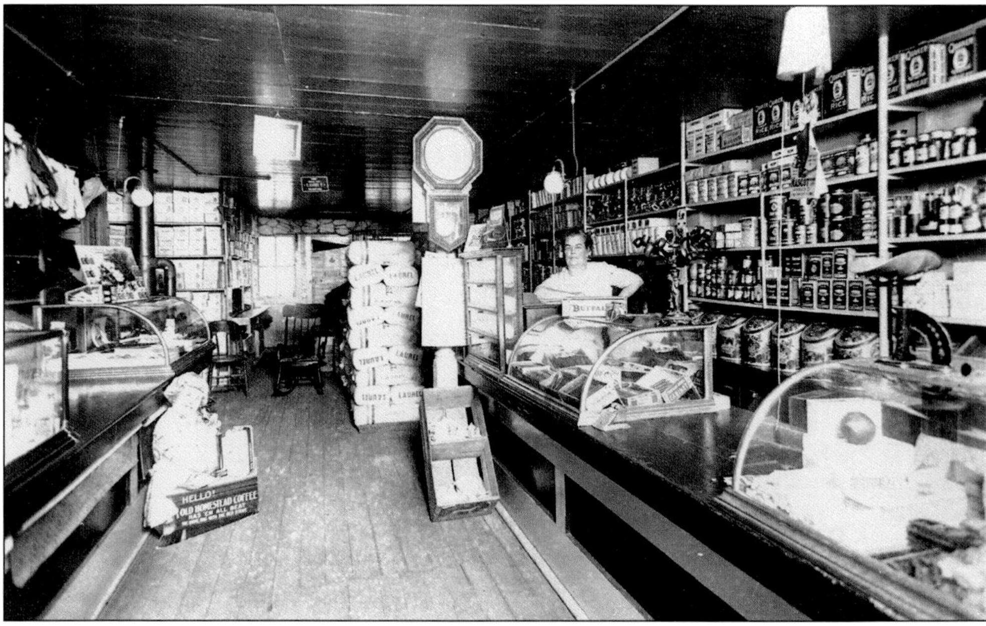

Lewis and Katherine Wilson ran this store at 1014 Main Street from about 1901 until 1929. Katherine Wilson is shown in this picture. Ashley Price was its first storekeeper. James McQueen operated it and was postmaster there in the 1860s. The Wilsons were succeeded by their son-in-law, A. J. Baldeck.

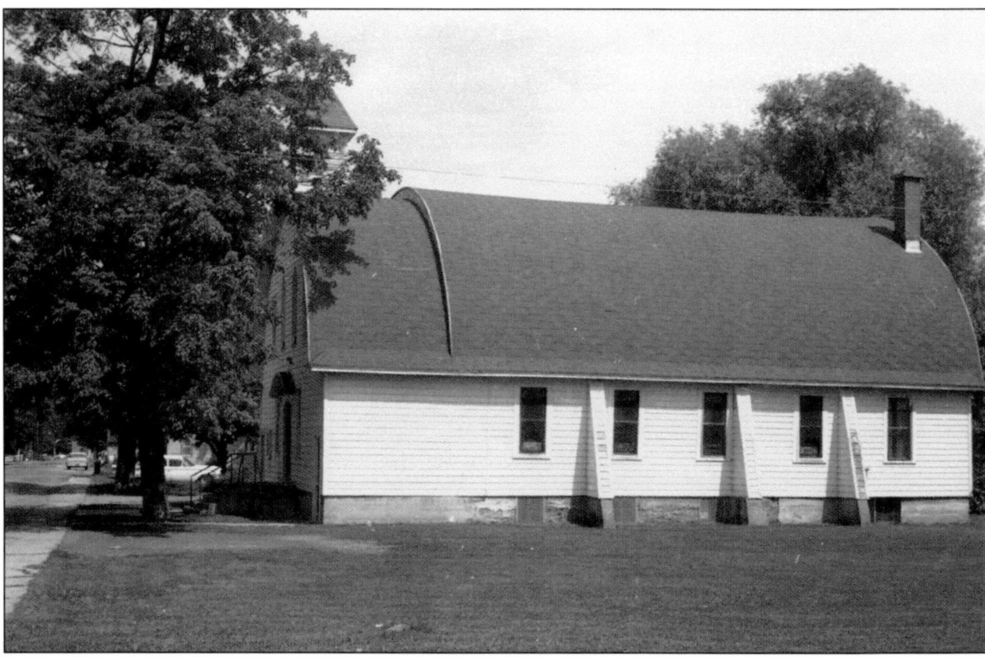

The Second Baptist Church of Mumford was actually started in Belcoda by the Reverend Clayton Coles, a former slave. After meeting for some time in the parsonage of the Belcoda Church, the African American congregation was able to construct a building, which was moved to George Street in Mumford in 1891. The church has been remodeled a number of times. This picture shows what it looked like in 1964.

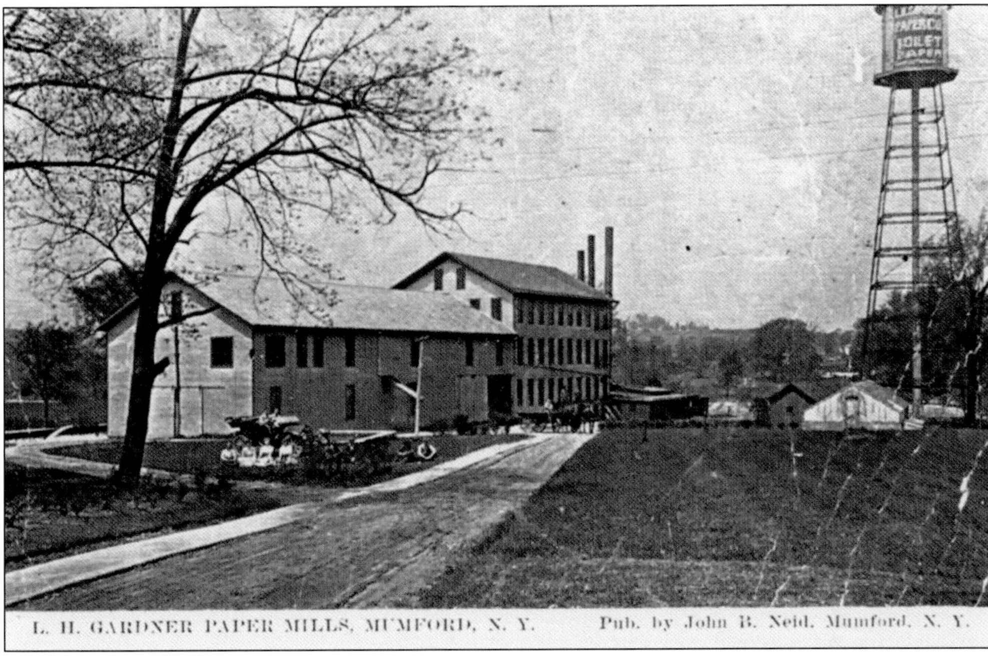

The business on Spring Creek in Mumford that made smoking pipes relocated to Elmira in 1904, and the former woolen mill and pipe factory was recycled into a paper mill. The L. H. Gardner Paper Company employed 20 to 30 people and produced 5,000 to 7,000 pounds of paper per day. In 1915, the company was reorganized as the Mumford Mills, which made toilet paper, embossed napkins, tablecloths, and towels. In 1939, the machinery and trade names were transferred to a southern company, and the doors were closed.

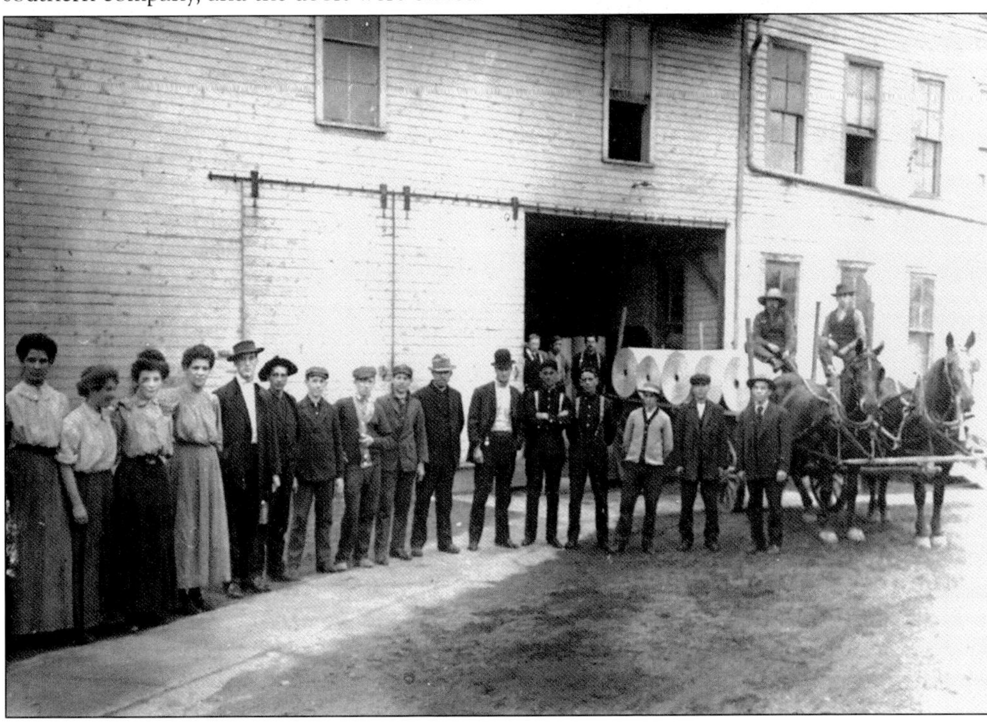

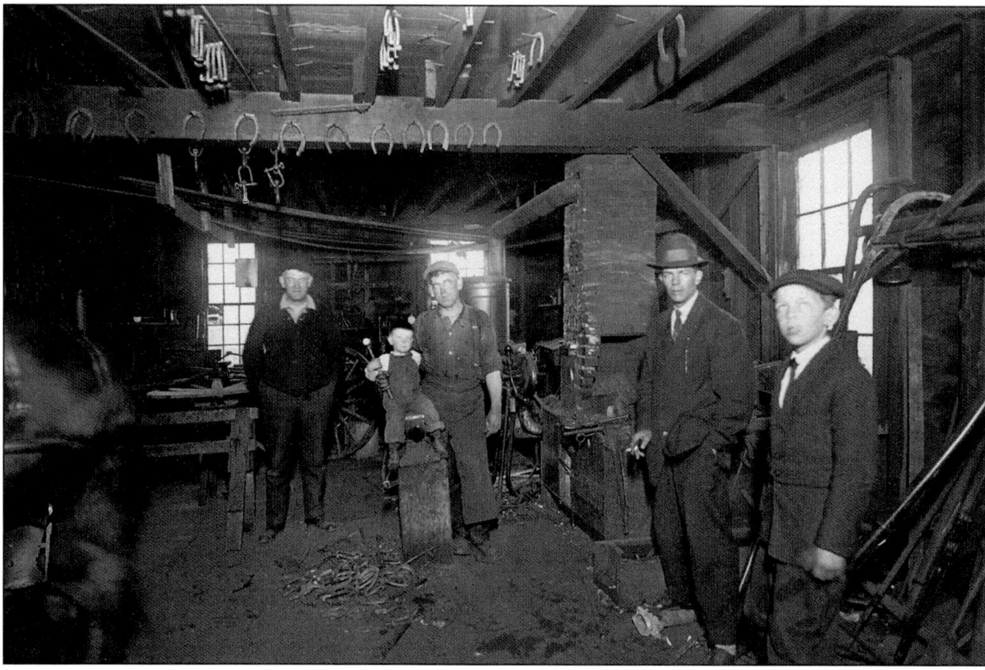

In 1884, the Nichols family built a new carriage shop on the corner of George Street and Brookside Drive with a blacksmith shop in the rear. In 1912, Robert Nichols and his partner, Neil Purdie, took over the blacksmith shop. Nichols continued the business into the 1920s. This photograph shows, from left to right, Bill Buckley; John Nichols, the boy; Rocky Nichols, his father; Harry Kinney; and David Belleau.

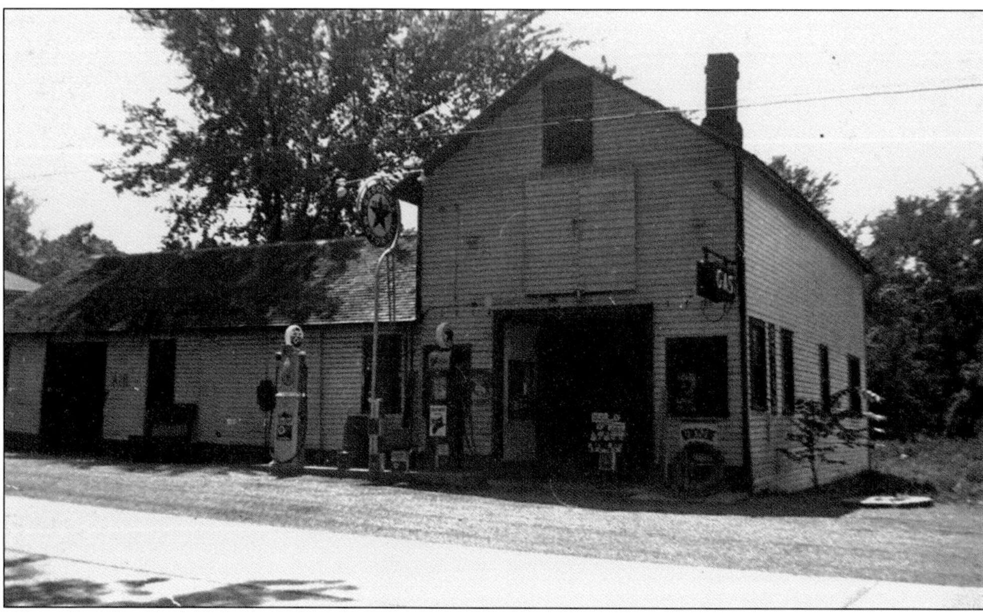

In 1899, Patrick Hickey built a blacksmith shop on the west side of Main Street, and in the early years of his business, he charged $1 to shoe a horse. Hickey had been born in Ireland, and, after coming to Mumford, he learned blacksmithing from James Freeman. After 47 years, the old smithy retired, and the shop became a gas station and automobile repair business.

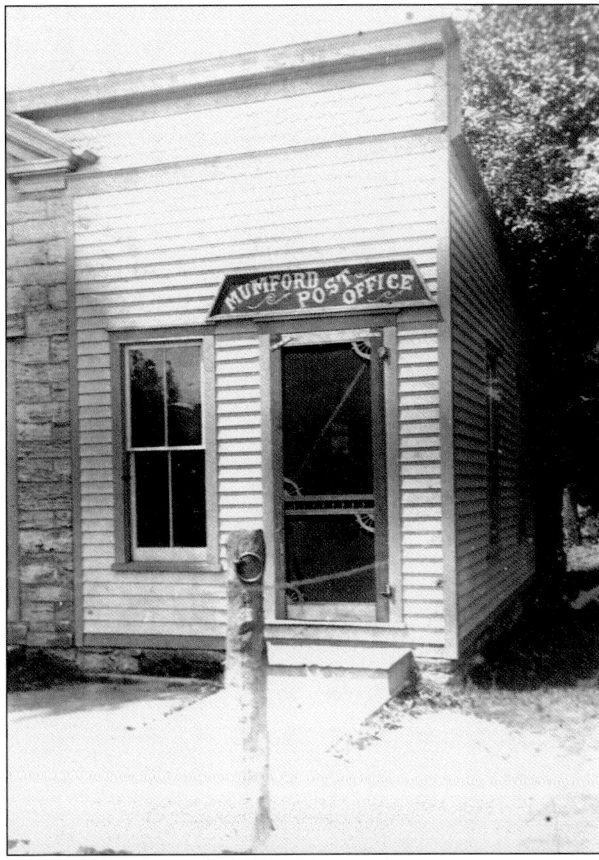

The Mumford Post Office has been located on each of the four corners of Main Street at some point in its history. In 1893, William Buckley was appointed postmaster and moved the post office from Harvey's Hardware to this little bog limestone and frame building on the west side, where it remained until it was moved to its present quarters on Dakin Street in 1962. Below is a photograph of John A. Campbell, who was postmaster from 1923 until 1938.

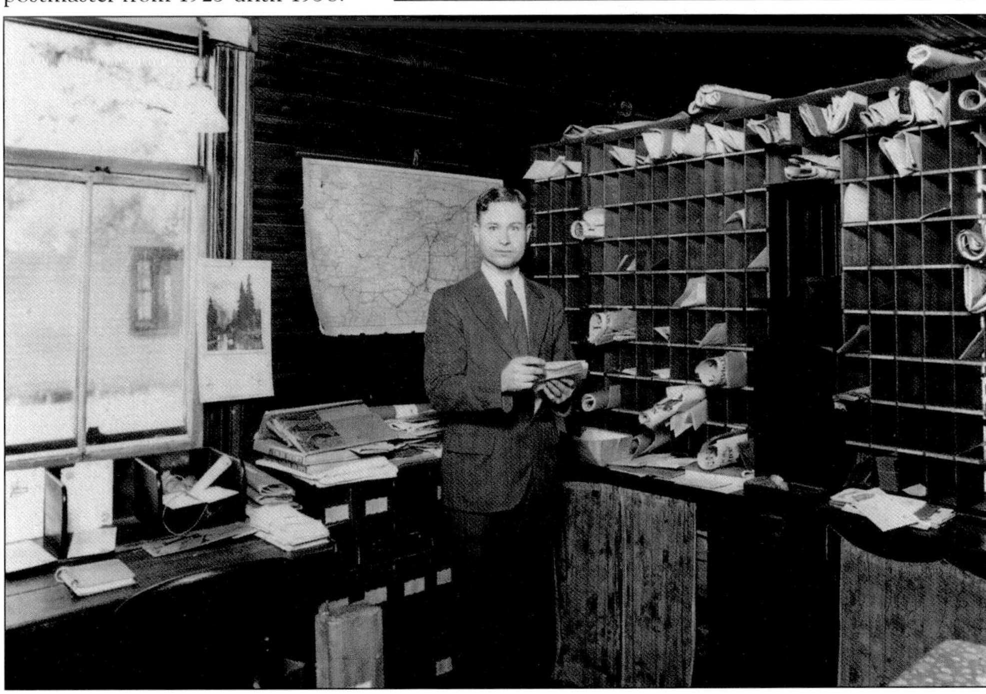

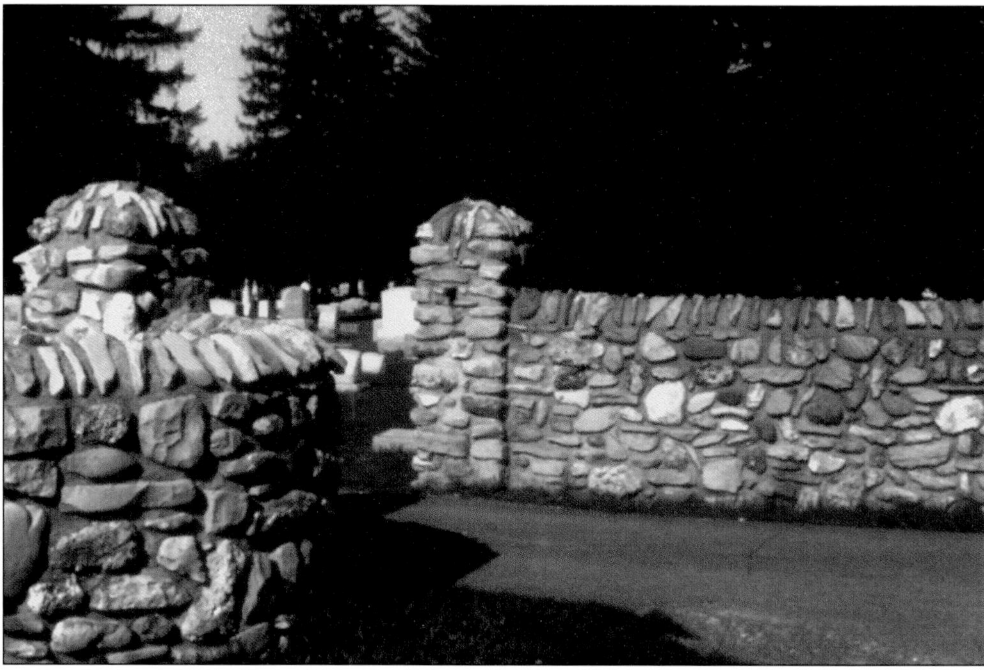

In 1929, Valance and Alexander Hamilton employed Wells Rulifson to build the beautiful stone wall at the Mumford Rural Cemetery. The stone wall, which serves as a memorial to the early citizens of the area, was dedicated on May 30, 1930, with Rochester judge Harvey Remington as the speaker. (Courtesy of Big Springs Historical Society and Museum.)

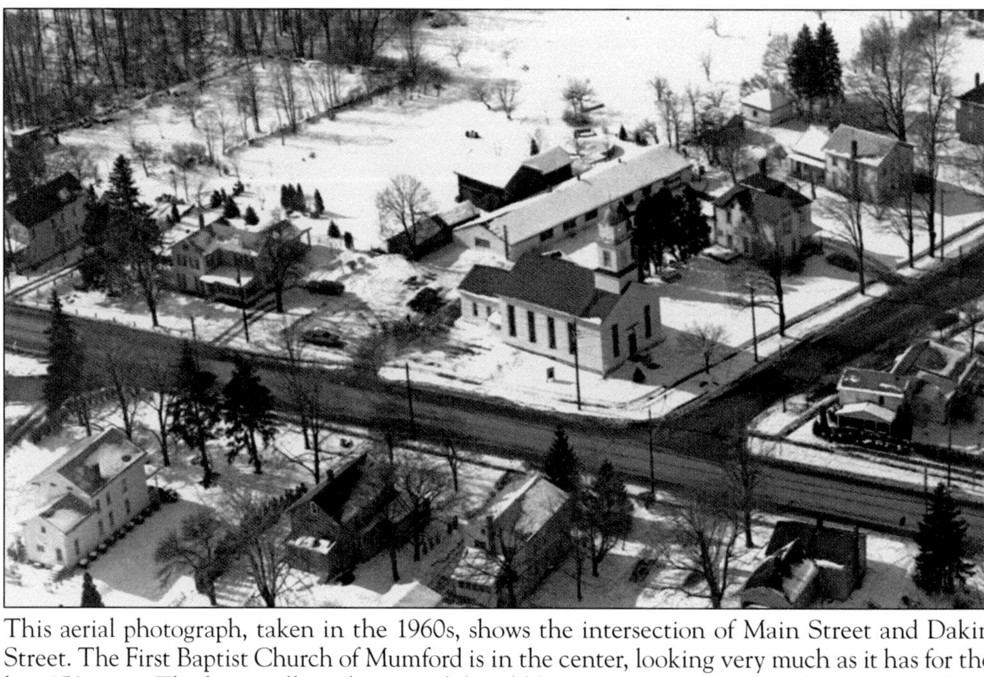

This aerial photograph, taken in the 1960s, shows the intersection of Main Street and Dakin Street. The First Baptist Church of Mumford is in the center, looking very much as it has for the last 150 years. The busy mills and many of the old businesses are gone, but the location of the Genesee Country Village and Museum nearby has made Mumford and the town of Wheatland a major tourist destination in western New York.

Four

North Road and South Road Settlements

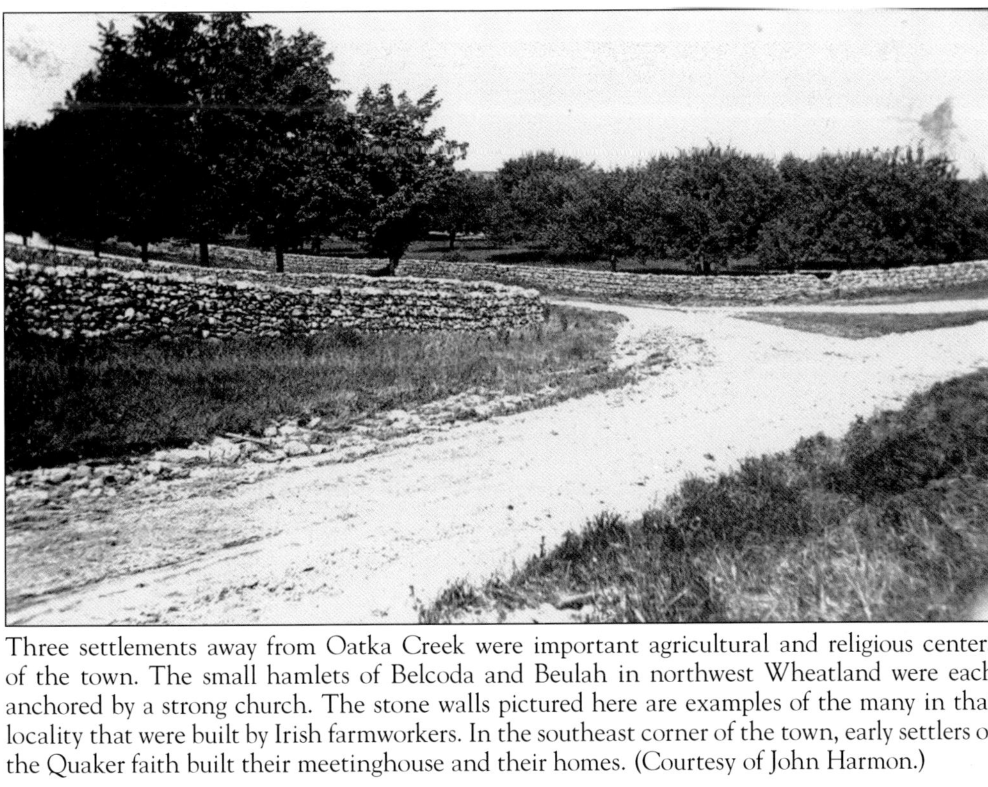

Three settlements away from Oatka Creek were important agricultural and religious centers of the town. The small hamlets of Belcoda and Beulah in northwest Wheatland were each anchored by a strong church. The stone walls pictured here are examples of the many in that locality that were built by Irish farmworkers. In the southeast corner of the town, early settlers of the Quaker faith built their meetinghouse and their homes. (Courtesy of John Harmon.)

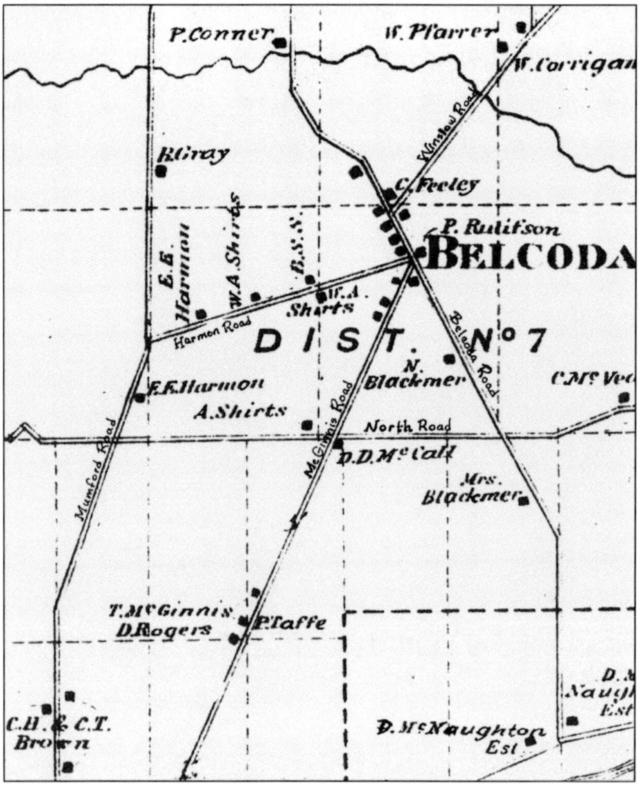

The settlement known as Belcoda is at the intersection of Harmon, Belcoda, and McGinnis Roads. The first settlers were the Farwells, who came in 1800. They built a brick kiln and a small mill on the stream that empties into Blue Pond. Names of later settlers are seen on this modified 1872 map: the Blackmers, the Shirts, and the Harmons.

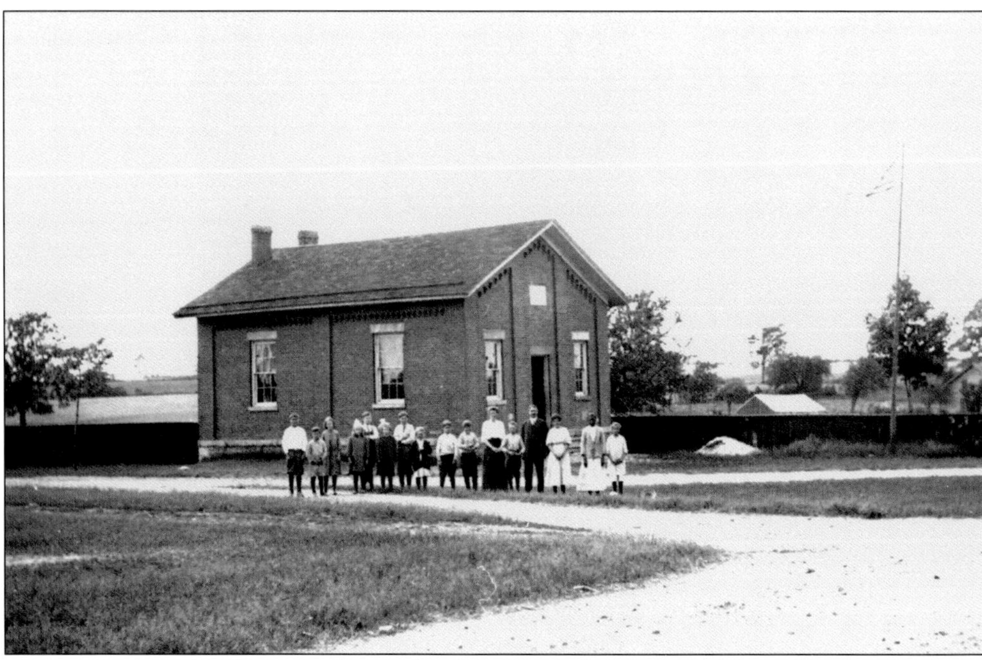

There was a log schoolhouse built in Wheatland District No. 7 in Belcoda before 1811. In 1867, this fine brick schoolhouse replaced an earlier brick building. Local children walked to school here until 1942 when the school closed, and they were transported to the Caledonia school by bus.

This boulder marking the site of the First Baptist Church of Wheatland was dedicated in 1917. Organized in 1811, the Belcoda church became one of the strongest in its denomination. Three other congregations, the Baptist Church of Clifton, the Baptist Church of Churchville, and the First Baptist Church of Mumford, were formed from it, which so weakened the mother church that it closed in 1870.

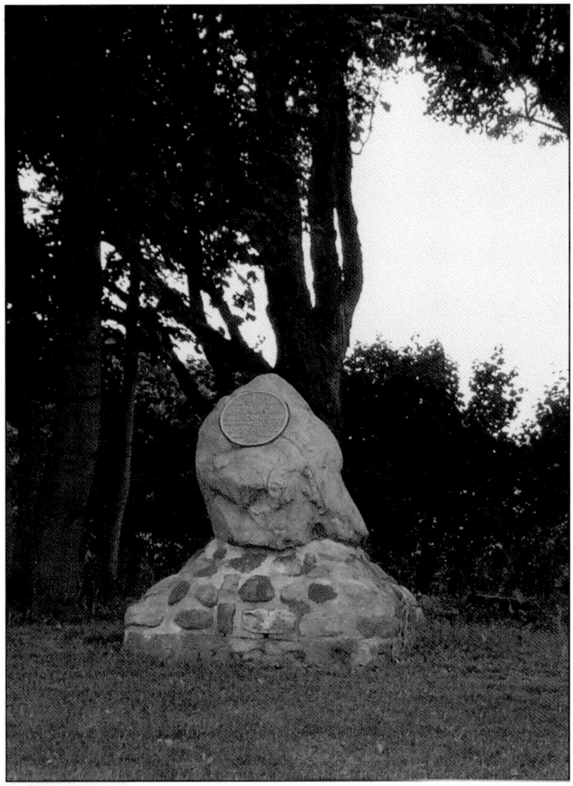

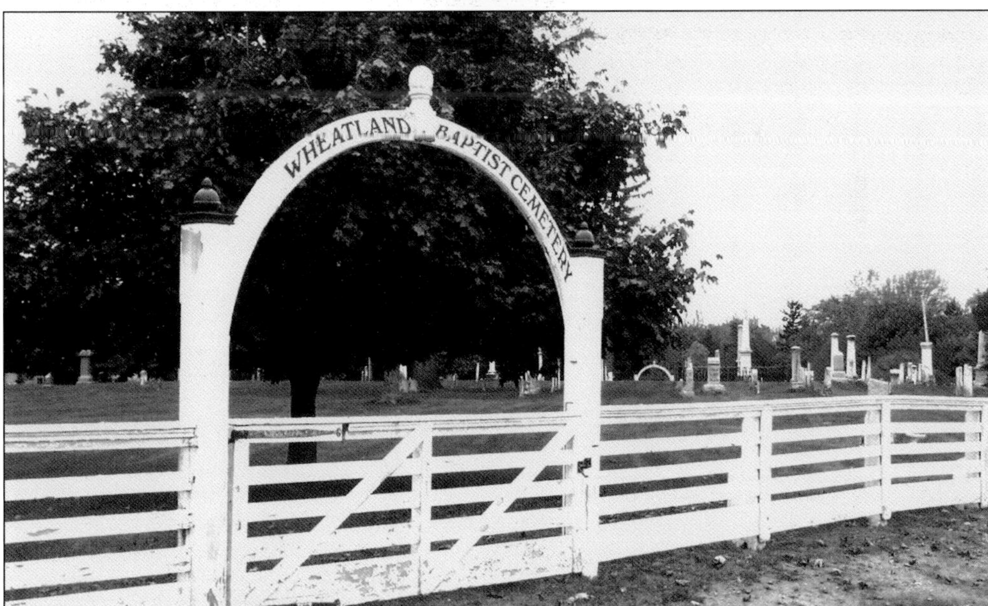

Opposite the church site on McGinnis Road is the Belcoda cemetery with its striking Greek Revival–style fence. After the church closed, the Wheatland Cemetery Association was formed in 1881, and is still active today. Rev. Clayton Coles, a former slave and body servant for Thomas Jonathan "Stonewall" Jackson, came to Wheatland after the Civil War and is buried here.

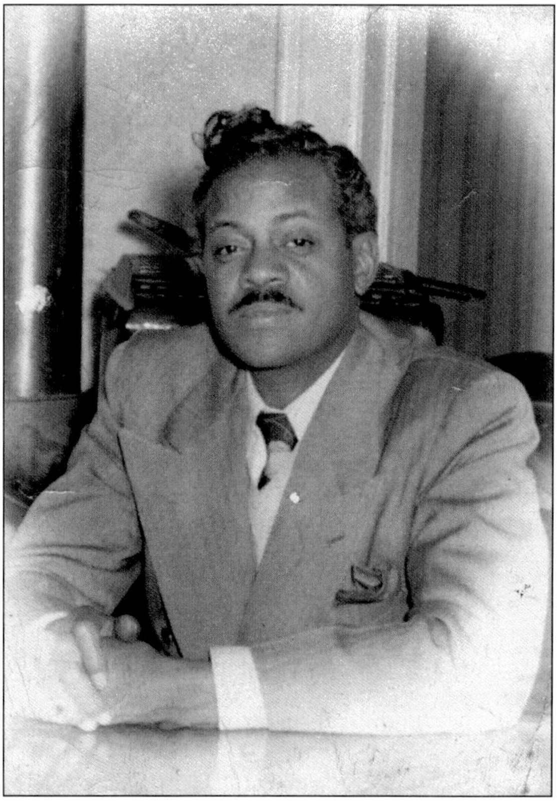

Howard Wilson Coles, grandson of Rev. Clayton Coles, was born in Belcoda in 1903. He became the publisher of an African American newspaper, the *Voice*, a radio personality, and a civil rights activist in Rochester. Howard Coles authored *The Cradle of Freedom*, which documented African American life in the city. He died in 1996 and is buried in the Belcoda Cemetery. (Courtesy of the Howard W. Coles Collection, Rochester Museum and Science Center.)

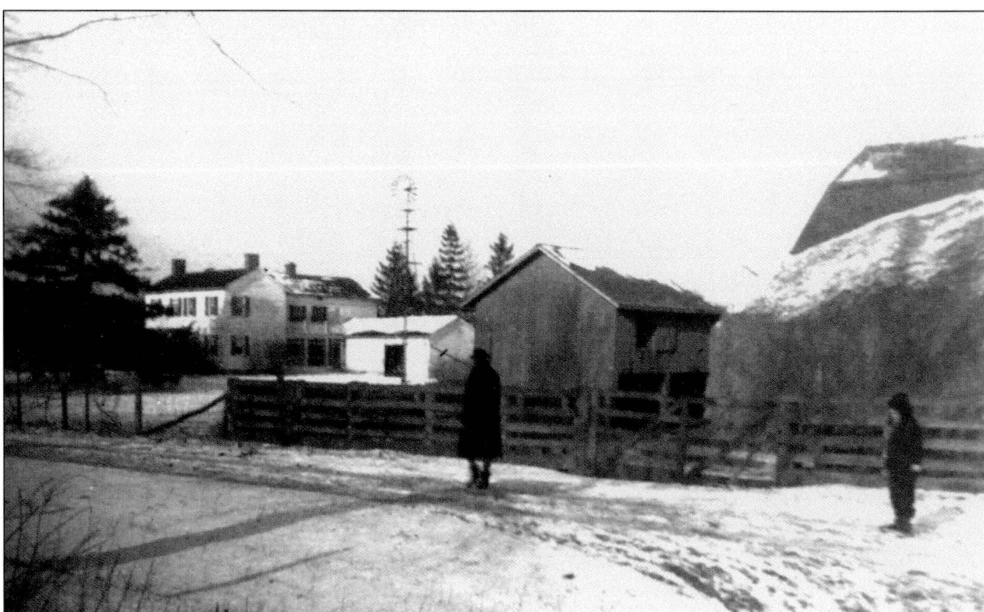

This large Federal-style house, at 196 Harmon Road, was built by William Shirts in 1825. He was a tanner and a staunch member and chorister of the First Baptist Church of Wheatland in Belcoda. Eugene E. Harmon purchased the property from the Shirts family, and his daughters named it Camperdown Farm. (Courtesy of John Harmon.)

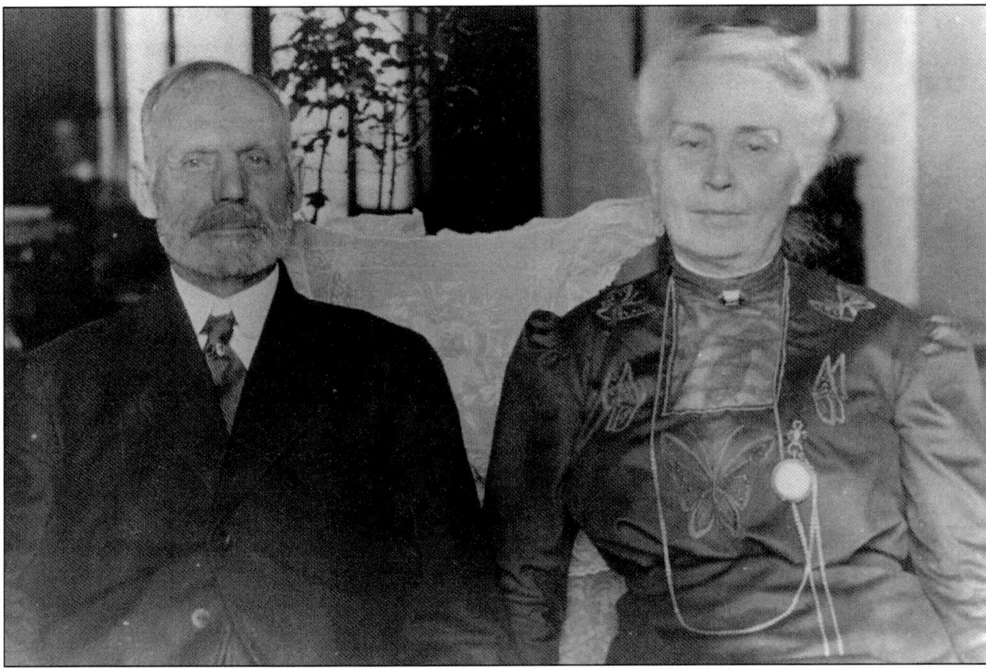

Eugene E. Harmon was the son of Ira Harmon, who had come to Wheatland in 1811 from Massachusetts with his parents, Deacon Rawson Harmon I and Lydia, and his five brothers and five sisters. Eugene's wife, Marion, was the granddaughter of early settler Duncan McPherson. (Courtesy of John Harmon.)

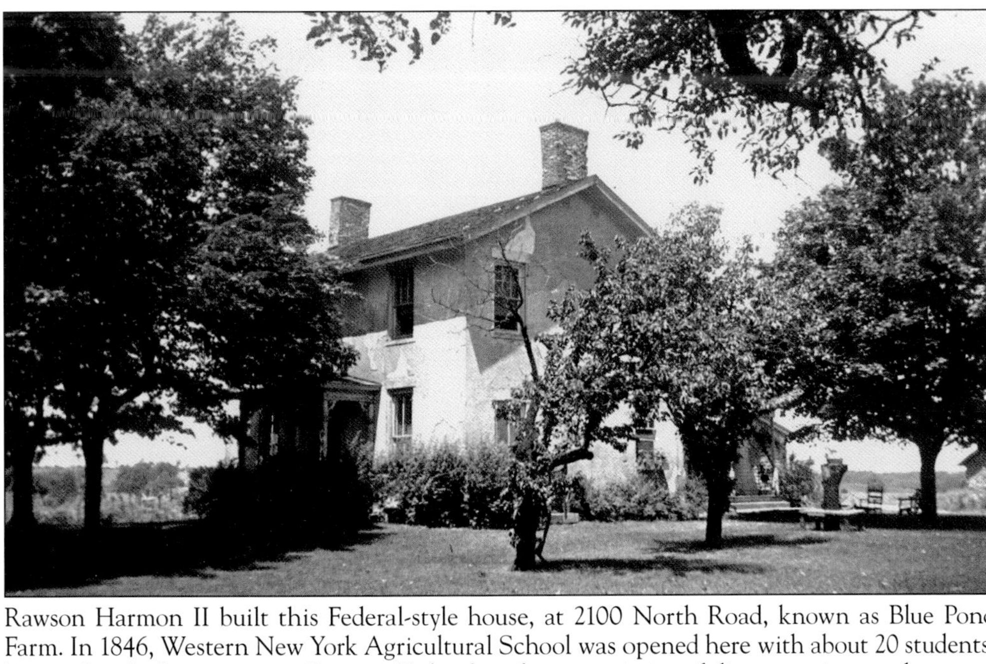

Rawson Harmon II built this Federal-style house, at 2100 North Road, known as Blue Pond Farm. In 1846, Western New York Agricultural School was opened here with about 20 students, but it closed after one year. Rawson II developed new varieties of disease-resistant wheat and won first prize for wheat entered in the Great Exhibition of the Works of Industry of All Nations, London's 1851 world's fair.

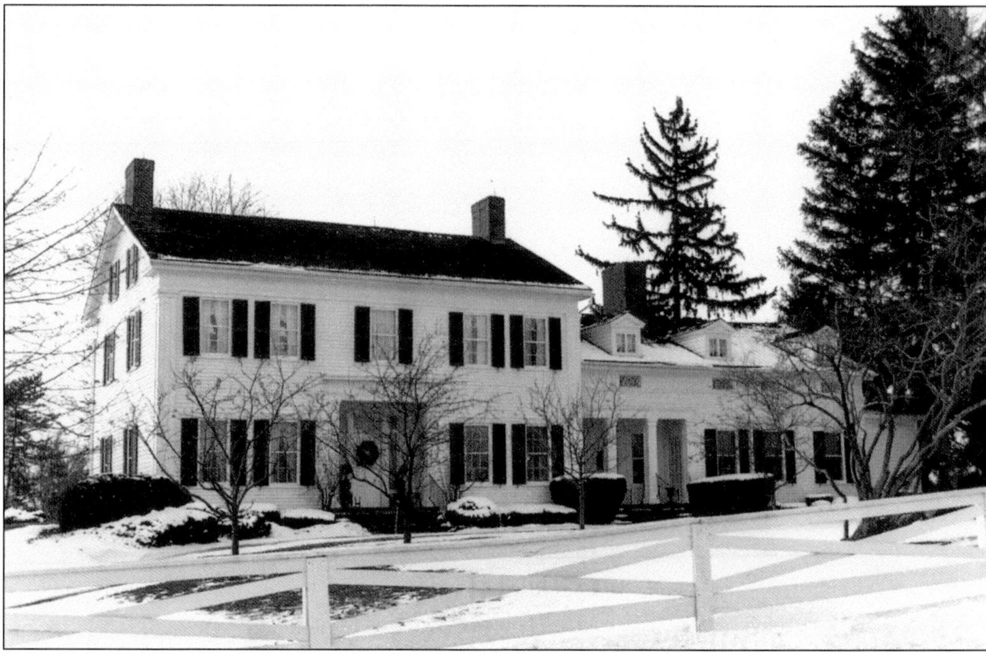

This important example of domestic Greek Revival architecture, at 2286 Mumford Road, was built by Theron Brown about 1840. Rev. Solomon Brown, Theron's father, was the first pastor of the Wheatland Baptist church at Belcoda from 1813 until his death in 1815. Theron was supervisor of Wheatland in 1837 and 1838. This property was later known as the Dow Farm. (Courtesy of the Landmark Society of Western New York.)

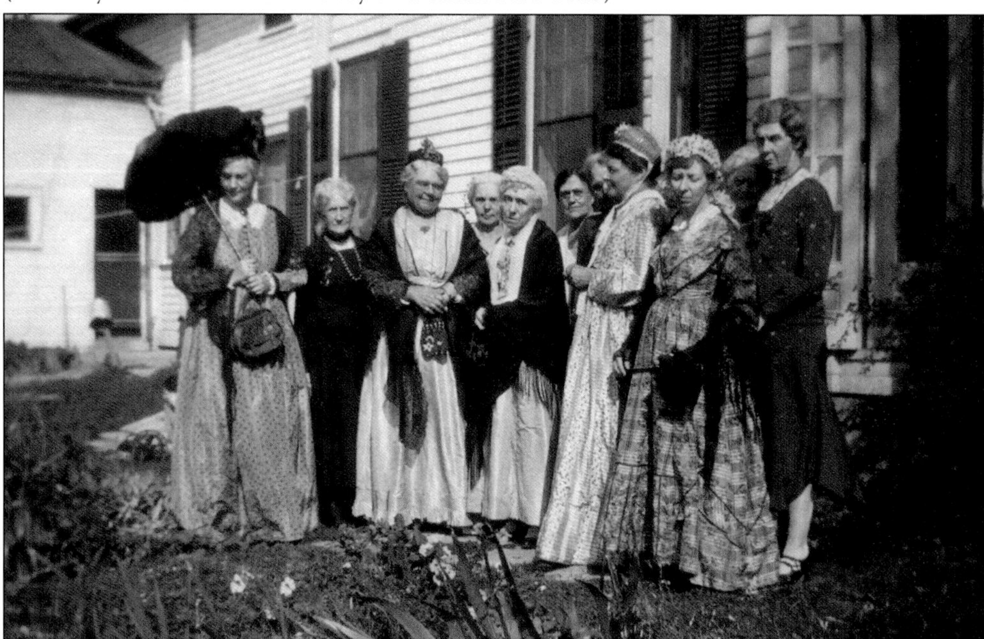

This photograph was taken at the Dow Farm in 1931. A group of Belcoda ladies are reenacting an old-time quilting party. A daughter of Eugene E. Harmon, Isabel is at the far left, and her sister, Mary, is fourth from the right. The hostess, Hattie Brown Dow, is second from the left.

Beulah is the name of a hamlet and a road that crosses North Road a few miles west of Belcoda. On the day of the "raising" of the Presbyterian church in 1851, the speaker quoted the Bible verse, Isaiah 62:4, about a place called Beulah, and the name stuck. It is shown in this modified section of the Wheatland map from the 1872 F. W. Beers *Atlas of Monroe County, N.Y.*

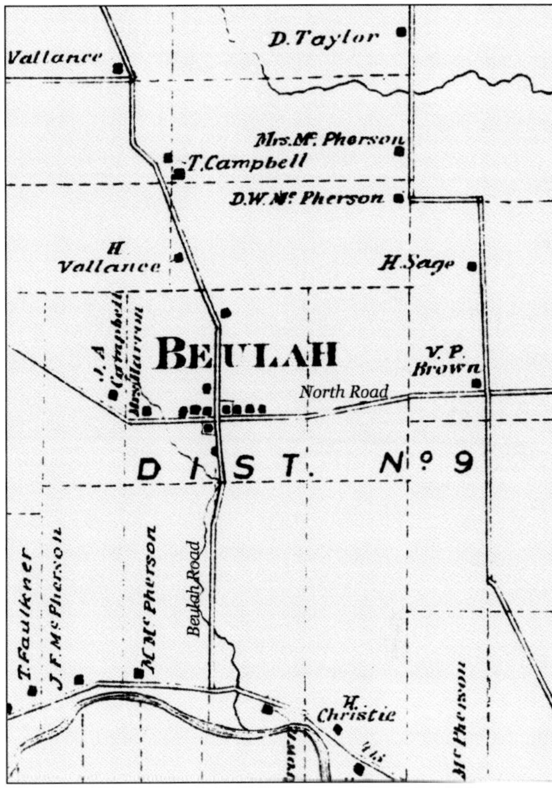

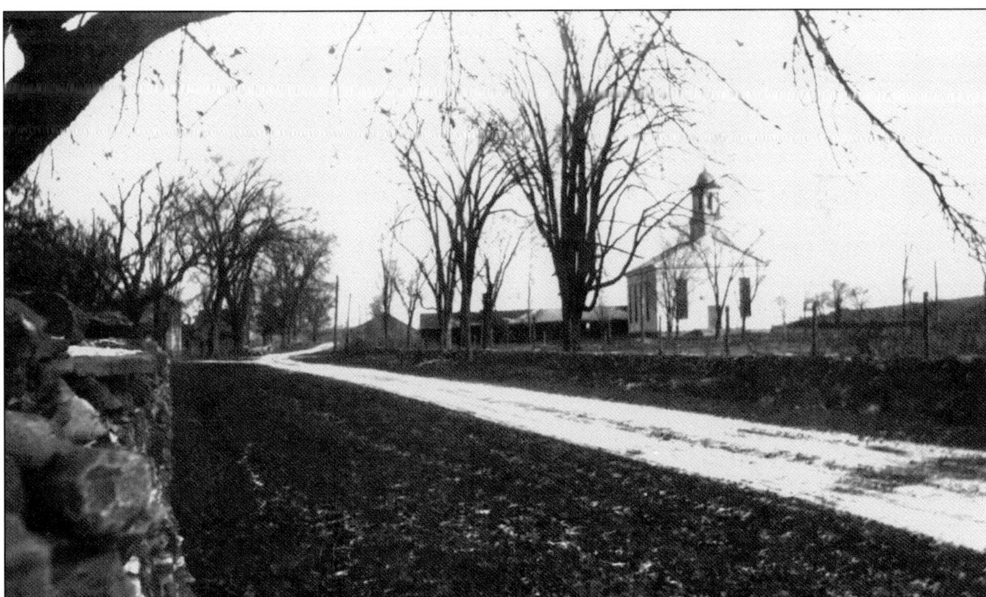

The United Presbyterian Church of Beulah was formally organized in 1852 with 27 members. Up until that time local descendants of the Scottish settlers had attended the Stone Presbyterian Church in Caledonia. For many years, it was a busy and active congregation, but during the 1920s, it gradually declined and was eventually disbanded. Note the low sheds that sheltered the horses and vehicles during church services. (Courtesy of John Harmon.)

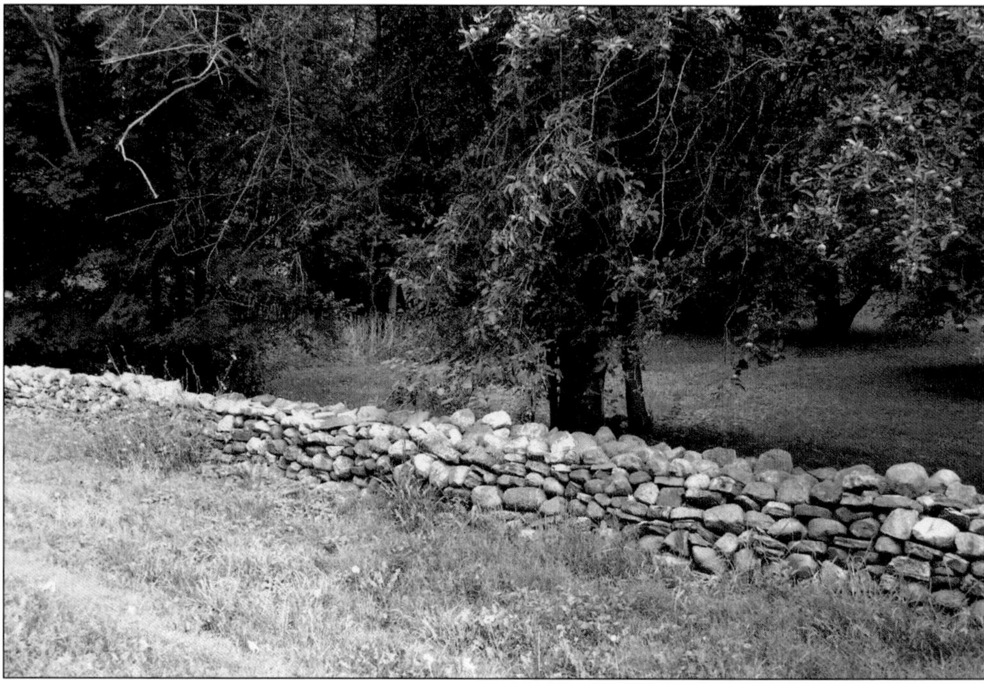

Wheatland has the most outstanding and extensive collection of these 19th-century stone fences in Monroe County. They were built by immigrants who had come to the area during the potato famine in Ireland. Some of those who learned the trade of farm-wall layer or dry wall mason were Owen Farmer, Peter Taffe, John and Thomas Callan, and Terrance McCall.

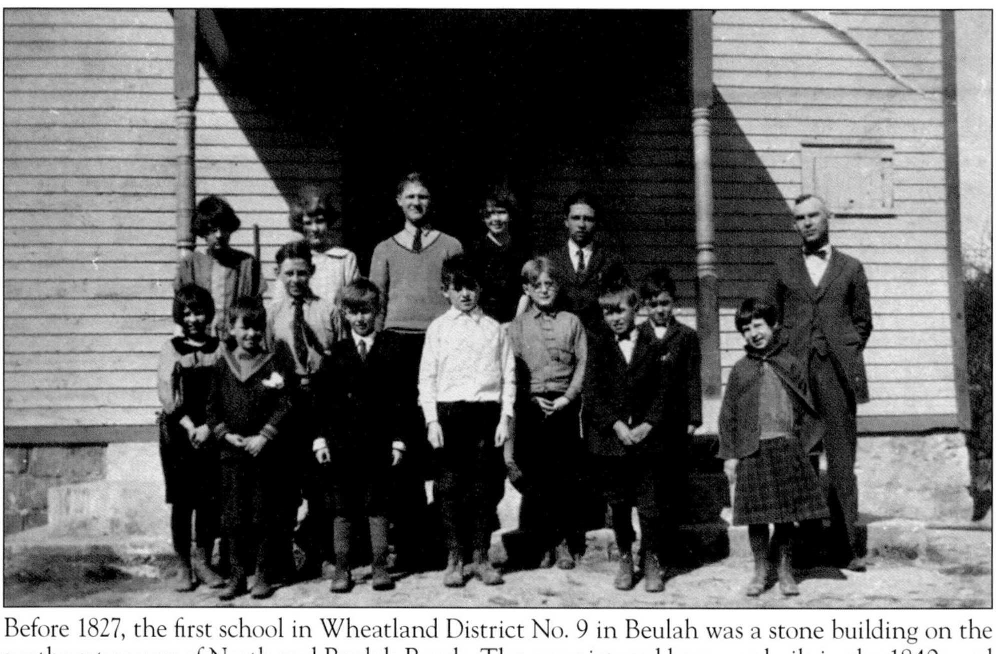

Before 1827, the first school in Wheatland District No. 9 in Beulah was a stone building on the southwest corner of North and Beulah Roads. The one pictured here was built in the 1840s and was moved across the corner to the north side of North Road in 1919. This 1924 photograph shows members of the Vink, Stoddard, and Kelly families with their teacher, Robert Sterling.

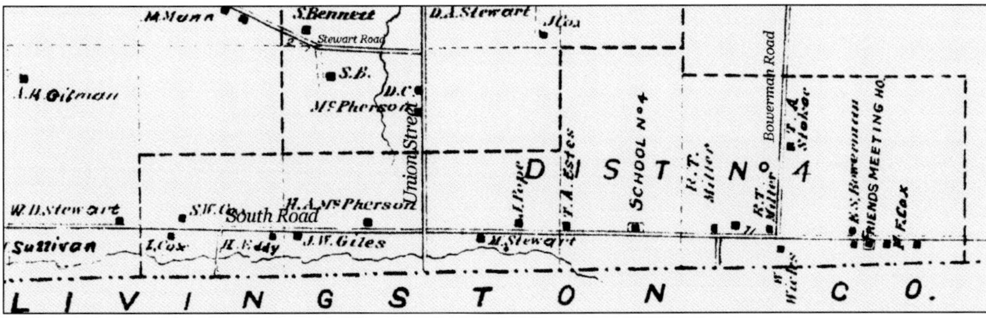

South Road runs along the southern boundary of Monroe County. A number of Quaker families had settled along this road and in the vicinity by 1820. They established a Meeting of Friends and built a meetinghouse on Quaker Road. In 1828, a schism occurred, and the Society of Friends, or Quaker denomination, was divided into factions known as the Hicksites and the Orthodox.

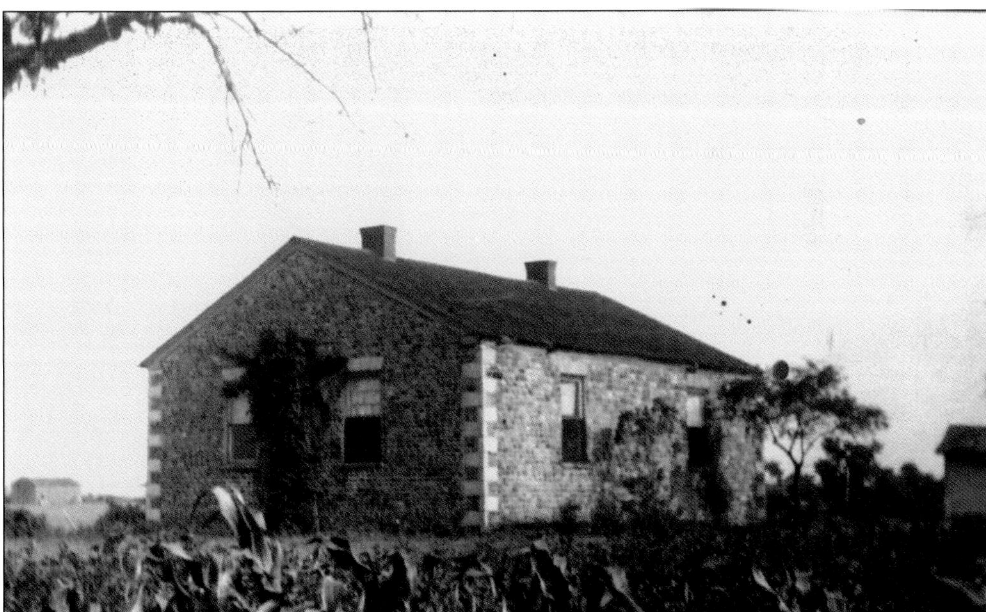

In 1834, the Orthodox Quakers sold their frame building, now demolished, to the Hicksites and built this cobblestone meetinghouse at 409 Quaker Road. It consisted of two rooms, one for men and the other for women, with a low lattice partition separating them. This view does not show the two entrances, which are on the other side of the building. The membership dwindled, and the Wheatland Meeting of Friends closed in 1873.

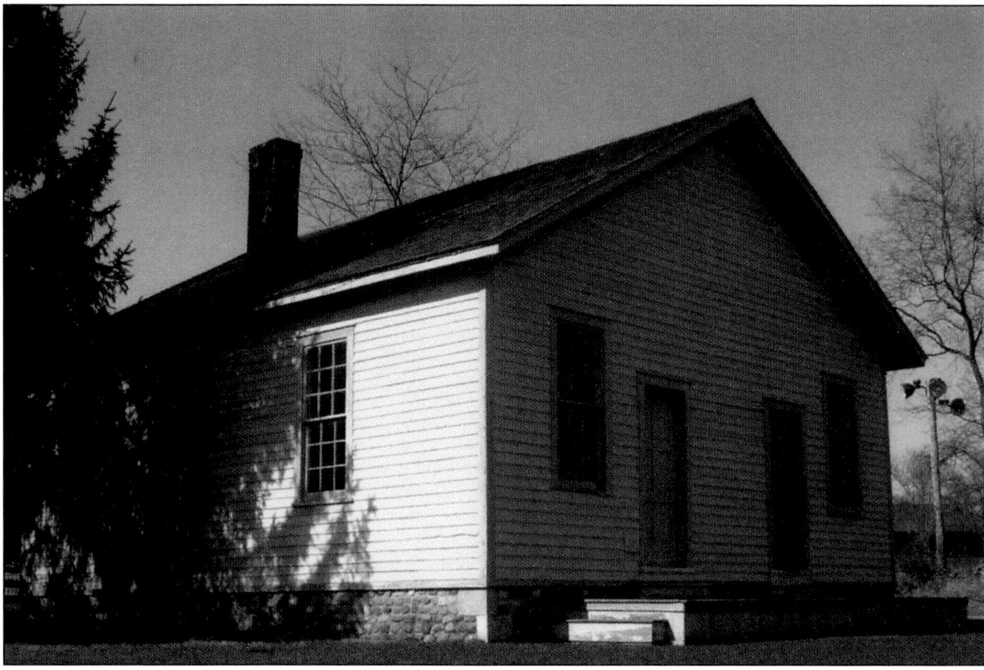

In 1854, the Orthodox Quakers constructed another building on South Road, and the Hicksites inherited the cobblestone meetinghouse. This photograph shows the South Road structure after it was moved to the Genesee Country Village and Museum and was restored as an example of a typical Quaker meetinghouse of the 19th century.

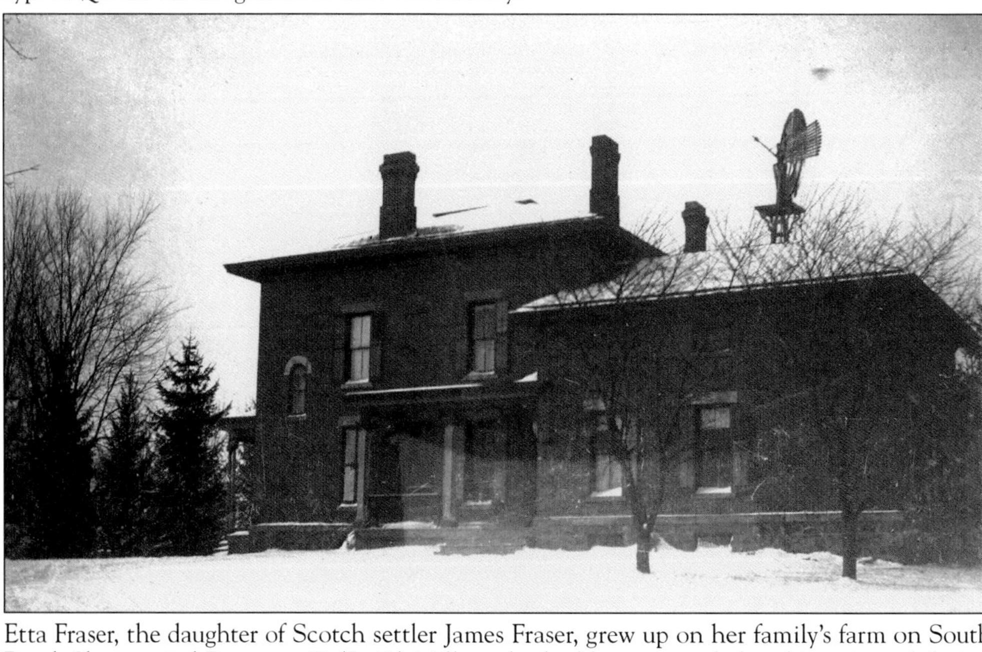

Etta Fraser, the daughter of Scotch settler James Fraser, grew up on her family's farm on South Road. She married Romanta T. (R. T.) Miller, who had been wounded and imprisoned during the Civil War. He was the son of Elijah T. Miller, an important businessman in Scottsville. In 1870, R. T. and Etta built this Italianate-style brick house, designed by architect Isaac Loomis, at 1089 Bowerman Road.

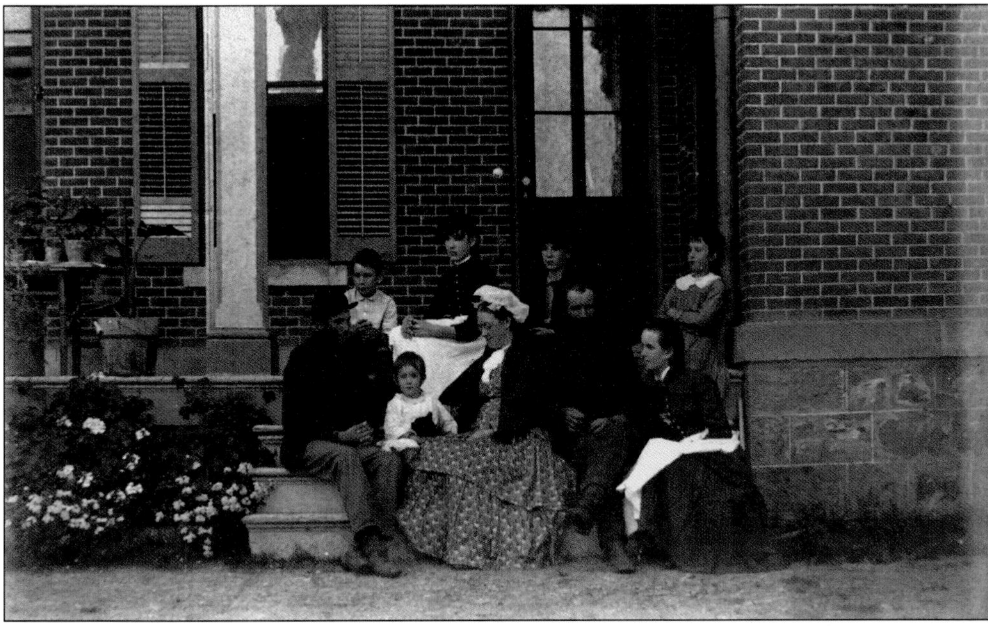

The Miller family is shown here about 1886 on the steps of their house. Etta and R. T. are in the center. Clockwise from left of Etta are: Ruth, James, Oliver, Sophia, Royal, Jeannette, and Laura. R. T. Jr. was not present. The Miller children were educated at the Wheatland District No. 4 School, and later some of them taught there. They all went on to become university graduates.

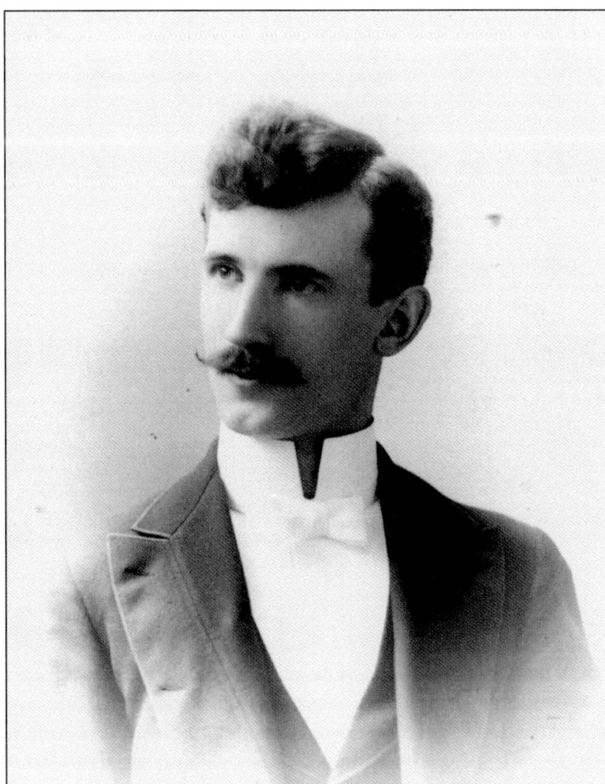

R. T. Miller Jr., who became a local philanthropist, is seen here as a young man. He graduated from Oberlin College in 1891 and founded the American School, a correspondence school in Chicago. R. T. Jr. contributed thousands of dollars to institutions, including the University of Rochester and the Memorial Art Gallery. He supported many projects in his hometown, particularly the Scottsville Free Library.

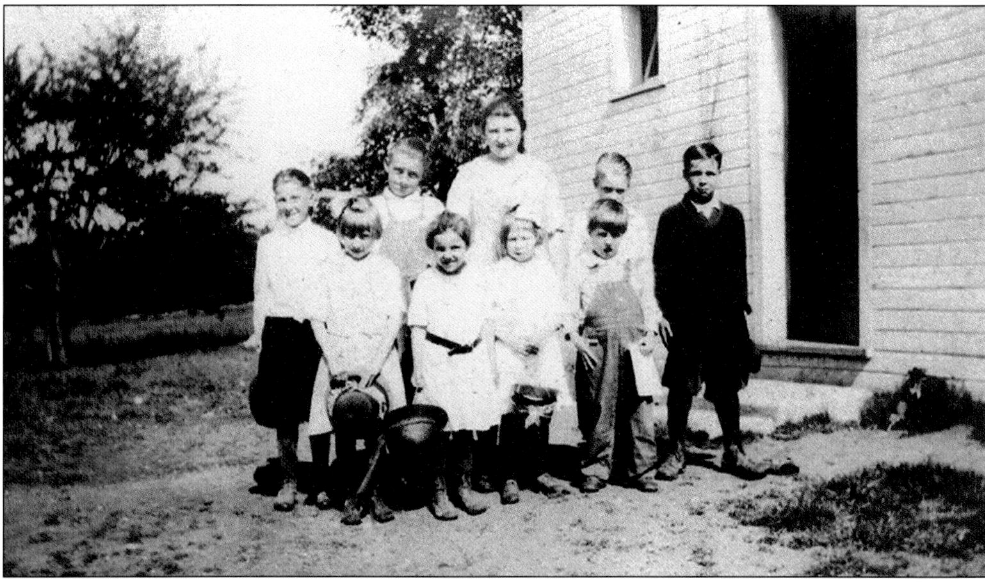

The Wheatland District No. 4 schoolhouse was built about 1850 and served the children who lived along South Road and in the surrounding area. This photograph was taken in the 1920s when Ethel Schillinger, in the center of the back row, was the teacher. Ethel Schillinger taught at the school for over 20 years. After it closed in 1947, the area students went to school in Scottsville. (Courtesy of Duncan Schillinger.)

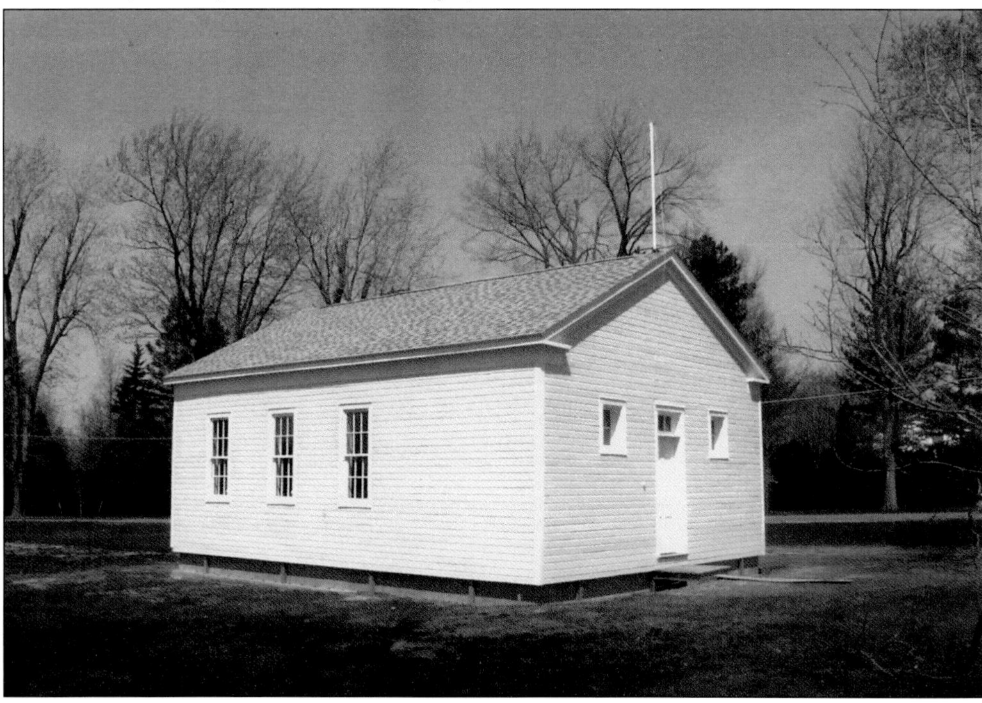

The District No. 4 schoolhouse was moved to the Giles farm on River Road, where it served as a storage building for nearly 50 years. In 2004, it was moved to the campus of the Wheatland-Chili Elementary School. It has been restored, and it now has a new life, as children are again learning inside its walls.

Five

Hamlets of Garbutt and Wheatland Center

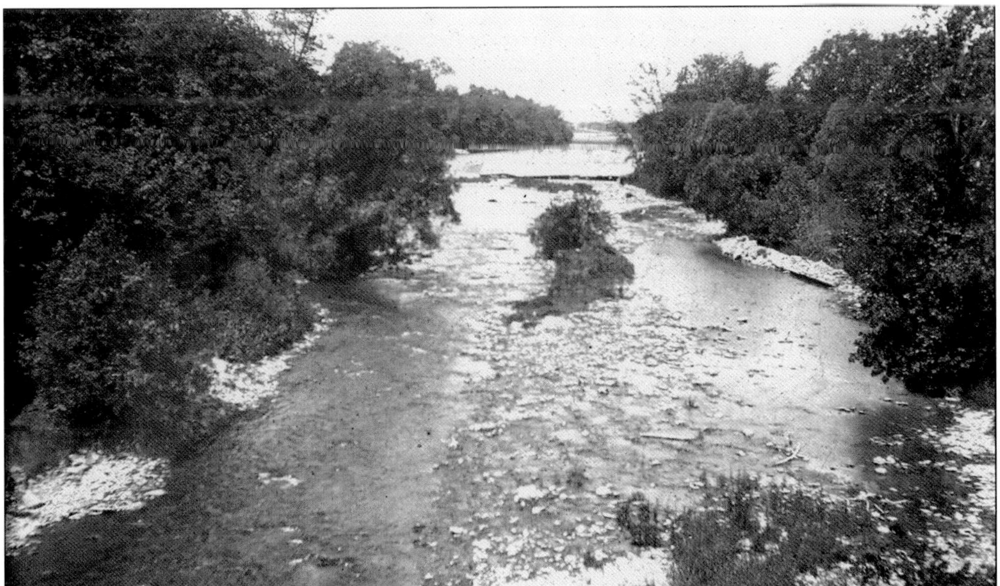

After flowing past Mumford, Oatka Creek next reaches the hamlets of Wheatland Center and Garbutt where, for 100 years, its current turned waterwheels and turbines that powered mills for grinding wheat to flour and gypsum to plaster. A few remnants of the millraces and structures remain today. Visitors to the area can observe them as they stroll through Oatka Park or stand on the Union Street bridge in Garbutt.

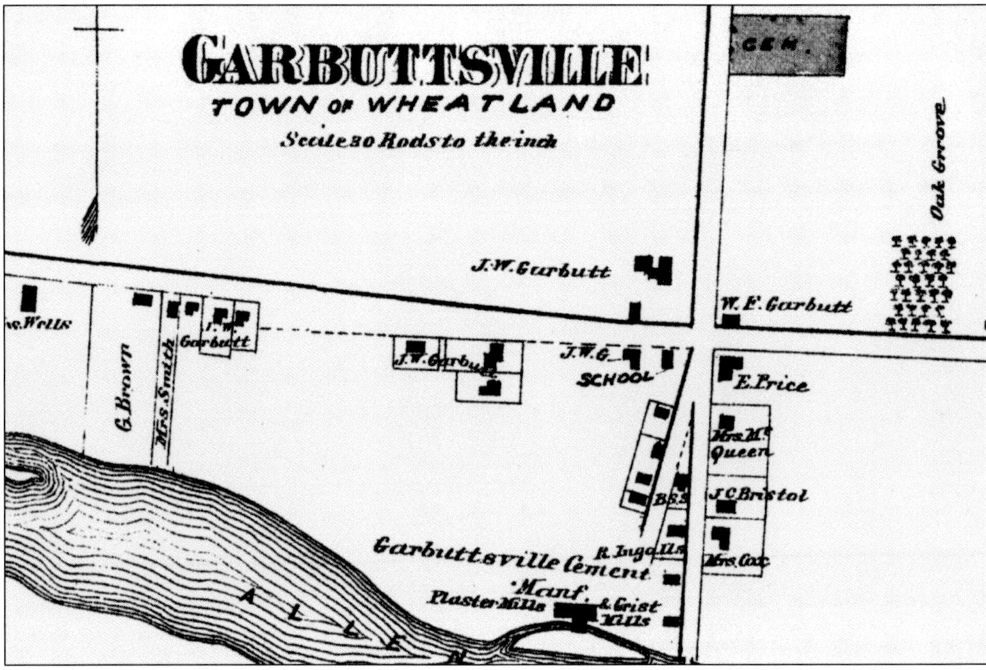

Garbuttsville was named for the first settlers in the area, Zachariah Garbutt and his sons, William, John W., and Philip. This inset map from the 1872 *Atlas of Monroe County, N.Y.* shows the locations of the mills started by Philip and continued by his son, John. By 1900 the name of the hamlet had been shortened to Garbutt.

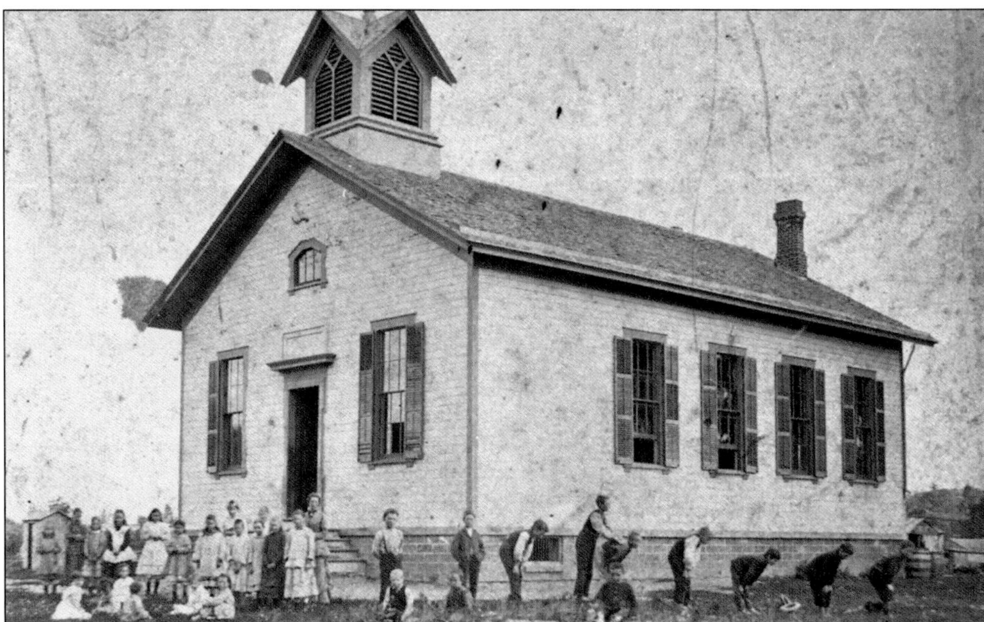

School District No. 3 at Garbutt had been in existence since 1821. In 1871, this stylish schoolhouse was built by John Talcott Wells at a cost of $2,200. For many years it was filled to overflowing with the local pupils, but by 1940, the numbers had dwindled, and the school closed. The remaining students were sent to the Scottsville School, and eventually the building was demolished.

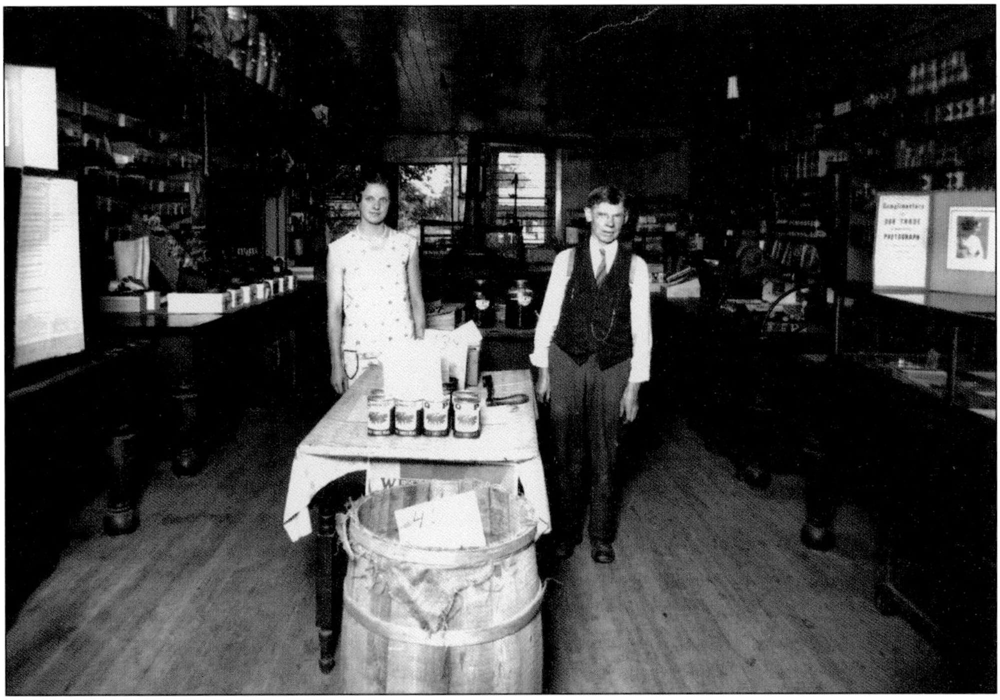

Philip Garbutt opened a general store about 1810, and in 1828, he moved the business to the stone building shown below on the north side of Scottsville-Mumford Road. For several decades, it was renowned for its city-made merchandise. The Wheatland Farmers' Library, one of the earliest libraries in Western New York, was founded in 1805. For more than 40 years, the library was housed at the Garbutt Store. The store passed through several owners until it was purchased by Frank Garbutt, grandson of Philip, who ran it from 1905 until 1943. Frank Garbutt and his employee are shown in the picture above.

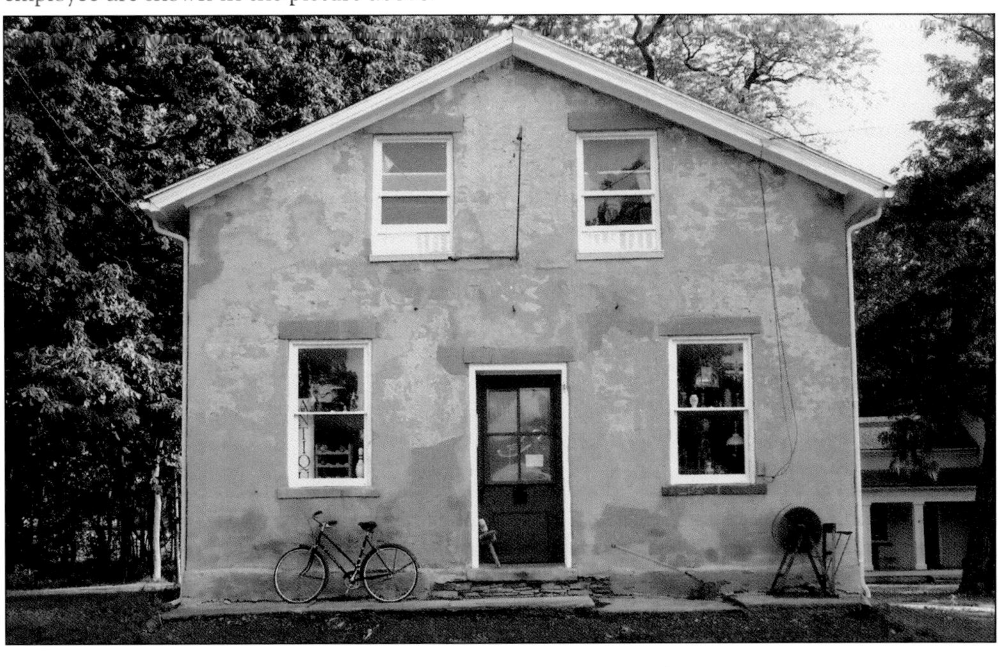

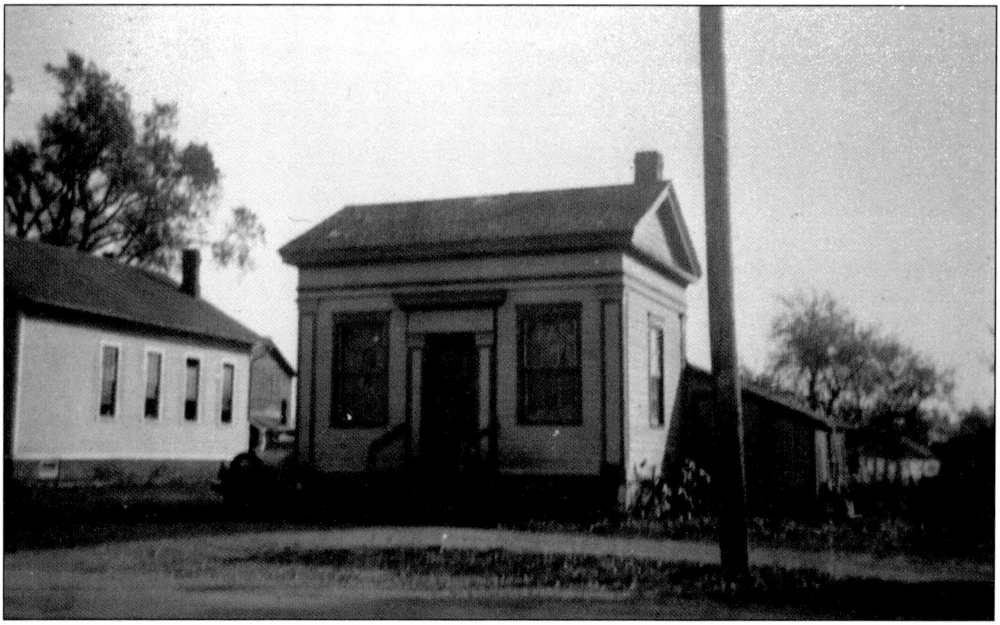

Located next door to the Garbutt schoolhouse, this charming little Greek Revival–style house was a tailor shop. It is said that the tailor here owned the first sewing machine in town but that he had to use it in secret as people were convinced that hand sewn garments were superior to machine work. The building was moved to the Genesee Country Village in 2006.

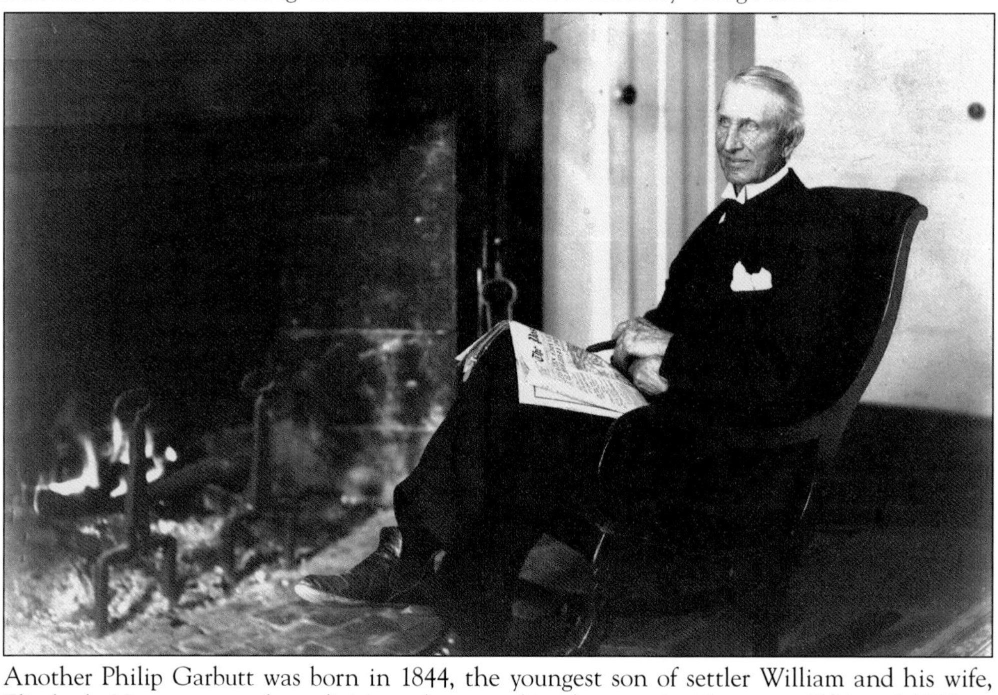

Another Philip Garbutt was born in 1844, the youngest son of settler William and his wife, Elizabeth. He was a popular politician who served in the state legislature in 1884 and 1885, as well as several terms as Wheatland supervisor. It is said that Philip was a friend of Theodore Roosevelt and that he entertained the future president at his home in Garbutt. (Courtesy of Richard LeRoy.)

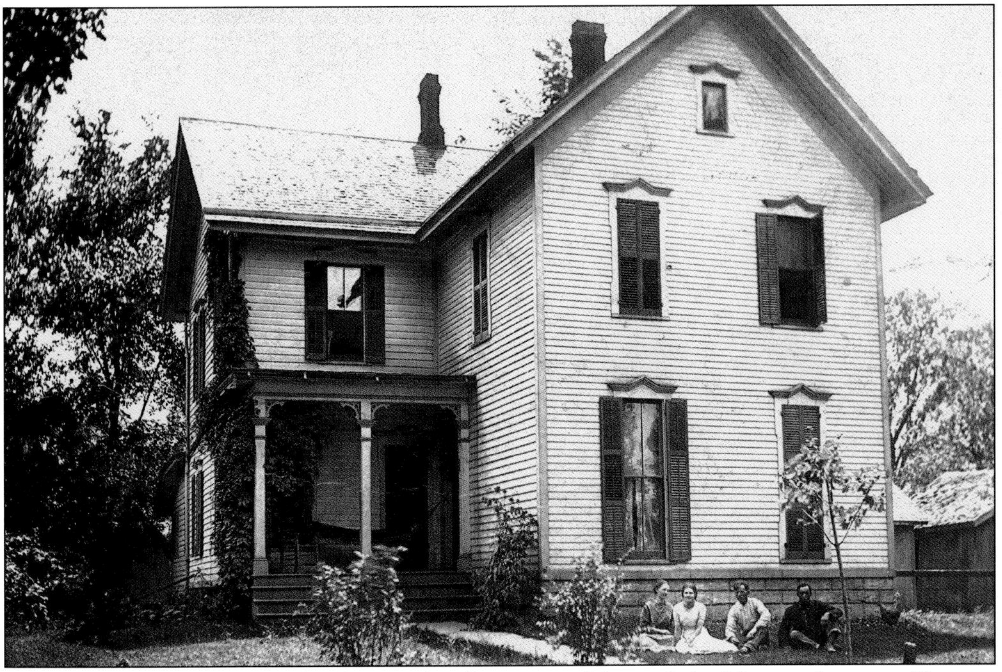

Moses Wells came to Wheatland in 1815 and was one of the early builders in the town. His son, John Talcott Wells, was the inventor of the well-known Wells Truss, which was widely used in the construction of barns. This is the Wells' home at 1151 Scottsville-Mumford Road, remodeled in the 1880s, which exhibits the Wells signature "Lazy W" over the windows.

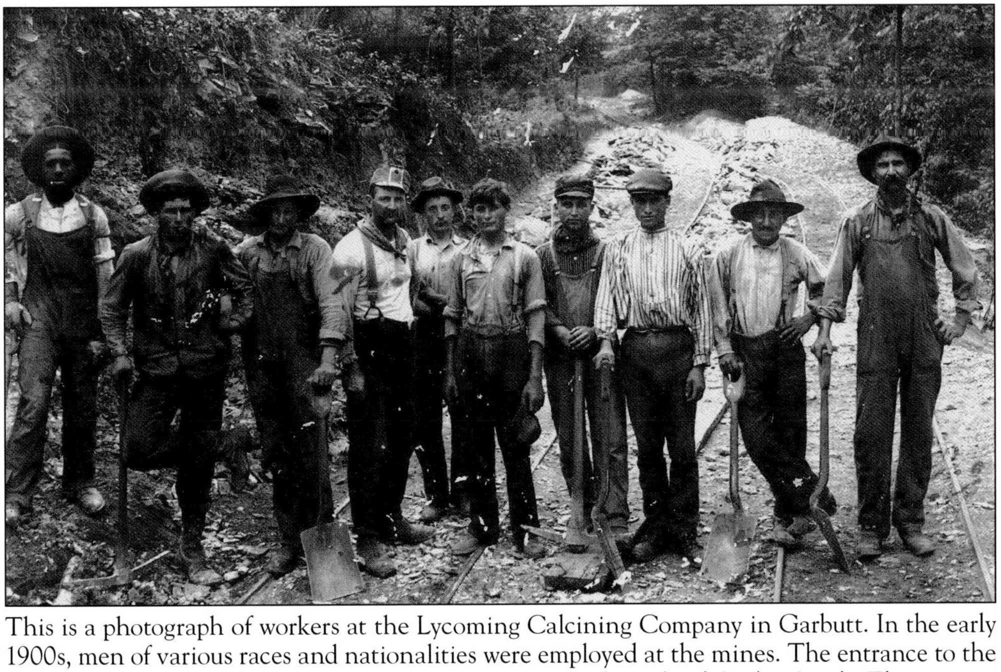

This is a photograph of workers at the Lycoming Calcining Company in Garbutt. In the early 1900s, men of various races and nationalities were employed at the mines. The entrance to the gypsum mine is behind them, west of Union Street and south of Oatka Creek. The gypsum was carried in carts pulled by mules along the tracks across the creek to the mill. (Courtesy of Joan Torpey Lenhardt.)

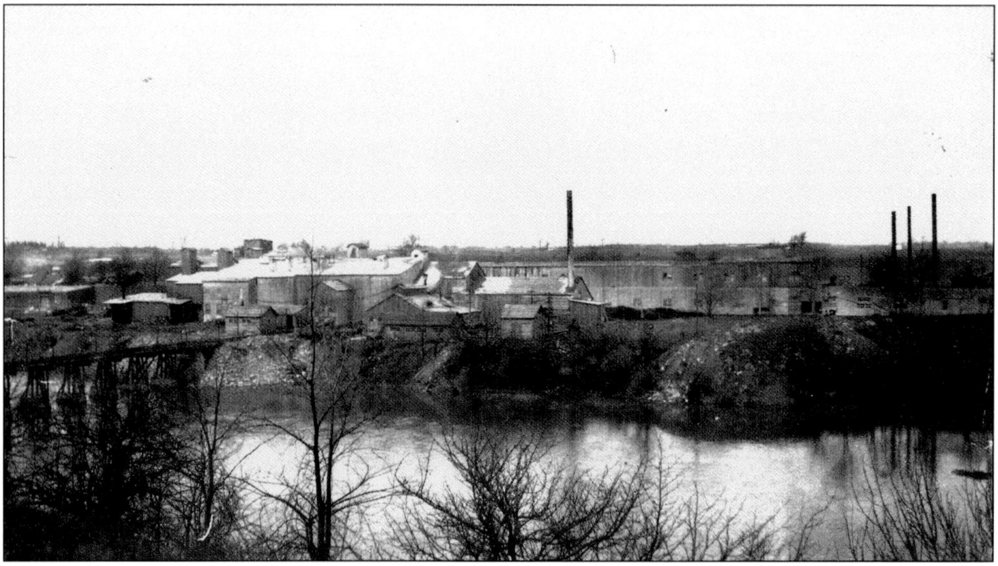

This photograph shows the Lycoming Calcining Company on the north side of Oatka Creek in Garbutt. Carts of gypsum rock were drawn across the bridge by mules from the mines on the south side of the creek. It was then ground into plaster in the mill. The operation enjoyed great success from about 1900 until the stock market crash in 1929.

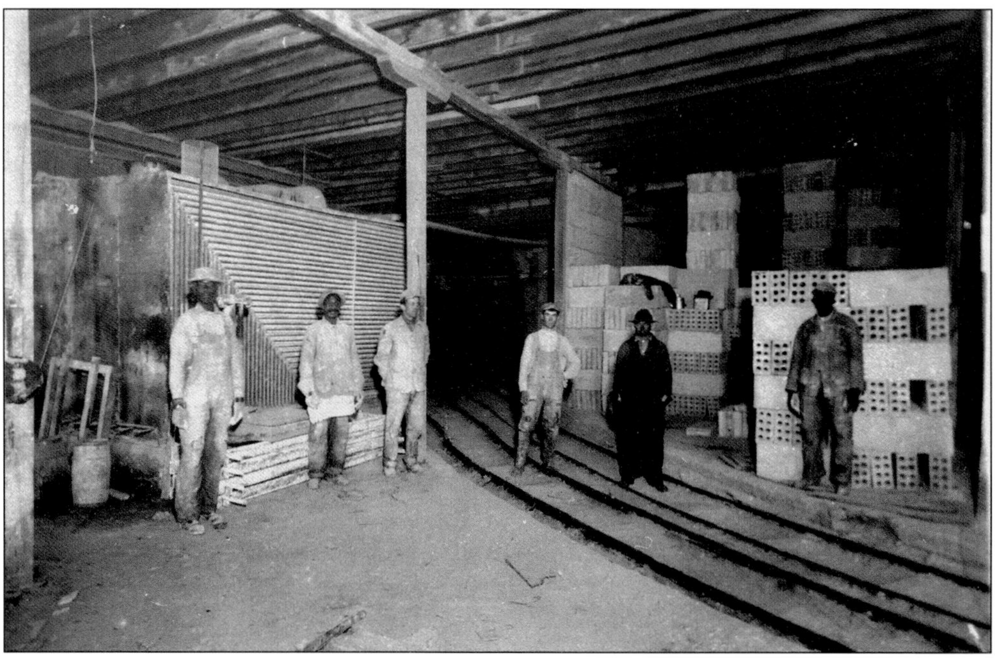

In 1911, the Ebsary Fire Proofing and Gypsum Block Company began production in Garbutt. They manufactured gypsum blocks for use as fireproof partitions in buildings. The gypsum was obtained from the Empire Gypsum Company, another industry with mines and a mill on the creek at Garbutt. This 1917 photograph shows some of the workers and the blocks made there. The Ebsary company moved to Wheatland Center in 1920.

This modified portion of the map of Wheatland from the 1872 F. W. Beers *Atlas of Monroe County, N.Y.* shows Wheatland Center and School Districts No. 5 and No. 6 that were in the vicinity. It also shows Oatka Creek and the location of the Smith Mill.

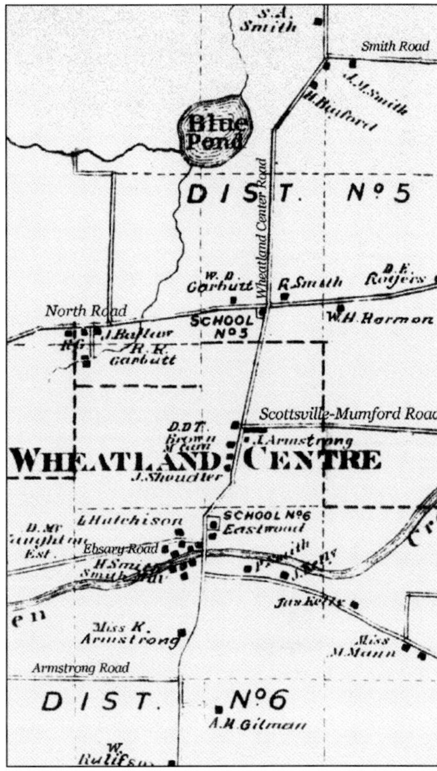

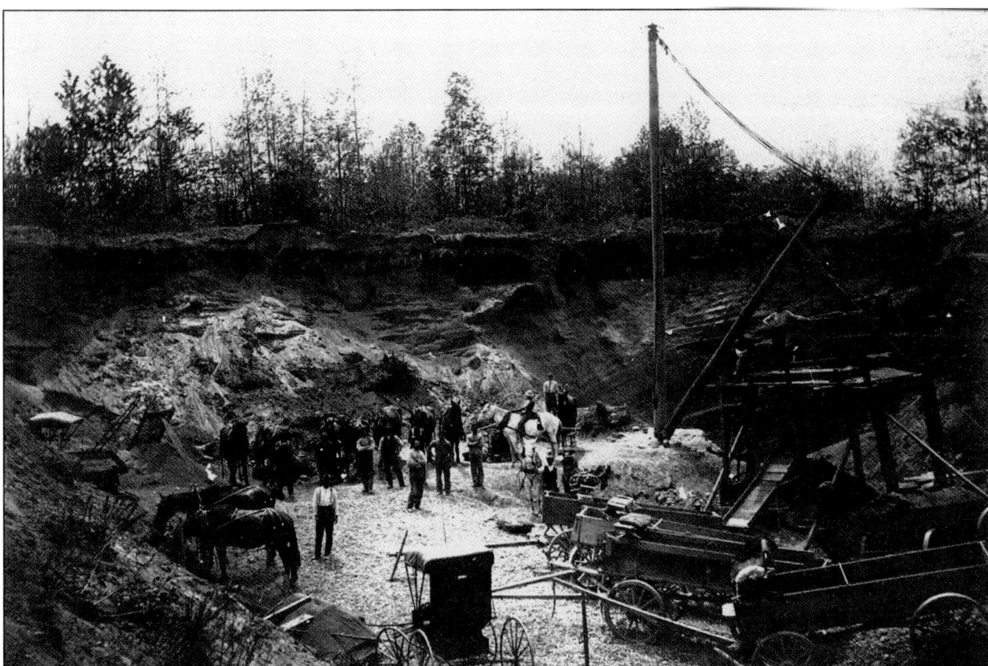

The sandpit pictured here was at the top of the hill between Wheatland Center Road and Scottsville-Mumford Road. During the late 1800s and early 1900s, sand was taken from this location and mixed with plaster to make wallboard. (Courtesy of Joan Torpey Lenhardt.)

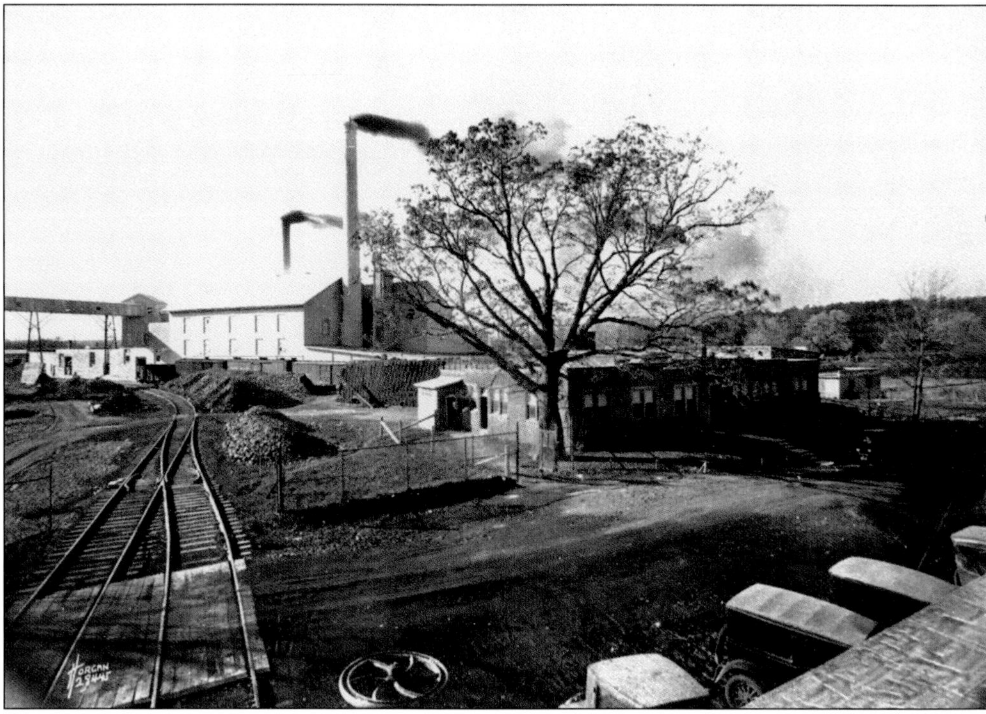

The Wheatland Land Plaster Company had occupied this site along Oatka Creek and the railroad during the 1890s. In 1920, Frederick G. Ebsary moved his gypsum plant from Garbutt to this location. Nearby they mined about 450 tons of gypsum a day and manufactured wallboard, wall plaster, and plaster block. The photograph above was taken in 1925 and the aerial view below about 1935. In 1971, the site was sold to the Sabin Metal Company, where precious metals are extracted from scrap metal.

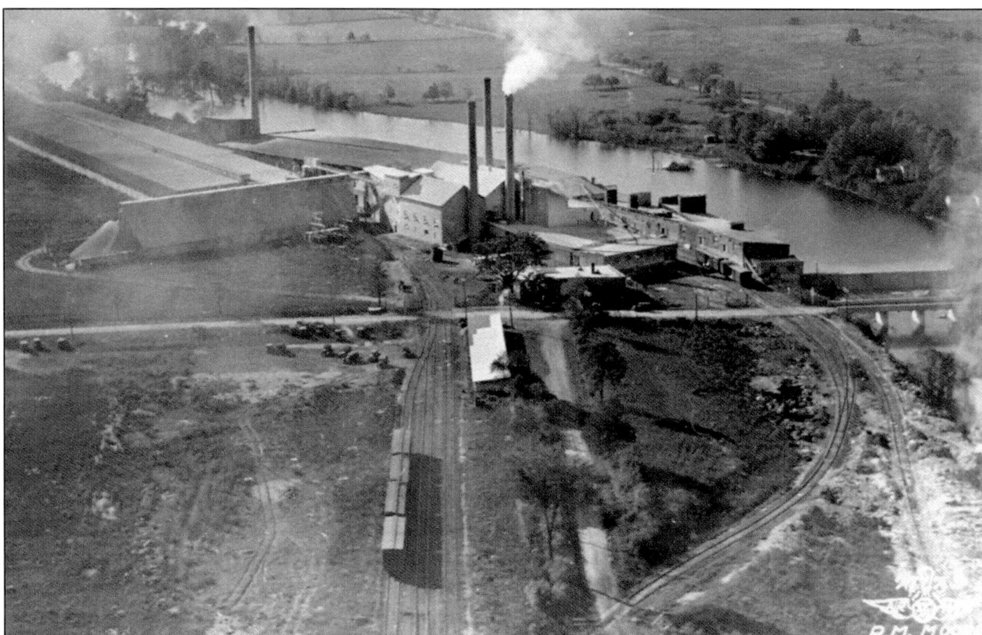

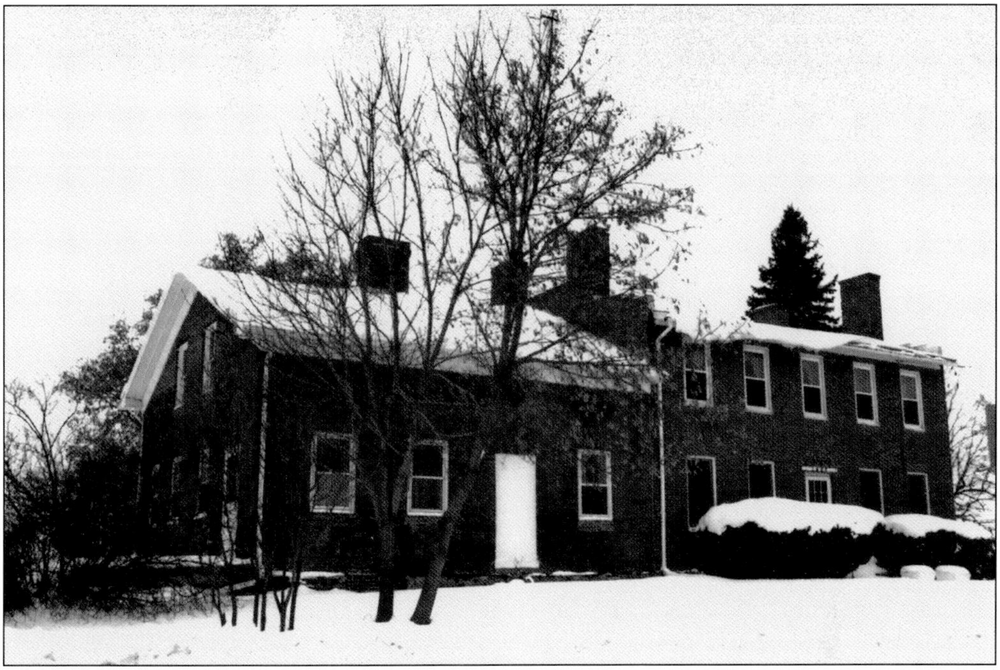

Clark Hall built this brick house, at the corner of Wheatland Center Road and Scottsville-Mumford Road, in about 1825. He opened it as a tavern and stagecoach stop, and because of its location in the center of town, it became a popular meeting place. For many years the area was known as Hall's Corners.

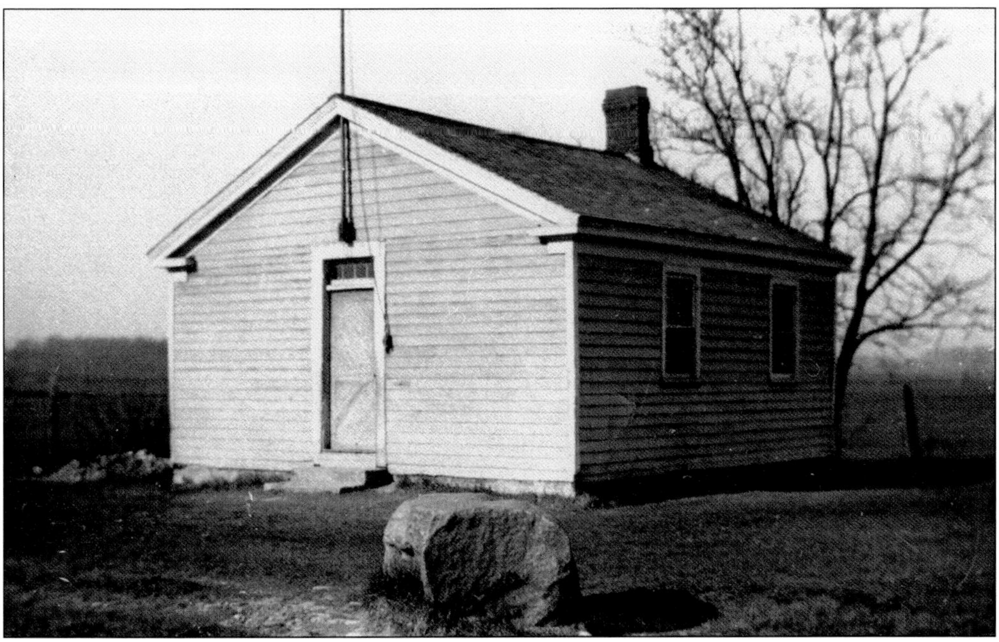

This tiny schoolhouse for Wheatland District No. 5 stood on the corner of Wheatland Center Road and North Road. It was built in 1838 and served the children of the area for 110, years until 1948 when it was closed. The building was then moved to Jack Miller's gravel pit on North Road where it is now part of the Gravel Ponds recreation area.

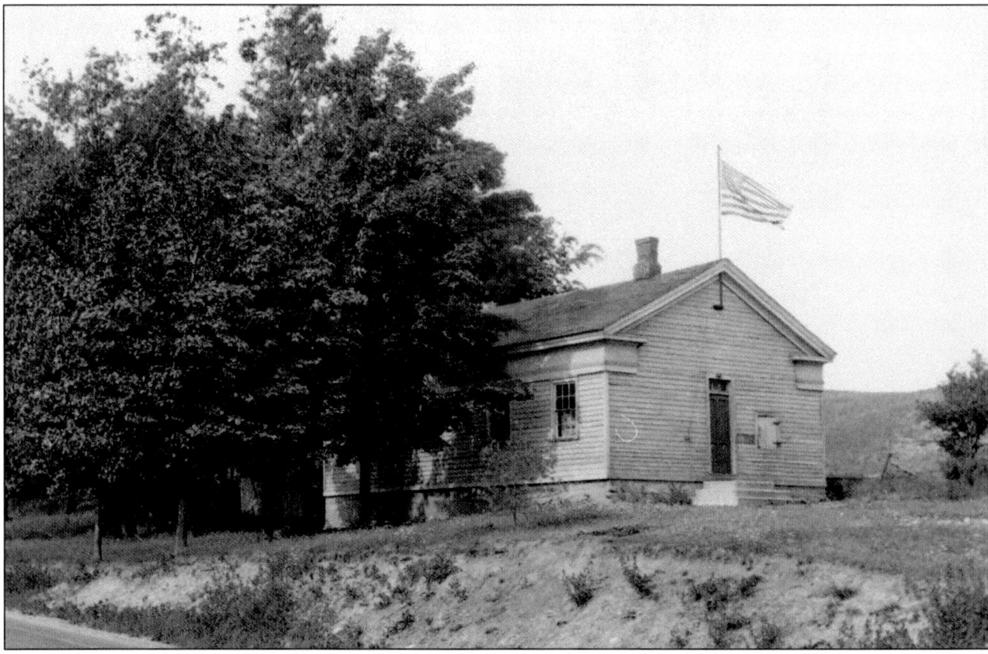

The Wheatland District No. 6 School was located just north of Oatka Creek at the present 1576 Wheatland Center Road. The building pictured was built in 1846 and closed at the same time as the District No. 5 school. This old schoolhouse is also still standing and has been made into a home. Notice the wide cornices and the returns on the gable end, characteristics of Greek Revival–style buildings.

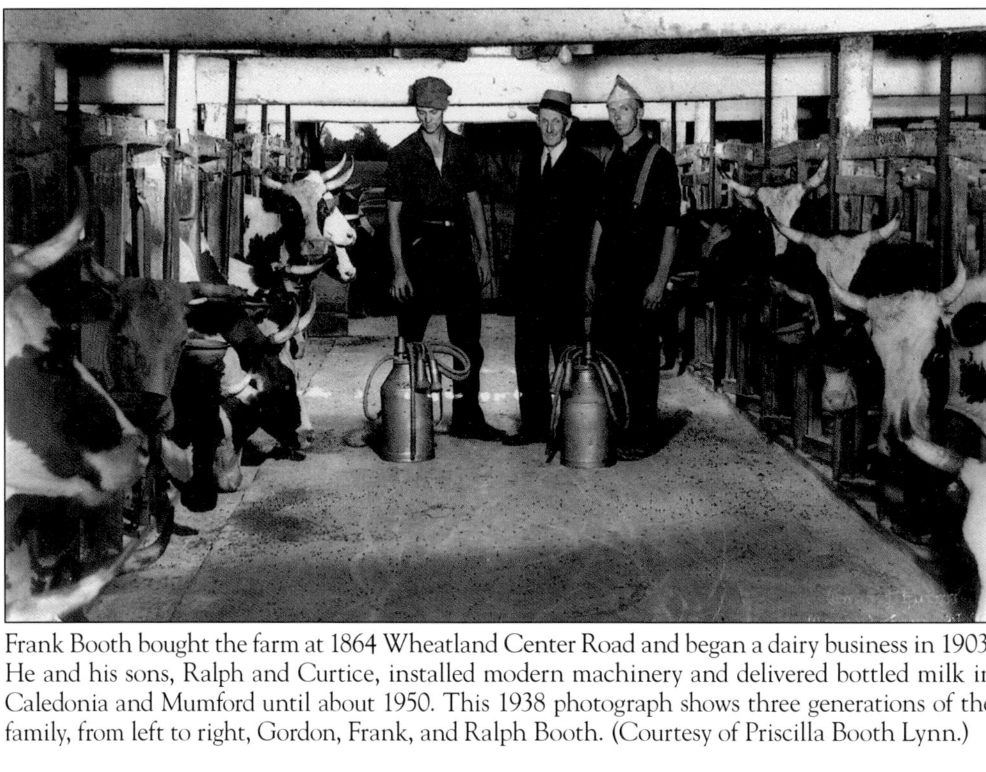

Frank Booth bought the farm at 1864 Wheatland Center Road and began a dairy business in 1903. He and his sons, Ralph and Curtice, installed modern machinery and delivered bottled milk in Caledonia and Mumford until about 1950. This 1938 photograph shows three generations of the family, from left to right, Gordon, Frank, and Ralph Booth. (Courtesy of Priscilla Booth Lynn.)

Six

Scottsville

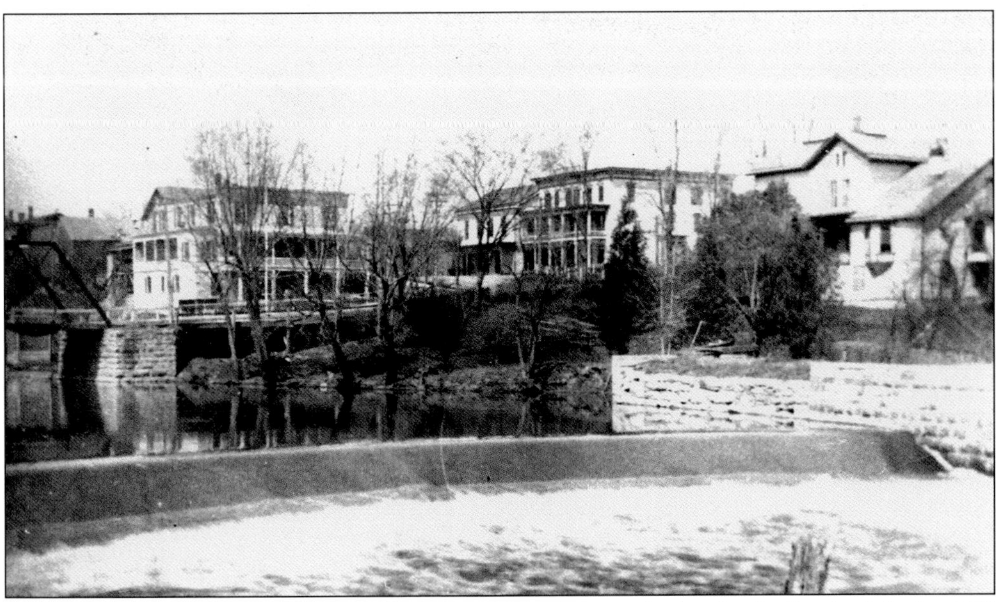

This 1890s view looking northwest shows Route 251 crossing Oatka Creek. On the left, the 1878 steel truss bridge replaced an earlier wooden structure. From left to right, the Salyerds' Block, the Cargill House, and the home of Mary M. Fraser are visible. The dam maintained the water at a sufficient level to feed the Genesee Valley Canal. This view today can be seen from the New York State Greenway Trail.

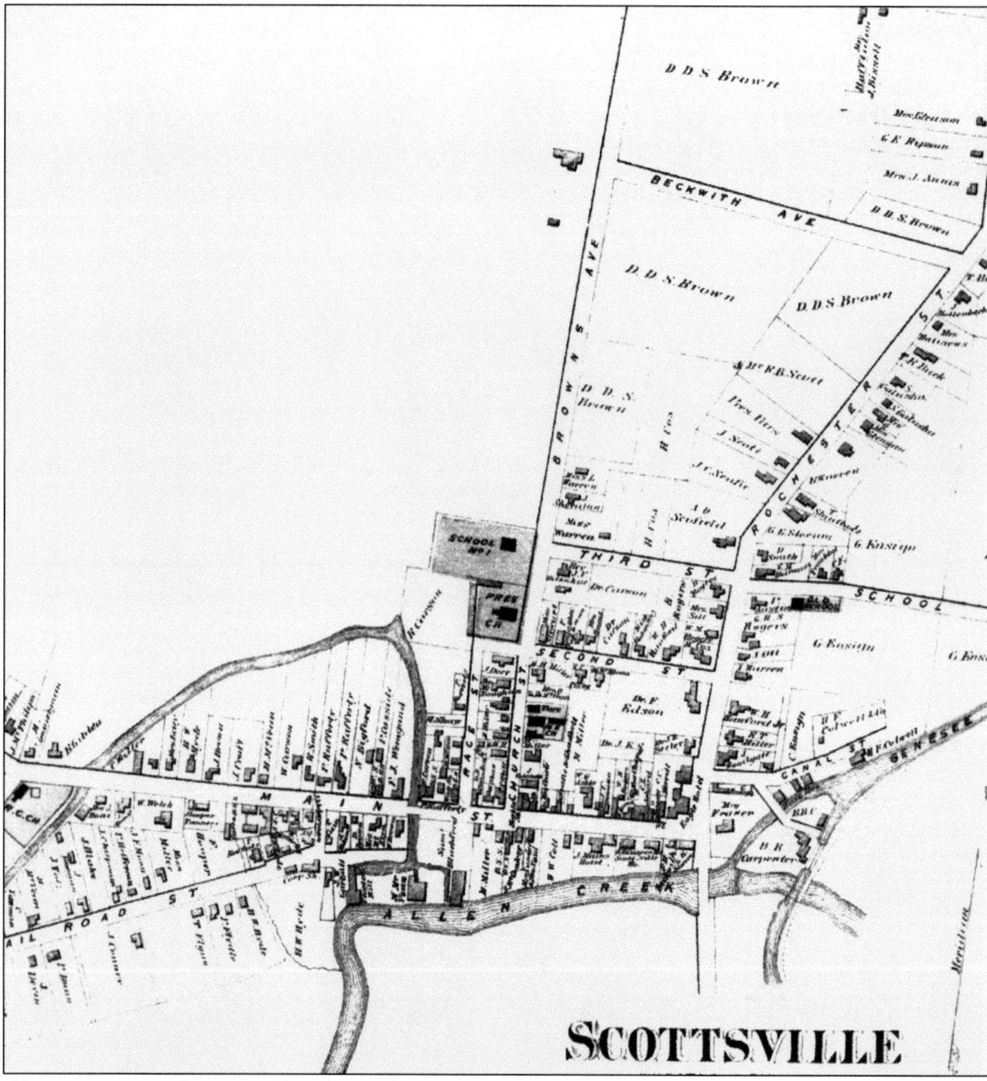

This 1872 map of Scottsville is from the *Atlas of Monroe County, N.Y.* by F. W. Beers. Buildings existing at that time and their owner's names were indicated. Allen was the early name of the local creek before the popular Native American word *Oatka* was used. On the right, the Genesee Valley Canal crossed the creek. On the left, the dug millrace provided waterpower for the mills. Beginning with early settler Isaac Scott, the village grew to be the largest population center in the town of Wheatland and was incorporated in 1914.

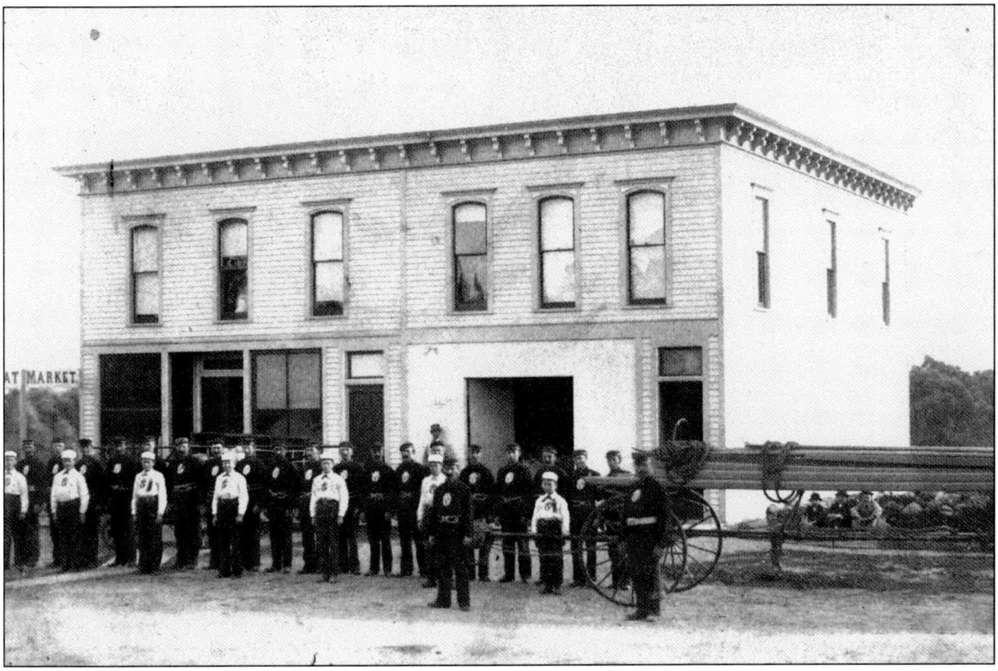

Isaac Salyerds purchased the site of a burned-out building on the corner of Main Street and Canawaugus Road, and in 1881, he built a two-story frame building using the first floor for a meat market. He also peddled groceries around the countryside with a horse and cart. The fire department was in the west half of this building.

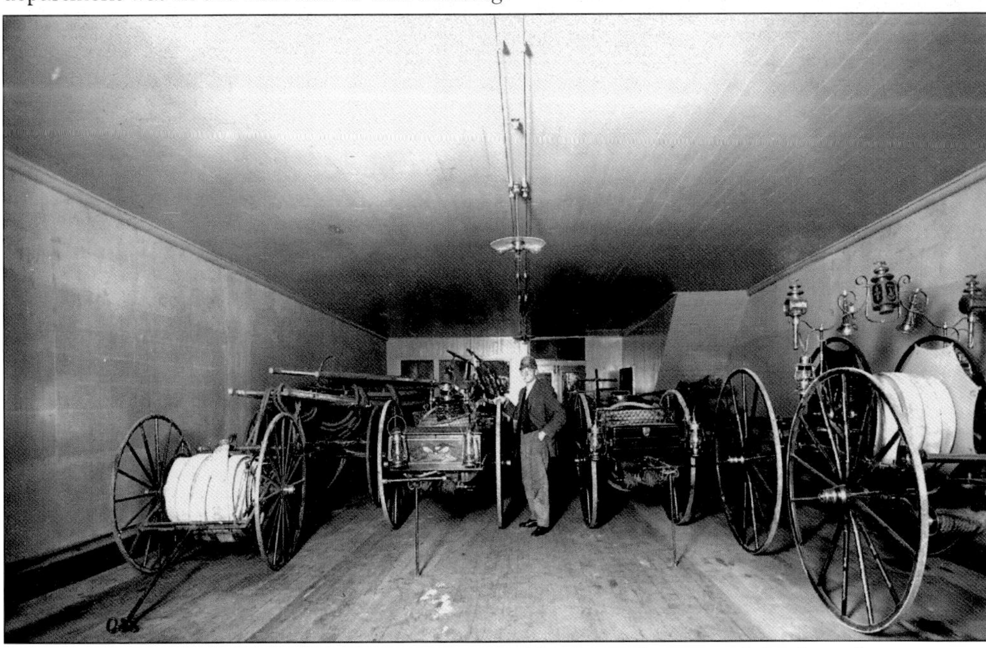

The Scottsville Fire Company of 60 members used buckets of water to fight fires when it started in the 1870s. In this 1890s photograph, Isaac Van Hooser is inspecting the equipment used by the hook and ladder and bucket brigade companies. He was a fire commissioner in 1913. Van Hooser was also a printer and bicycle repairman and was active in support of Windom Hall.

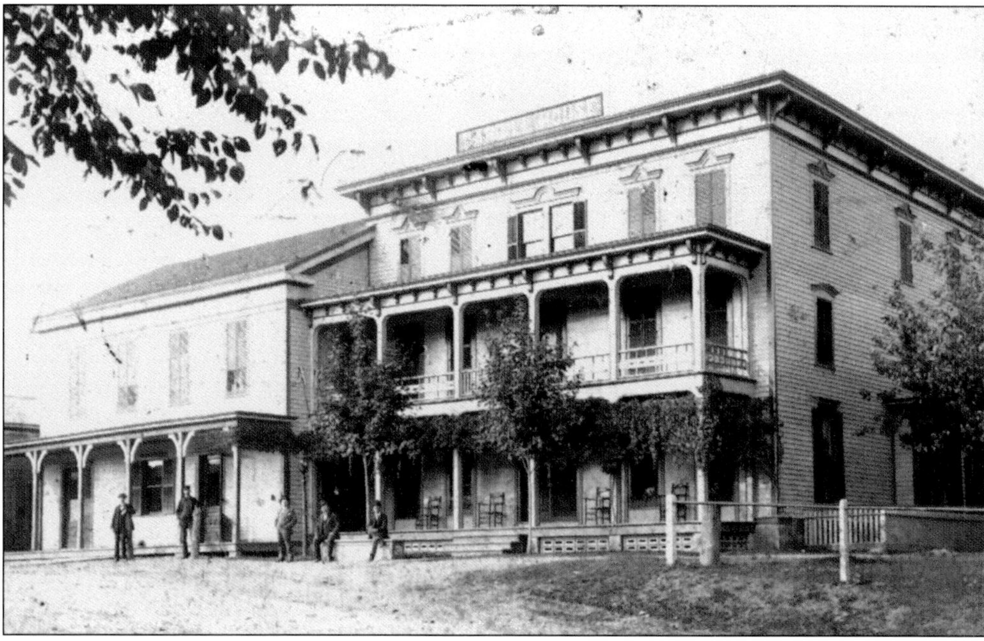

In 1820, Powell Carpenter erected the Eagle Hotel on the corner of Main and Rochester Streets. Later he enlarged it by adding a 20-by-40-foot section. In 1830, the hotel was sold to George Ensign and in 1846 to Elijah T. Miller, who added a bar and ballroom. In 1887, Norman Cargill renamed it the Cargill House. It was razed in 1930. (Courtesy of Richard LeRoy.)

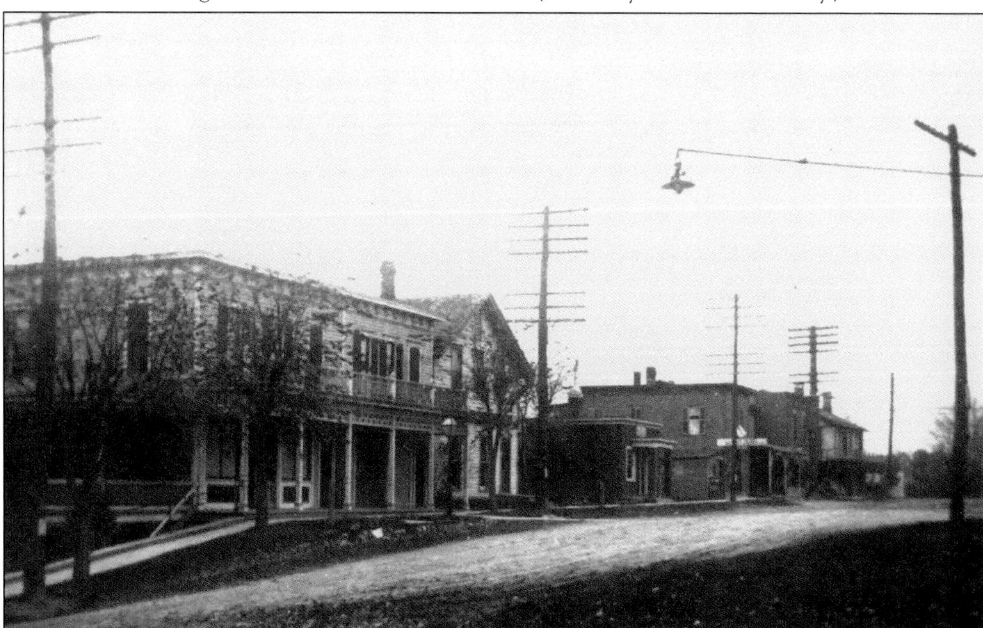

In this Main Street view, looking west, are some of the early buildings. Beginning on the left is the Salyerds' Block, the Tucker house, Thomas Brown's office, Slocum's Hardware store, and the Oatka Hotel. The street was unpaved but had streetlights and utility poles. In 1903, a concrete sidewalk was installed from Brown's Grove along Rochester and Main Streets to the Holy Angels Cemetery on Caledonia Avenue.

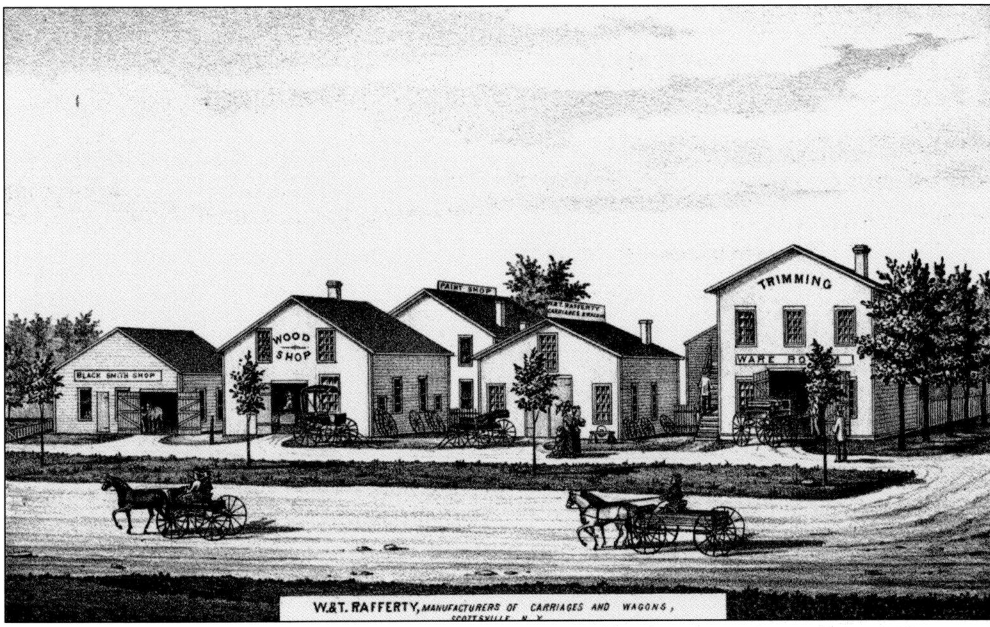

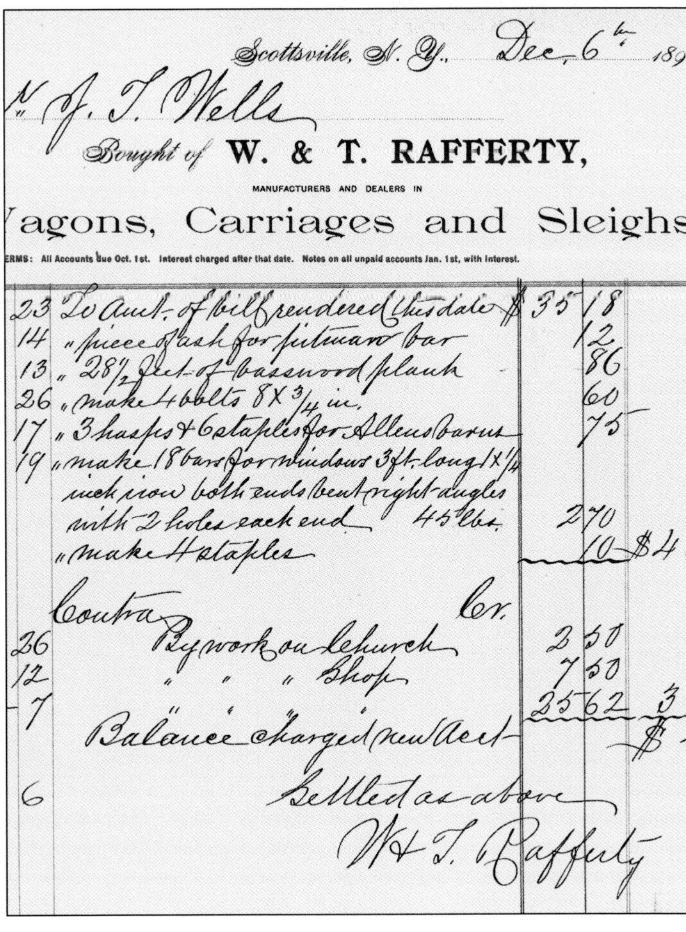

Scottsville, N. Y. Dec. 6th 189

M J. T. Wells

Bought of **W. & T. RAFFERTY,**

MANUFACTURERS AND DEALERS IN

Wagons, Carriages and Sleighs

TERMS: All Accounts due Oct. 1st. Interest charged after that date. Notes on all unpaid accounts Jan. 1st, with interest.

23	To Amt. of bill rendered this date	$ 35	18	
14	" piece of ash for pitman bar		12	
13	" 28½ feet of basswood plank		86	
26	" make 4 bolts 8 X ¾ in.		60	
17	" 3 hasps & 6 staples for Allens barn		75	
19	" make 18 bars for windows 3 ft. long 1 X ¼ inch iron both ends bent right angles with 2 holes each end 45 lbs.	2	70	
	" make 4 staples		10	$ 4
	Contra Cr.			
26	By work on church	2	50	
12	" " " Shop	7	50	
7	" " "	25	62	3
	Balance charged new Acct			$ 4
6	Settled as above			
	W & T. Rafferty			

The Rafferty Carriage Shop was on the north side of Main Street between Race Street and the millrace. Patrick Rafferty came to Scottsville in 1837 to work as a wagon and carriage maker. By 1841, he had established his own shop. When he retired in 1871, his sons, William and Thomas, succeeded him. Later they expanded the business into neighboring buildings. In 1908, the property was used as a repair and blacksmith shop, and in later years, it was an automobile garage. This sketch is from the 1877 *History of Monroe County, New York*, by W. H. McIntosh. The lower image shows materials purchased by John Talcott Wells from the W. and T. Rafferty Company in December 1892 for Oliver Allen's barn.

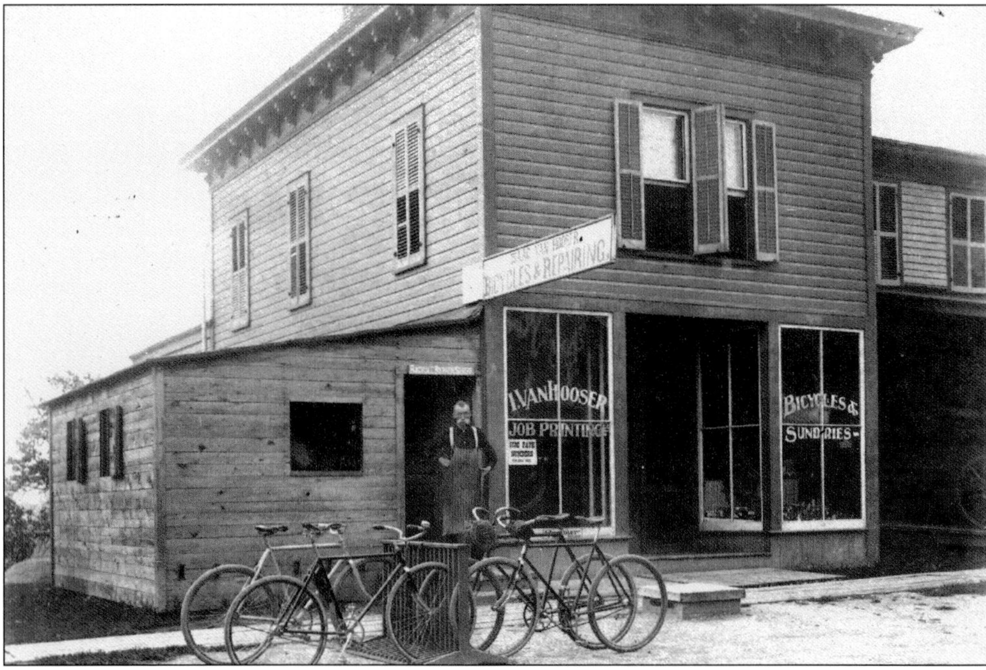

Isaac Van Hooser came to the village of Scottsville in the 1880s, where he conducted a printing business at his home at 8 Rochester Street. In 1894, he purchased the property at 11 Main Street for a bakery and ice-cream shop. He also moved his printing press there. When bicycles became popular, he closed the bakery and ice-cream shop and switched to selling and repairing bicycles.

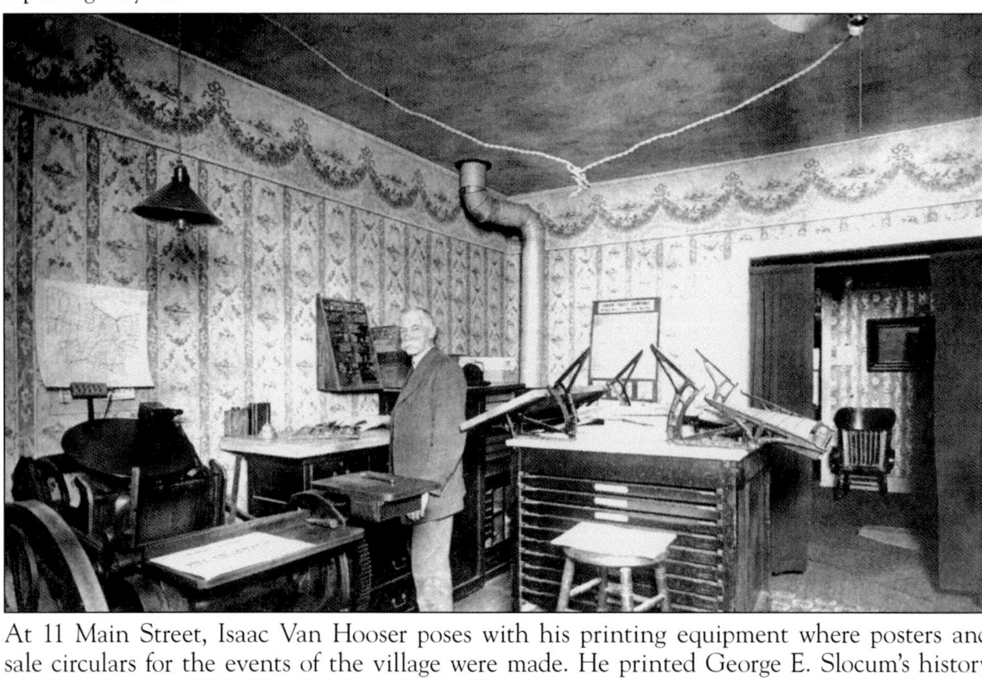

At 11 Main Street, Isaac Van Hooser poses with his printing equipment where posters and sale circulars for the events of the village were made. He printed George E. Slocum's history of Wheatland in 1908. His daughter, Stella Van Hooser, who later married Chester Harmon, worked in the print shop with him.

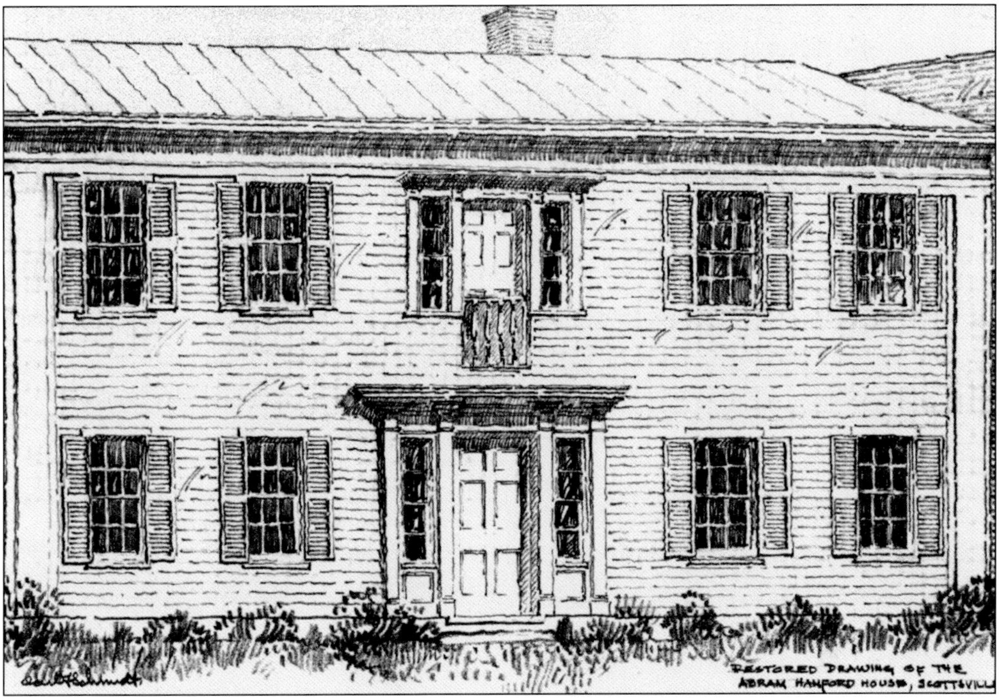

Abraham Hanford built this Greek Revival house about 1823 on the south side at 13 Main Street. He lived there for 20 years. Then it became the parsonage for the Presbyterian church. In later years, it has been converted for various uses, including the Slocum Hardware, and most recently, a laundromat. (Sketch by Carl F. Schmidt from *The Early Architecture of the Genesee Valley*.)

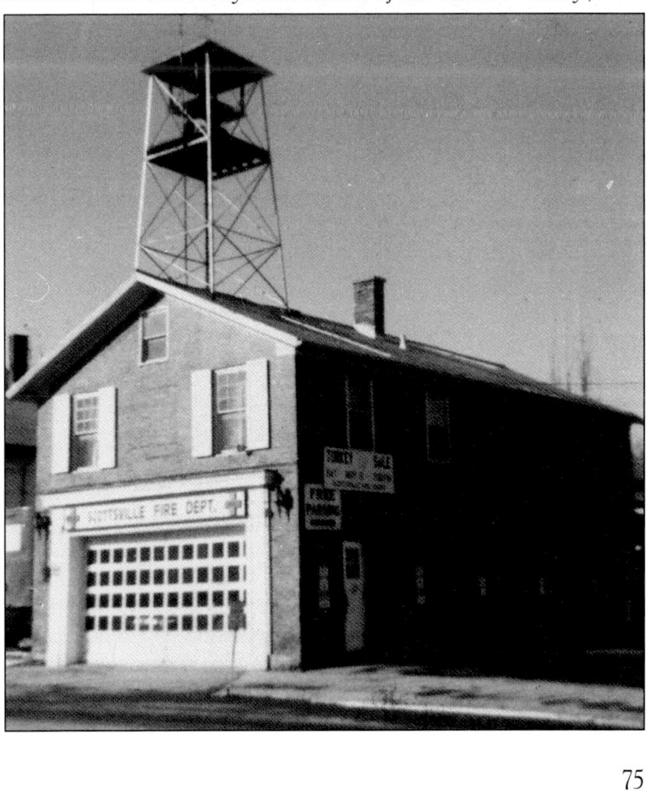

In 1911, Scottsville enlarged its fire district and purchased the brick building at 22 Main Street for the firehouse. The first motorized equipment was purchased in 1924, and in 1953, ambulance service was added. By 1968, larger facilities were needed and existing buildings were cleared for a new seven-bay building erected on this site. In 2006–2007, it was renovated for municipal offices of both the town and village.

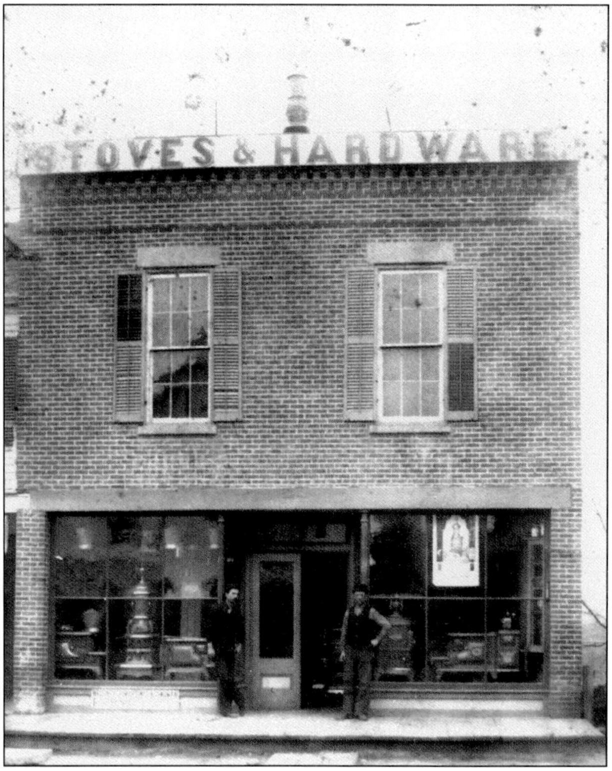

George E. Slocum and his wife, Lydia, came from Delhi, Onondaga County, to Scottsville in 1849 by packet boat on the Genesee Valley Canal. Slocum, a skilled tinsmith by trade and an astute businessman, opened a hardware store in the Beckwith block on the southwest corner of Main Street and River Road. When his building burned to the ground in 1878, he purchased the vacant brick Scottsville Hotel at 15 Main Street and immediately remodeled it into a new store and shop. In this photograph, employees Jim Tobin and William Smith stand with a display of stoves.

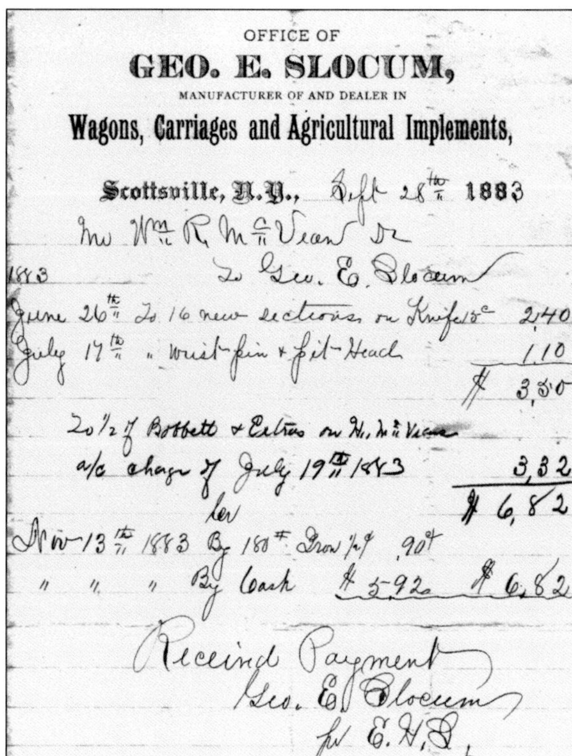
OFFICE OF

GEO. E. SLOCUM,

MANUFACTURER OF AND DEALER IN

Wagons, Carriages and Agricultural Implements,

Scottsville, N.Y., Sept 28th 1883

Mr Wm R McVean Dr

1883 To Geo. E. Slocum

June 26th To 16 new sections on Knife 15c 2,40

July 17th " wrist pin & pit Head 1,10

$ 3,50

20% of Bobbett & Extras on H. McVean

a/c charge of July 19th 1883 3,32

$ 6,82

Cr

Nov 13th 1883 By 180# Iron 1/2¢ ,90

" " " By Cash $ 5,92 $ 6,82

Received Payment

Geo. E. Slocum

per E.H.S.

Slocum's talents were much in demand. He made a wide range of products from utensils for the home to parts for the village industries. Later he obtained the 1814 Hanford frame building to the east and expanded his store. In 1886, his son LeRoy M. joined him in the hardware business and the name was changed to G. E. and L. M. Slocum. One of his ventures, overseen by another son, Earl, was the Scottsville Agricultural Works that made wagons and farm implements that were sold at the store.

George E. Slocum sold hardware for 40 years, and then the business continued for three more generations with LeRoy I, LeRoy "Morg" II, and LeRoy "Roy" III. George was a founder of the Scottsville Literary Society. He gathered historical information and research for the book *Wheatland, Monroe County, New York* that was published after his death in 1908.

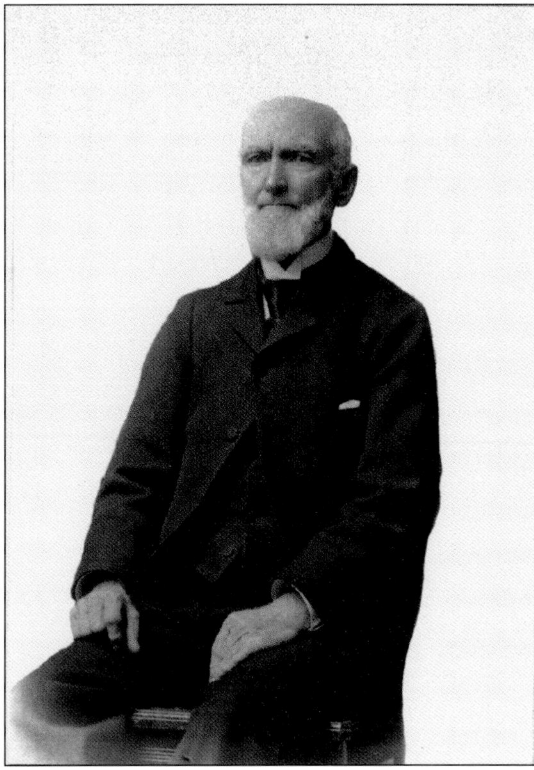

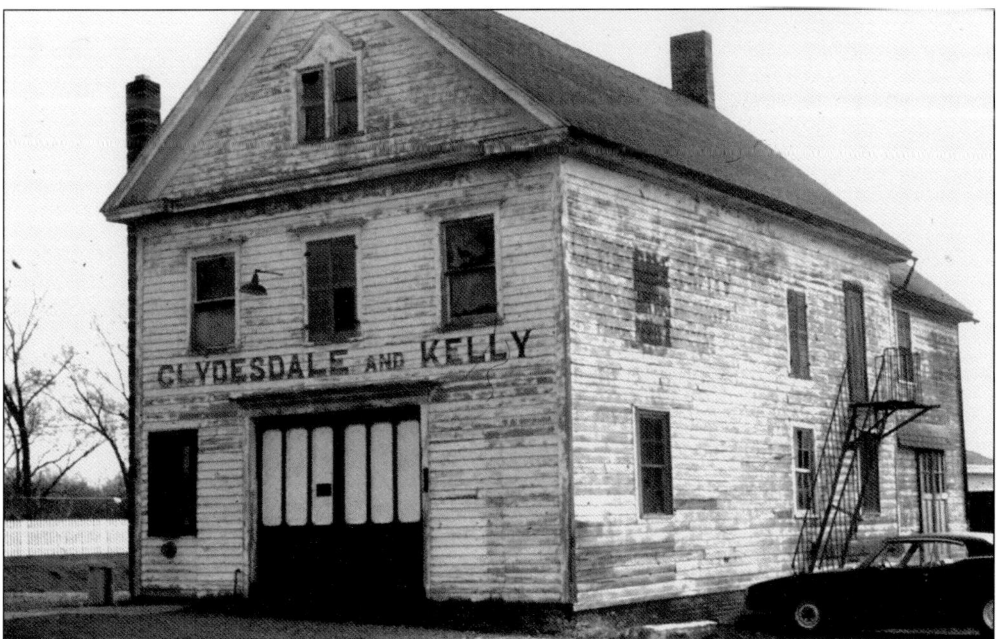

Elijah Talcott Miller constructed this building in 1832 as a mercantile business at 35 Main Street. Later it was used as a stagecoach station, a miller's residence, the fire department, and the Masonic lodge. In 1934, the structure was purchased by Roger Clydesdale and Agnes Kelly for a grain business. As town clerk, Kelly had her office here until 1967.

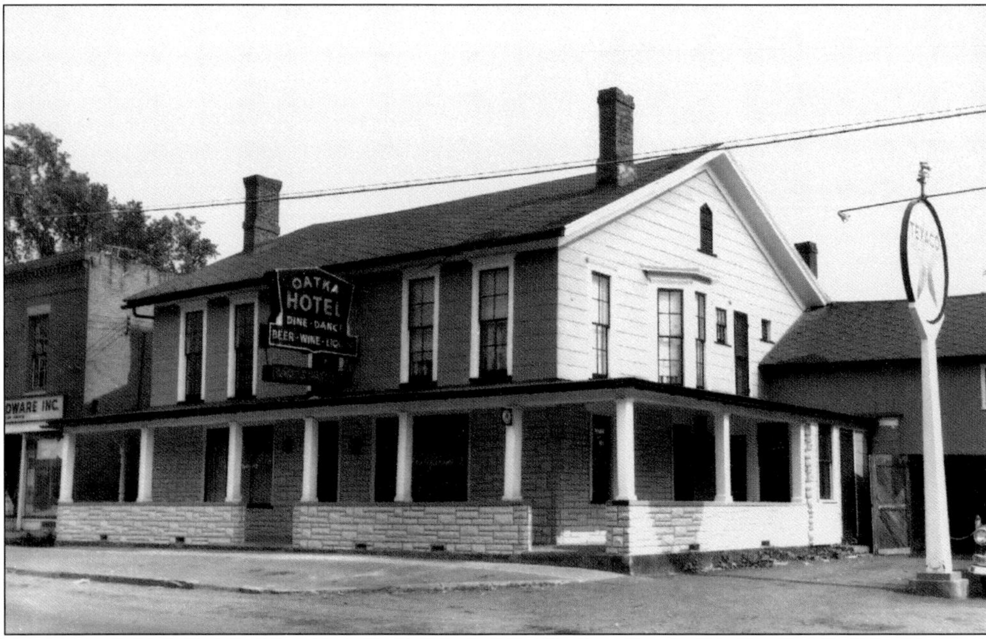

The Oatka Hotel was built in 1824 by James Brown and has changed owners many times over the years. About 1921, the hotel was sold to Mathew McConville, who remodeled and made a dance hall across the front of the building. During the Prohibition era, McConville sold only cider. The old porch overlooking Oatka Creek was made part of the dining room in 1974–1975.

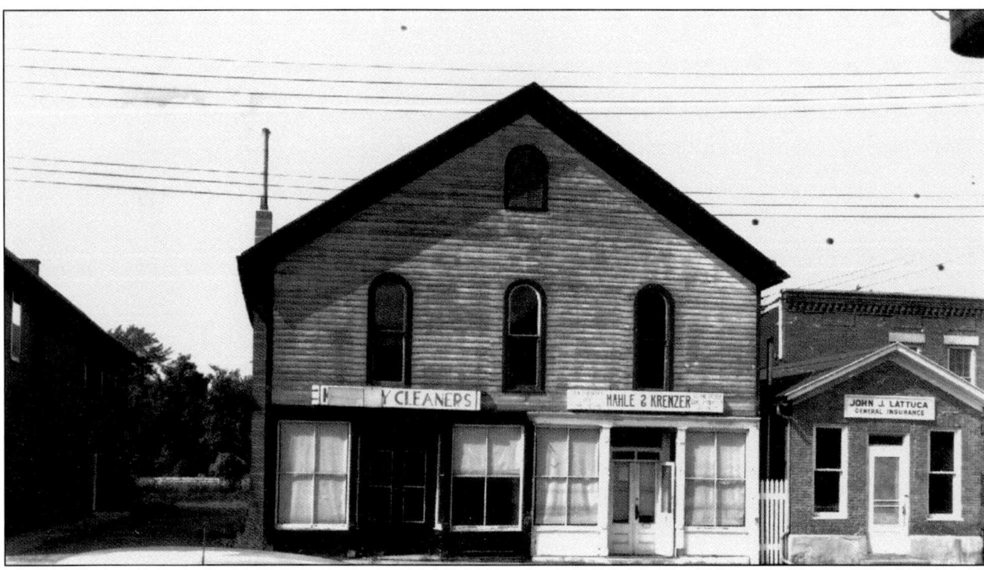

The firm of Colwell and Austin operated a general store here in 1875 and joined two small buildings together. A second story was added to serve as a meeting room called St. Joseph's Hall. Recitals, plays, and dances were held there. This building was razed in 1966 to make room for the new fire hall. (Courtesy of the family of Fredrick W. and Mary R. Kentner.)

This cobblestone general store, constructed about 1838 for Osborn Filer, is shown in a pencil sketch drawn by Carl F. Schmidt. The Keys brothers, John and William Keys, bought the property in 1890 and continued in the business until 1944. John Lattuca purchased the Keys Brother's Store at 14 Main Street and the brick building at 16 Main Street in 1950 and remodeled them into an office and apartments.

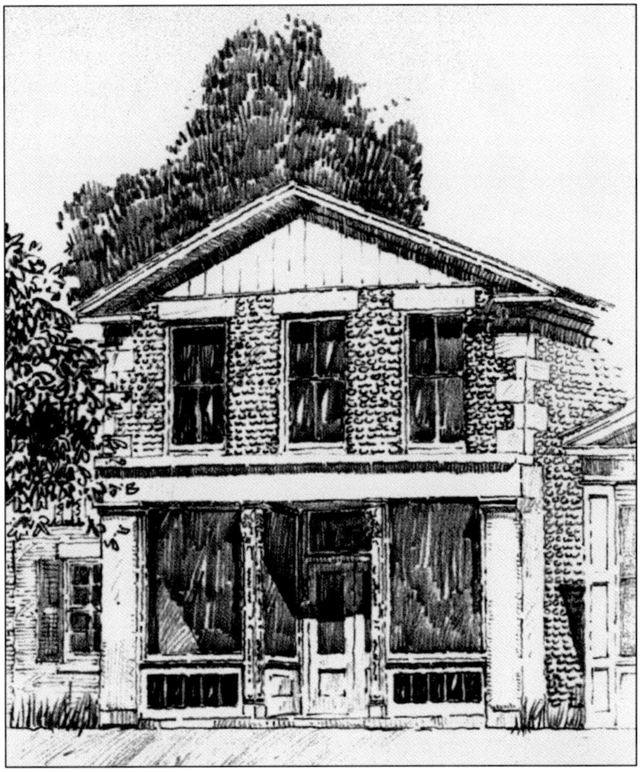

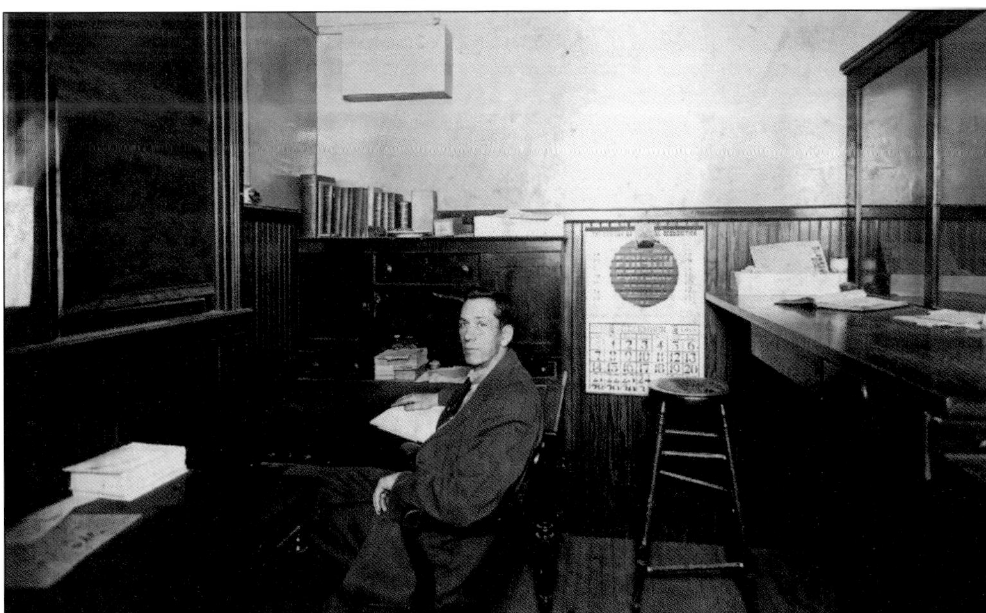

In 1904, Thomas Brown III organized a bank in the west room of Windom Hall. He then had a small frame building constructed at 7 Main Street. The bank was not a success and closed after two years. The building became the office of the Scottsville Coal Company of Everett Darrohn. Later, in 1929, the Mathews Insurance Company occupied the building. In 1971, it became the Burton Brown Insurance agency.

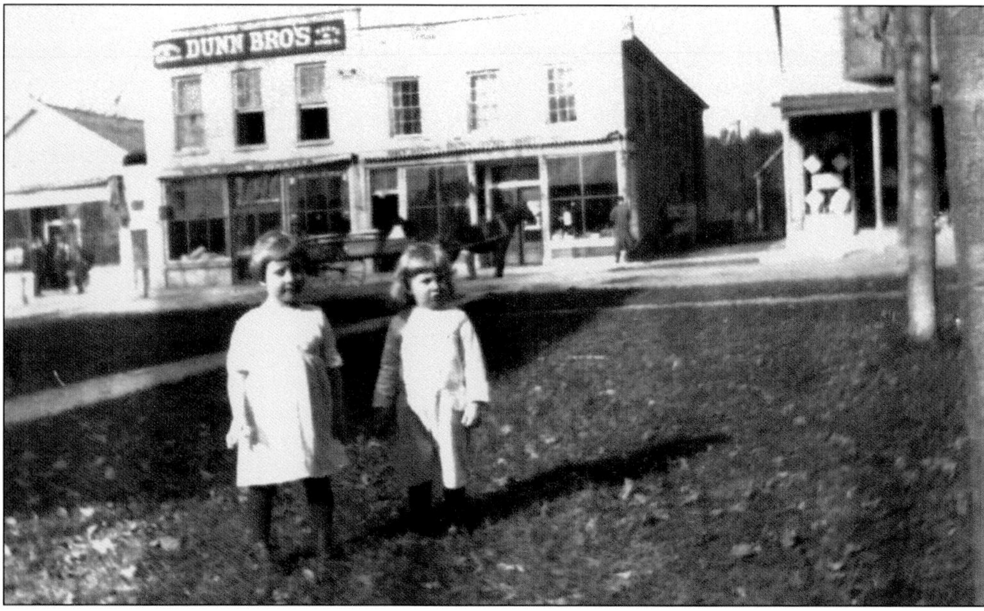

In 1903, William Dunn returned from the Alaskan gold fields and bought out Marvin Williams to join his brother, Frank W. Dunn, in a mercantile business. The brothers purchased 32 and 34 on the north side of Main Street from Phillip Garbutt. The children in the photograph are Frank W. Dunn's daughter Annis (left) and his niece Ruth Hanford. (Courtesy of Richard LeRoy.)

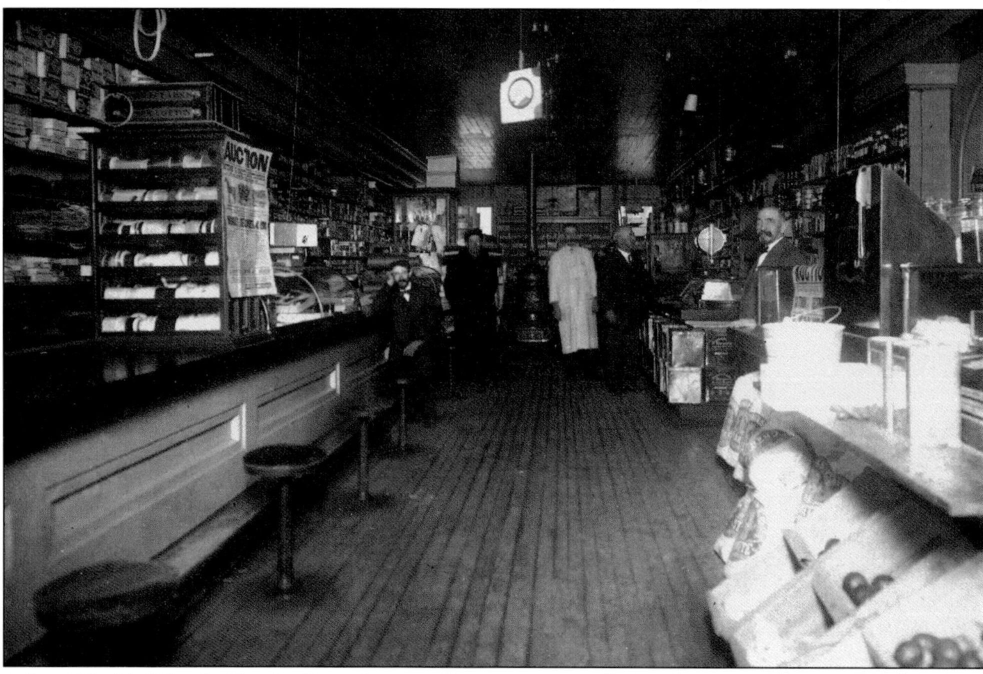

After World War I, Frank Dunn's son, Romeyn, joined the business. Dunn Brothers was Scottsville's last old-time general store. Shown here are, from left to right, William Stokoe, Robert Cox, William Dunn, Leland Horton, and Frank Dunn. In 1944, Romeyn Dunn rented 32 Main Street to the post office. In 1947, he sold the business at 34 Main Street to Harts Food Stores of Rochester. (Courtesy of Richard LeRoy.)

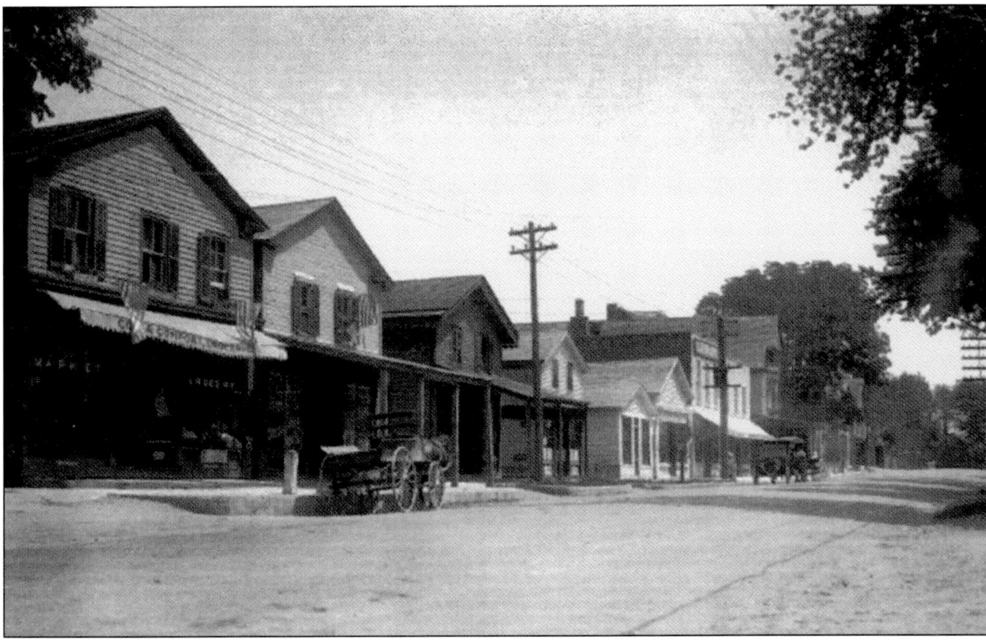

The store on the extreme left at 46 Main Street was, in 1851, the marble and tombstone business of Herman Miller and O. P. Simmons with Thomas Gildea as the marble cutter. In 1908, Theron Cox started a bakery and grocery here, and in 1910, he was joined by Mr. Comfort, who bought a half interest in the business. Donato Grassi and Son Grocery occupied the store from 1930 to the 1960s.

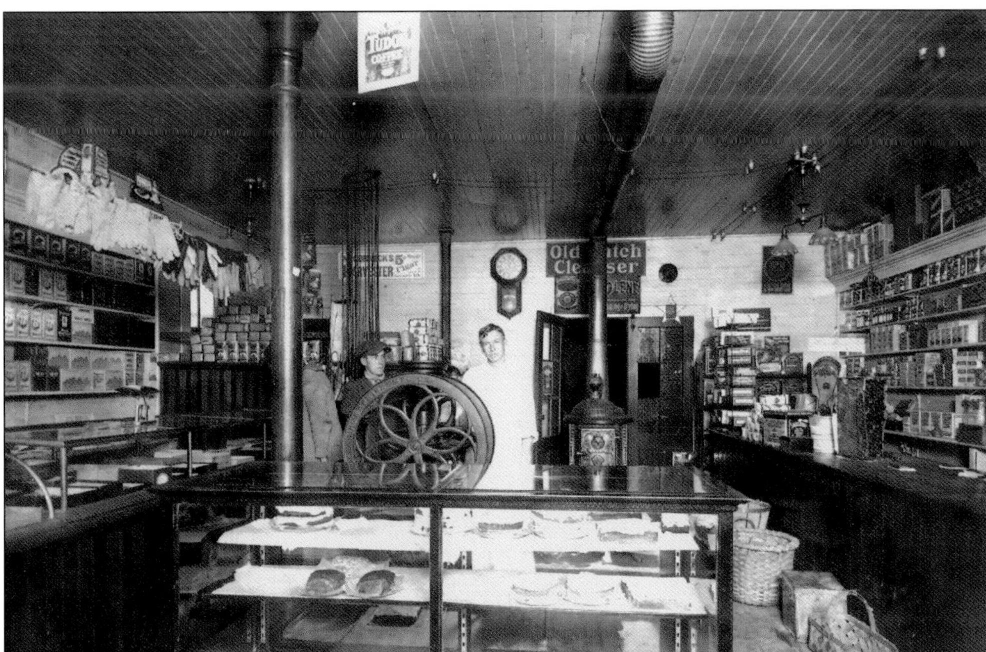

In this photograph, Theron Cox waits on Peter White in his grocery at 46 Main Street. From 1908 until 1929 he sold many products from baked goods to tobacco. Since the 1960s, this building has housed a popular diner. (Courtesy of Walter Cushman.)

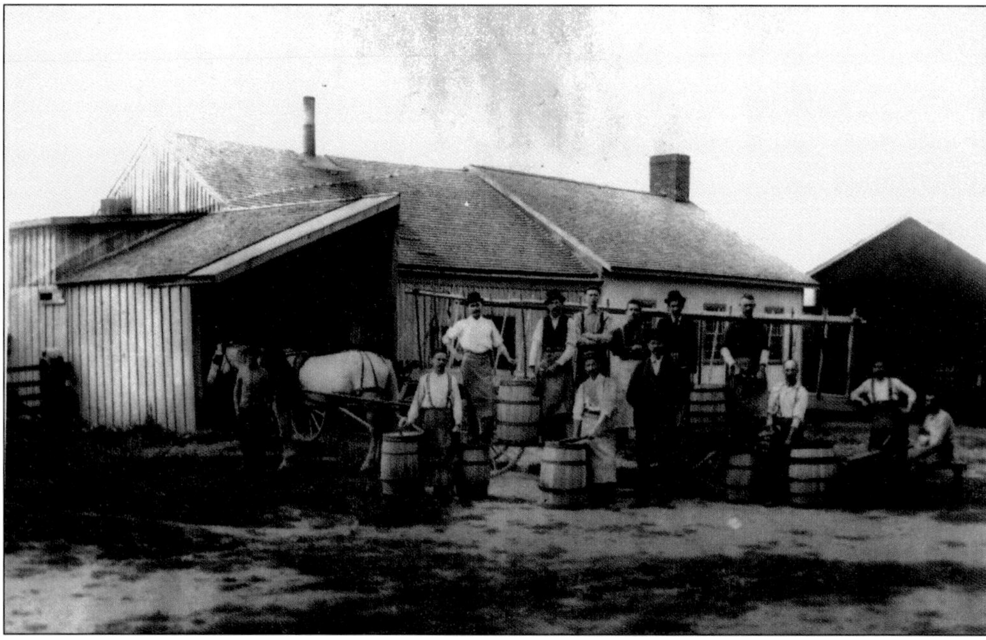

In 1886, Peter Freidell and his son, Goodard J. Freidell, purchased the Harvey Hyde cooper shop on Railroad Street, now called Scott Crescent Drive. They made flour and apple barrels and employed up to 17 coopers. After his father died in 1889, Goodard conducted the business until 1917. Other coopers in the village were George Ensign and Christian Walter, who made tight barrels for vinegar and whiskey.

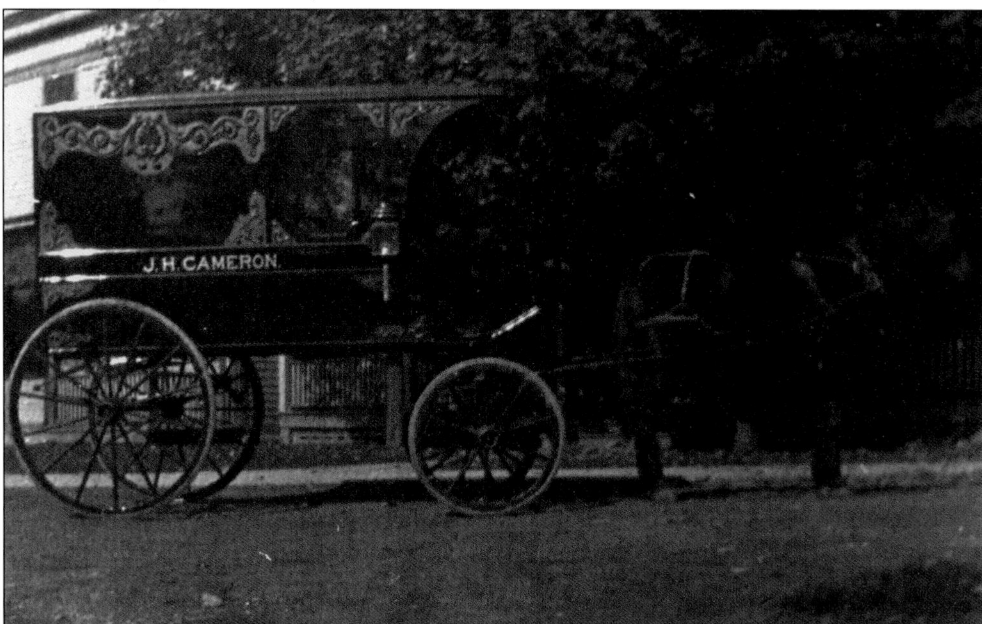

The J. H. Cameron Funeral Home is the oldest business in Scottsville, continuing for four generations. James Cameron Sr. started an undertaking service in 1907 in a storefront on Main Street. He built a home at 35 Rochester Street, where the first funeral calling hours were held. In 1926, the business moved to 26 Rochester Street. Joe Davey was employed to drive the hearse.

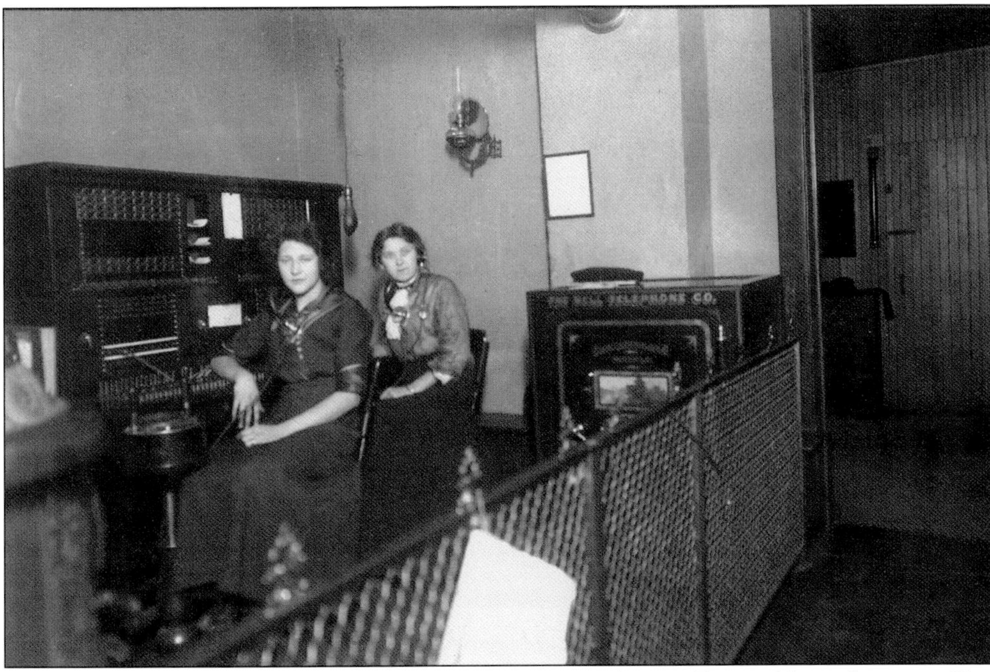

The brick building at 16 Main Street was Dr. Freeman Edson's office and later the post office. In 1902, the Scottsville telephone exchange was moved here from 30 Main Street. In this 1905 photograph, Ruth Clydesdale is the operator on the right. The last exchange in Scottsville was in a frame building at 25 Main Street, which was built by the Rochester Telephone Company in 1924. (Courtesy of Roberta R. Dunn.)

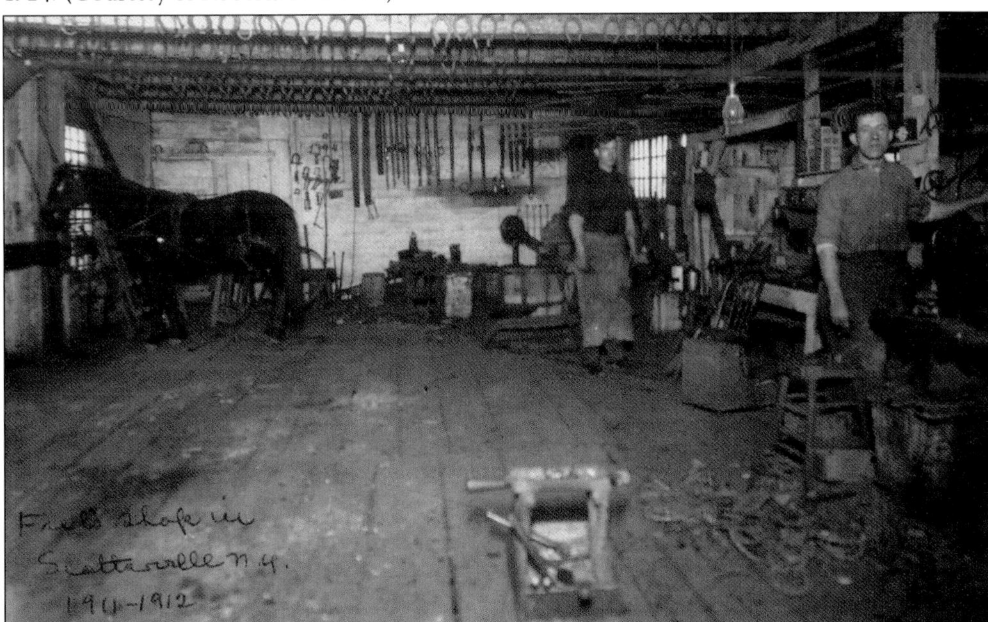

Fred Guernsey operated this blacksmith shop near the millrace at 58 Main Street from 1911 to 1912. Other blacksmiths, over the years, included John French, William Carson, James Quinlan, and Ellsworth Carver. (Courtesy of Walter Cushman.)

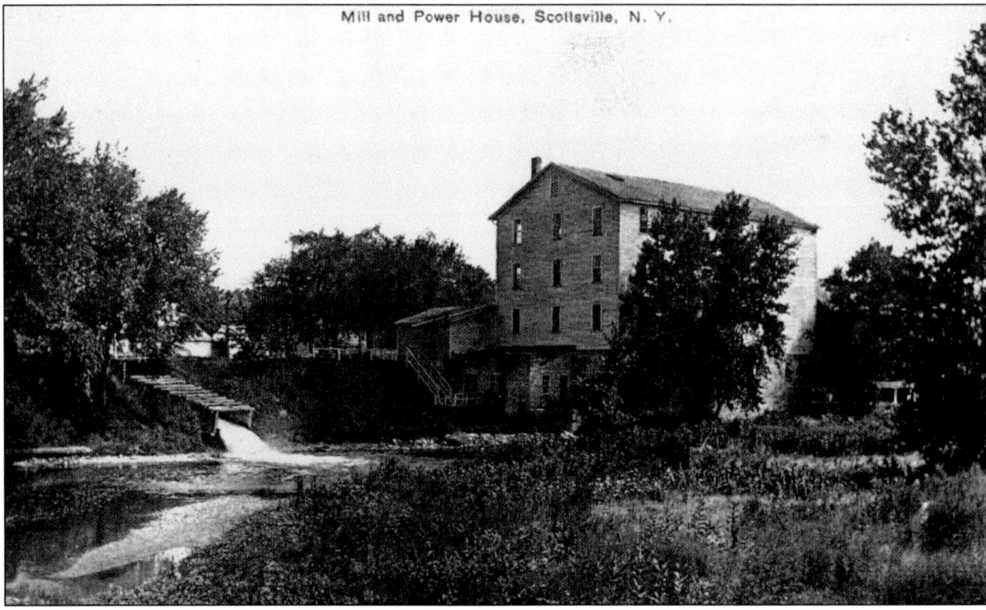

Early activity at this historic mill site, where the race emptied into Oatka Creek, was discussed in chapter 2. In 1904, a wood frame mill was built for Isaac Salyerds by John Talcott Wells. The Wheatland Milling and Power Company produced Scottsville's first electricity here in 1905. Adjacent to the millrace, this site has been the location of several buildings with a variety of uses. In 1947, the Dorey Corrugated Paper Products building, at 39 Main Street, was remodeled and equipped with machinery to manufacture special packages and boxes. It has been the Rodwin Industrial Center since 1970.

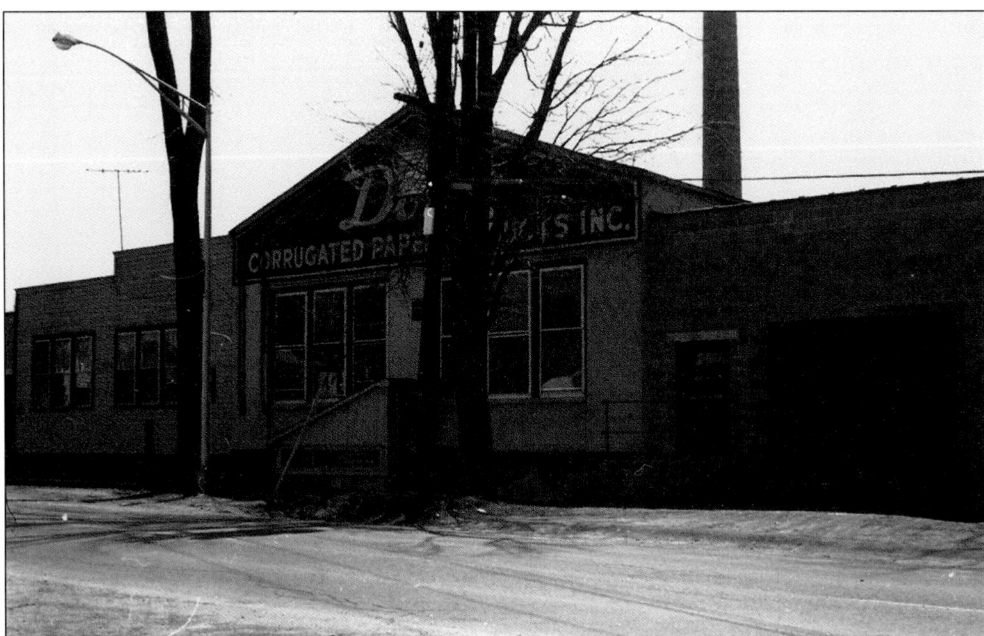

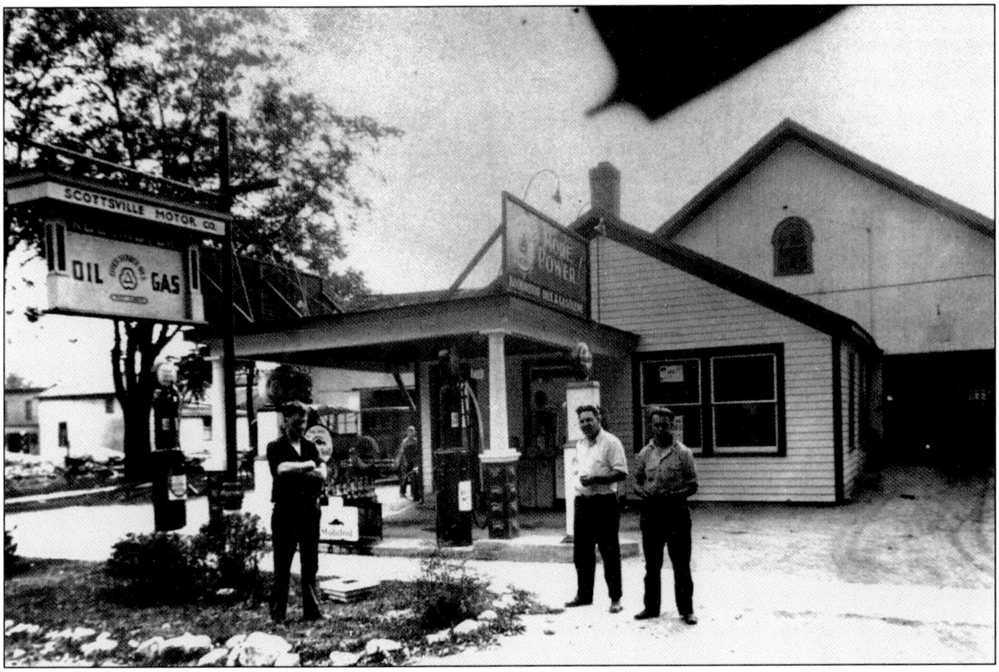

Arthur Torpey and George Rosenworth purchased an automobile repair garage in 1928 from Leo Rossiter and called it the Scottsville Motor Company. The business originated in barns at the rear of the Cargill Hotel. Torpey sold his interest to his partner in 1937. A year later, Rosenworth sold the business to William Jarret. Shown here from left to right are Arthur Torpey, George Rosenworth, and James Baker.

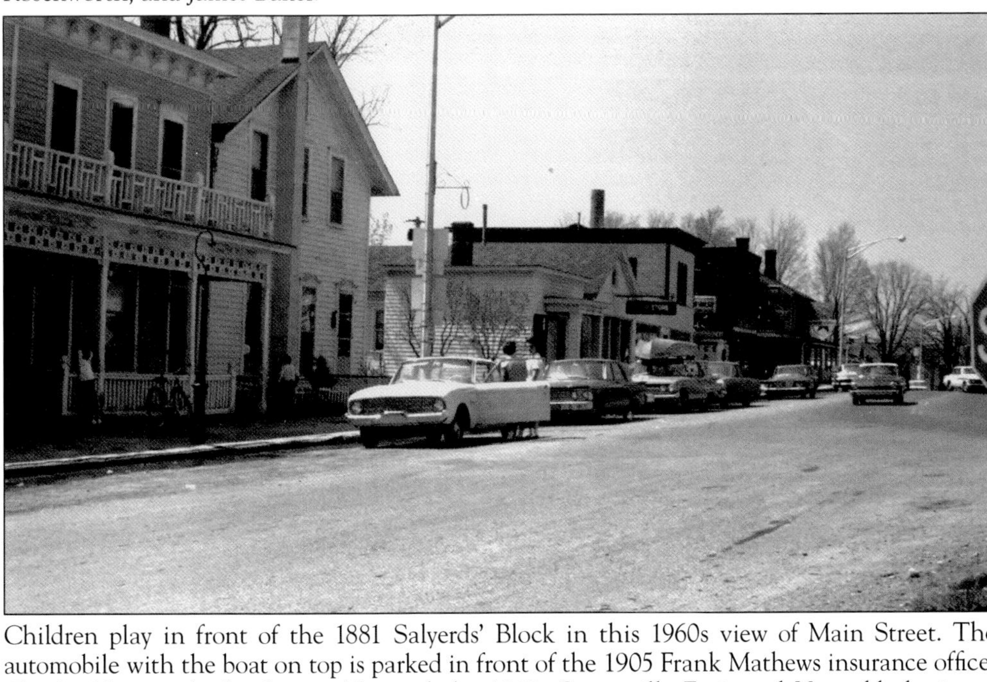

Children play in front of the 1881 Salyerds' Block in this 1960s view of Main Street. The automobile with the boat on top is parked in front of the 1905 Frank Mathews insurance office. The building with the flat roof housed the 1940s Scottsville Fruit and Vegetable business, commonly called Shortie's. The Oatka Hotel, dating from 1824, is the last building visible.

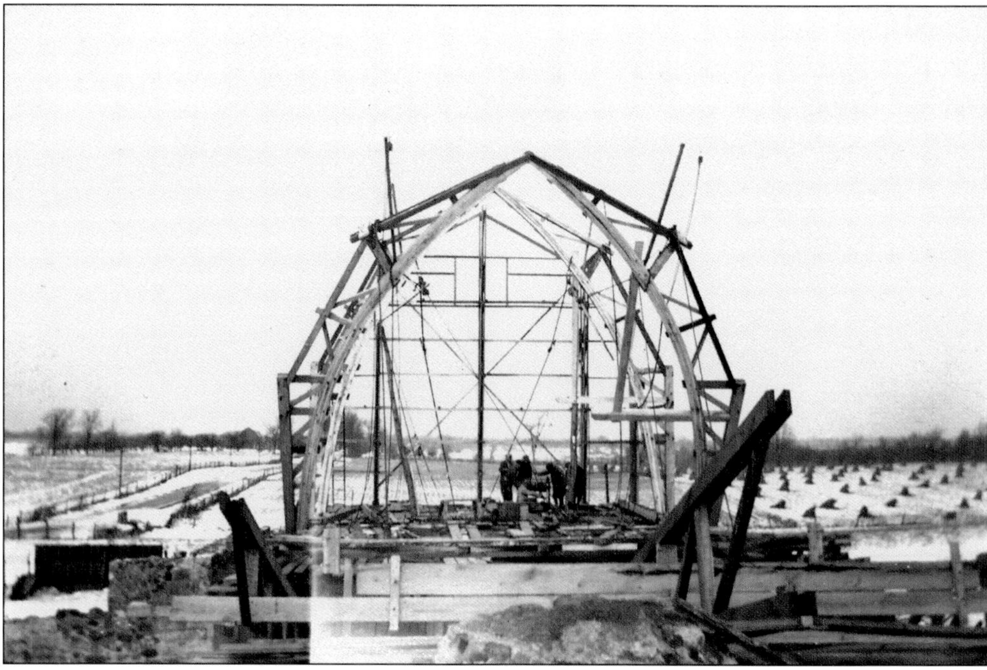

In 1888, John Talcott Wells Sr. invented a truss design for barns. By strengthening the roof and eliminating supporting posts, it was possible to drive a hay wagon into the barn. Over 50 Wells barns were constructed in western New York. In this 1942 picture, the last traditional Wells truss barn is being built by John T. Wells Jr. for Selden Stokoe at 940 Bowerman Road. (Courtesy of Richard Stokoe.)

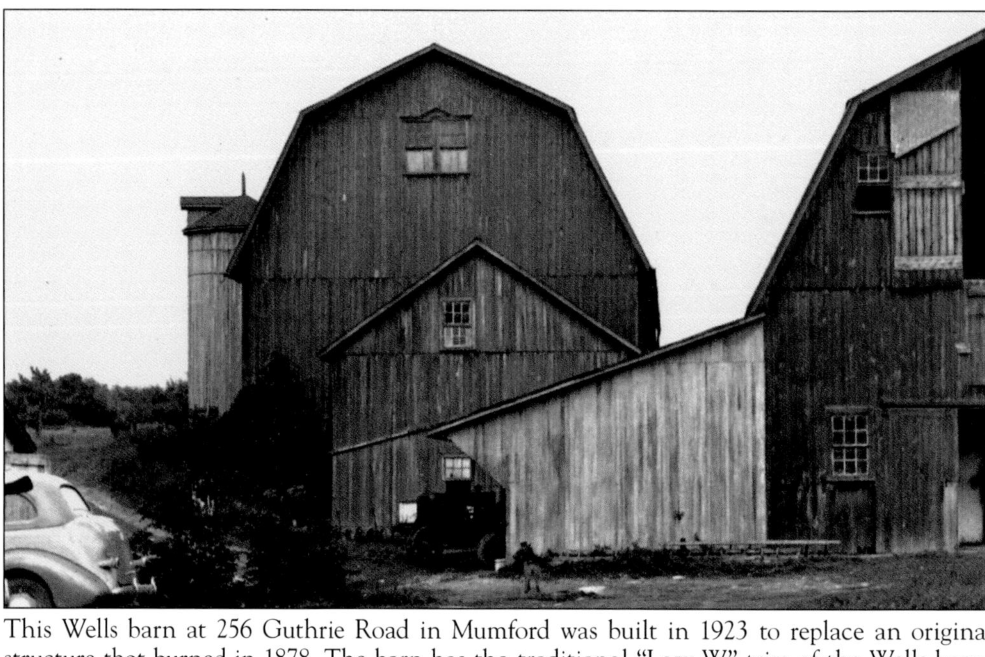

This Wells barn at 256 Guthrie Road in Mumford was built in 1923 to replace an original structure that burned in 1878. The barn has the traditional "Lazy W" trim of the Wells barns over the windows. The Guthrie farm was established in 1830 and is now owned by Marion Guthrie. (Courtesy of Jean Guthrie.)

After studying medicine at Yale, Dr. Freeman Edson traveled to Scottsville on horseback in 1814. He came to visit his uncle, Isaac Scott, but stayed to practice medicine in the village for nearly 70 years. He was the first Scottsville postmaster, a school commissioner, and a stockholder in the Scottsville and LeRoy Railroad and the Scottsville-Genesee River Canal. Dr. Edson was admired for his fine character and contributions to the community.

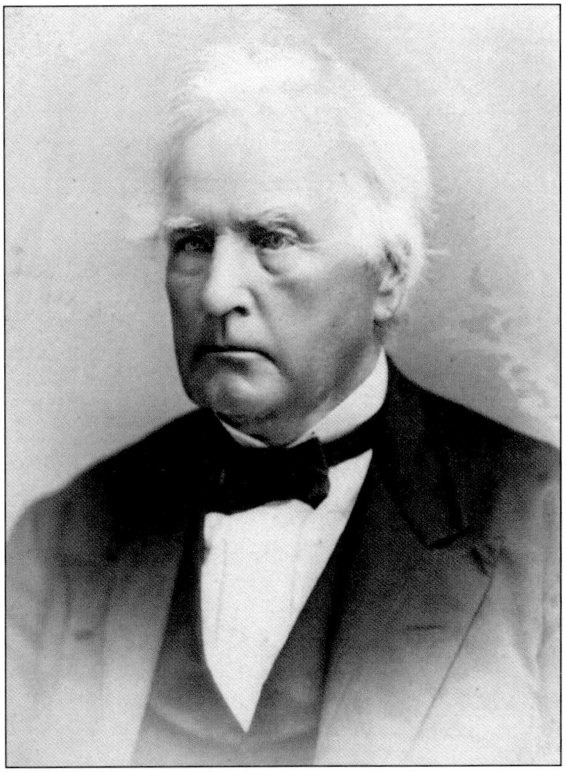

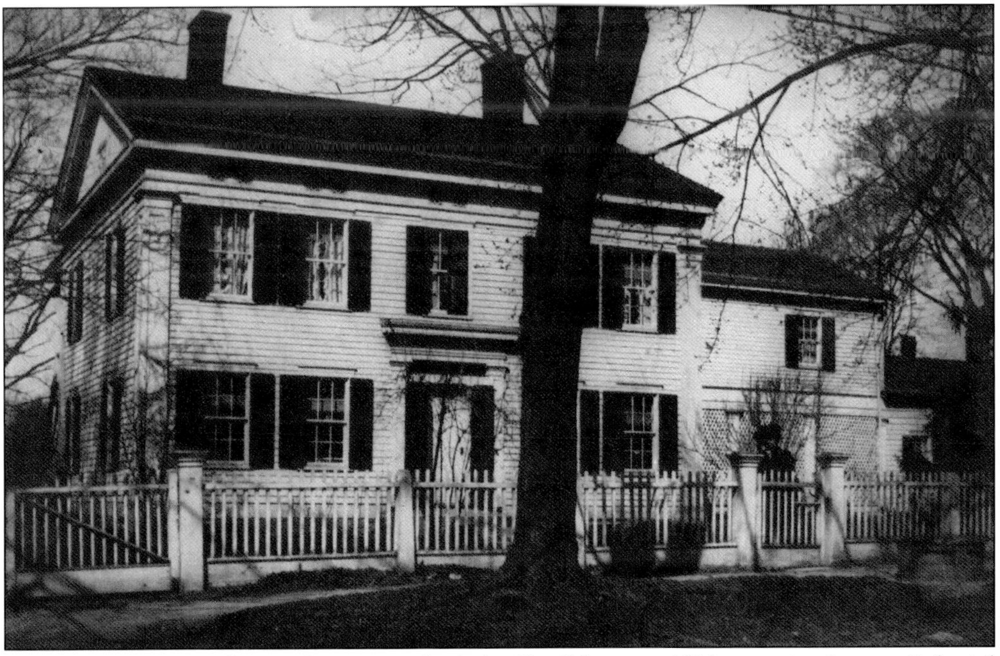

This house at 7 Rochester Street was built by Dr. Edson in 1816 in a simple post-Colonial style. In 1846, the house was completely remodeled with the main cornice, corner pilasters, and entrance in the Greek Revival style. It became the home of the George and Lucy Skivington family in 1923 and then the John and Dolores Loftus family in 1963.

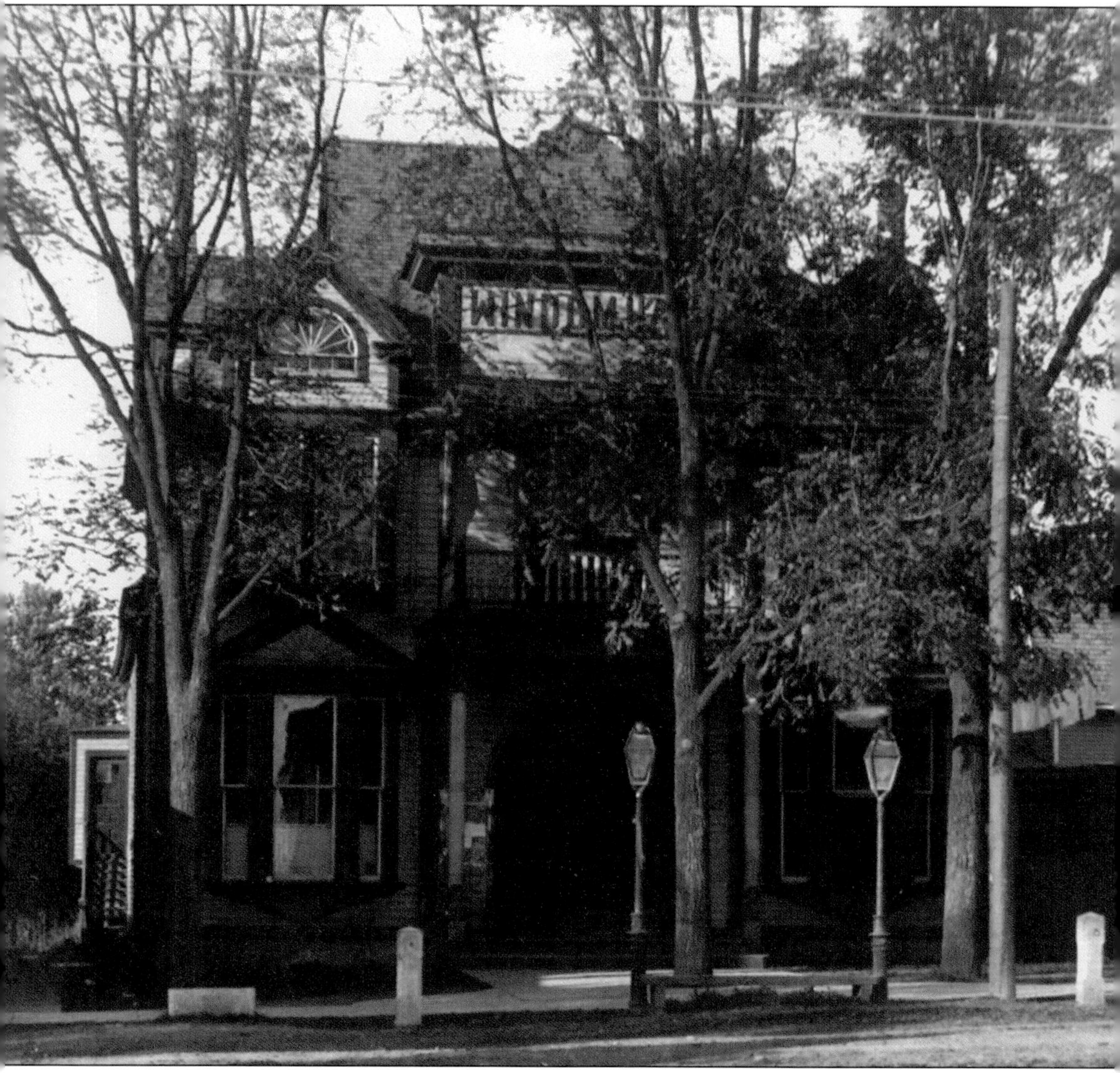

Windom Hall was built in 1891 to provide a space for community activities. A group of local private investors was headed by James Kelly. Designed by noted architect Charles Ellis, Windom Hall is in the Queen Anne style, and today retains virtually all its original features. Myron Pope was the builder of this distinctive building. The auditorium had a seating capacity of 468 including a 100-seat balcony. On the left of this photograph, the stairway to the backstage can be seen. This view is rarely shown, and that entrance has been eliminated. The balcony over the front doors deteriorated over the years and was also removed. Windom Hall was a busy hub of cultural activity around the dawn of the 20th century, playing host to performances of the local drama club, school and church activities, dances, and library facilities. By 1916, public use of the rooms had decreased, and the building was donated to the Scottsville Free Library. The building was listed with the National Register of Historic Places in 1994.

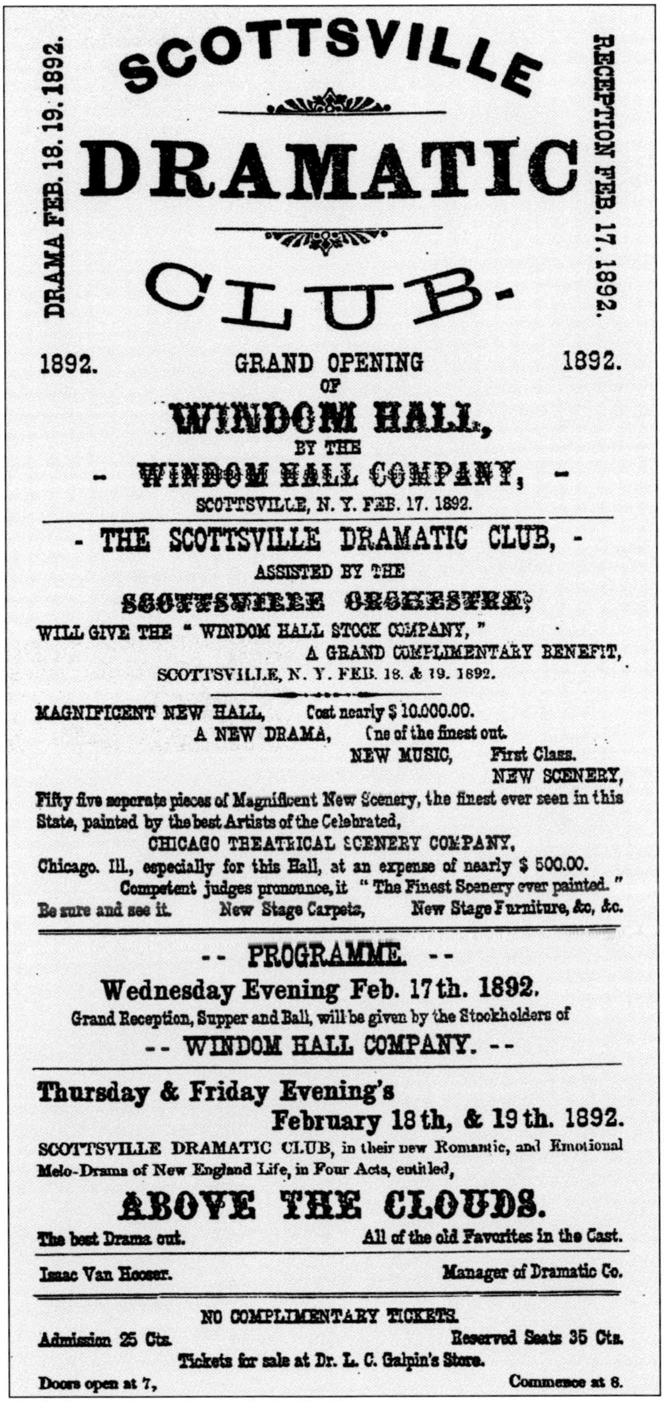

DRAMA FEB. 18. 19. 1892.

SCOTTSVILLE DRAMATIC CLUB.

RECEPTION FEB. 17. 1892.

1892. GRAND OPENING 1892.

OF

WINDOM HALL,

BY THE

- **WINDOM HALL COMPANY,** -

SCOTTSVILLE, N. Y. FEB. 17. 1892.

- **THE SCOTTSVILLE DRAMATIC CLUB,** -

ASSISTED BY THE

SCOTTSVILLE ORCHESTRA,

WILL GIVE THE " WINDOM HALL STOCK COMPANY, "

A GRAND COMPLIMENTARY BENEFIT,

SCOTTSVILLE, N. Y. FEB. 18. & 19. 1892.

MAGNIFICENT NEW HALL, Cost nearly $ 10.000.00.

A NEW DRAMA, One of the finest out.

NEW MUSIC, First Class.

NEW SCENERY,

Fifty five seperate pieces of Magnificent New Scenery, the finest ever seen in this State, painted by the best Artists of the Celebrated,

CHICAGO THEATRICAL SCENERY COMPANY,

Chicago. Ill., especially for this Hall, at an expense of nearly $ 500.00.

Competent judges pronounce, it " The Finest Scenery ever painted. "

Be sure and see it. New Stage Carpets, New Stage Furniture, &c, &c.

-- **PROGRAMME.** --

Wednesday Evening Feb. 17th. 1892.

Grand Reception, Supper and Ball, will be given by the Stockholders of

-- **WINDOM HALL COMPANY.** --

Thursday & Friday Evening's

February 18th, & 19th. 1892.

SCOTTSVILLE DRAMATIC CLUB, in their new Romantic, and Emotional Melo-Drama of New England Life, in Four Acts, entitled,

ABOVE THE CLOUDS.

The best Drama out. All of the old Favorites in the Cast.

Isaac Van Hooser. Manager of Dramatic Co.

NO COMPLIMENTARY TICKETS.

Admission 25 Cts. Reserved Seats 35 Cts.

Tickets for sale at Dr. L. C. Galpin's Store.

Doors open at 7, Commence at 8.

This 1892 poster advertises the grand opening of the new Windom Hall at 28 Main Street and gives details of the celebration. It was printed by Isaac Van Hooser on his printing press. The Scottsville Dramatic Club made its first appearance in the play *Above the Clouds*. The community was pleased with the large auditorium and looked forward to future programs and entertainments there.

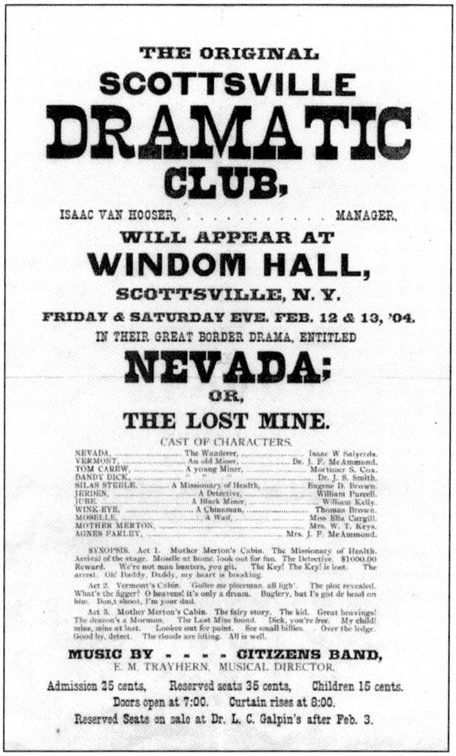
THE ORIGINAL

SCOTTSVILLE

DRAMATIC

CLUB,

ISAAC VAN HOOSER, ... MANAGER.

WILL APPEAR AT

WINDOM HALL,

SCOTTSVILLE, N. Y.

FRIDAY & SATURDAY EVE. FEB. 12 & 13, '04.

IN THEIR GREAT BORDER DRAMA, ENTITLED

NEVADA;

OR,

THE LOST MINE.

CAST OF CHARACTERS.

NEVADA,	The Wanderer,	Isaac W Salyerds.
VERMONT,	An old Miner,	Dr. J. F. McAmmond.
TOM CAREW,	A young Miner,	Mortimer S. Cox.
DANDY DICK,	" " "	Dr. J. S. Smith.
SILAS STEELE,	A Missionary of Health,	Eugene D. Brown.
JERDEN,	A Detective,	William Purcell.
JUBE,	A Black Miner,	William Kelly.
WINK-EYE,	A Chinaman,	Thomas Brown.
MOSELLE,	A Waif,	Miss Ella Cargill.
MOTHER MERTON,		Mrs. W. T. Keys.
AGNES FARLEY,		Mrs. J. F. McAmmond.

SYNOPSIS. Act 1. Mother Merton's Cabin. The Missionary of Health. Arrival of the stage. Moselle at home, look out for fun. The Detective. $1000.00 Reward. We're not man hunters, you git. The Key! The Key! is lost. The arrest. Oh! Daddy, Daddy, my heart is breaking.

Act 2. Vermont's Cabin. Goller me pleeman, all ligh'. The plot revealed. What's the figger? O heavens! it's only a dream. Buglery, but I's got de bead on him. Don,t shoot, I'm your dad.

Act 3. Mother Merton's Cabin. The fairy story. The kid. Great heavings! The deacon's a Mormon. The Lost Mine found. Dick, you're free. My child! mine, mine at last. Lookee out for paint. See small billies. Over the ledge. Good by, detect. The clouds are lifting. All is well.

MUSIC BY - - - - CITIZENS BAND,

E. M. TRAYHERN, MUSICAL DIRECTOR.

Admission 25 cents, Reserved seats 35 cents, Children 15 cents.

Doors open at 7:00. Curtain rises at 8:00.

Reserved Seats on sale at Dr. L. C. Galpin's after Feb. 3.

The 20-by-40-foot stage at Windom Hall was outfitted with 55 separate pieces of scenery purchased from the Chicago Scenery Company at a cost of $500. Inside and outside exits, a trap door, drawbridge, and drop curtains were used for dramatic entrances and disappearances. Carpets and furniture completed the grand setting.

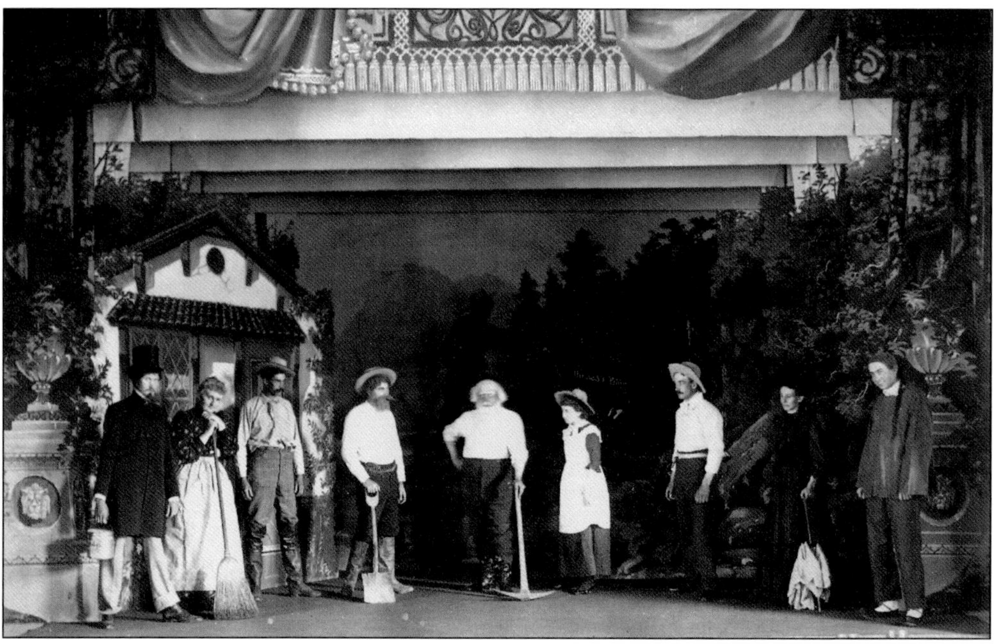

The Scottsville Dramatic Club presented the play *Nevada; or, The Lost Mine* on February 12–13, 1904. It was a popular 1882 melodrama by George M. Baker. The leading roles were played by Isaac Salyerds as the wanderer, William Purcell as the detective, and Isabelle Stewart Keys as Mother Merton. Isaac Van Hooser was the manager, and music was provided by the Citizens Band with Eli M. Trayhern as director.

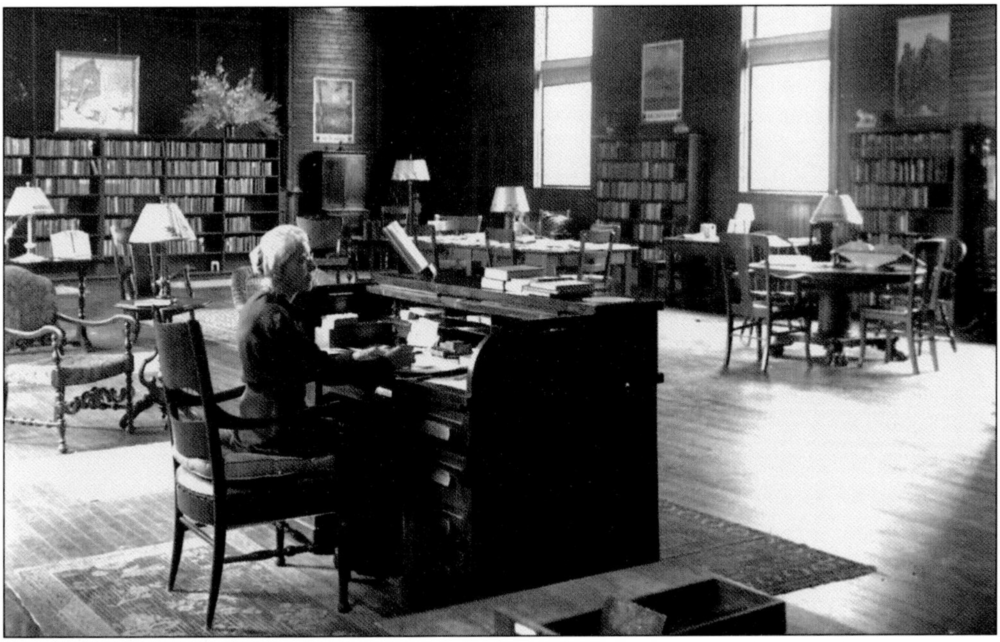

In Scottsville, a reading room opened in 1912 at 29 Main Street and in 1916 moved across the street to Windom Hall. In 1935, the Scottsville Village Improvement Society deeded the building to the Scottsville Free Library, and in 1936, New York State granted a permanent charter. Shown here is Ida Chambers, librarian from 1912 until 1944.

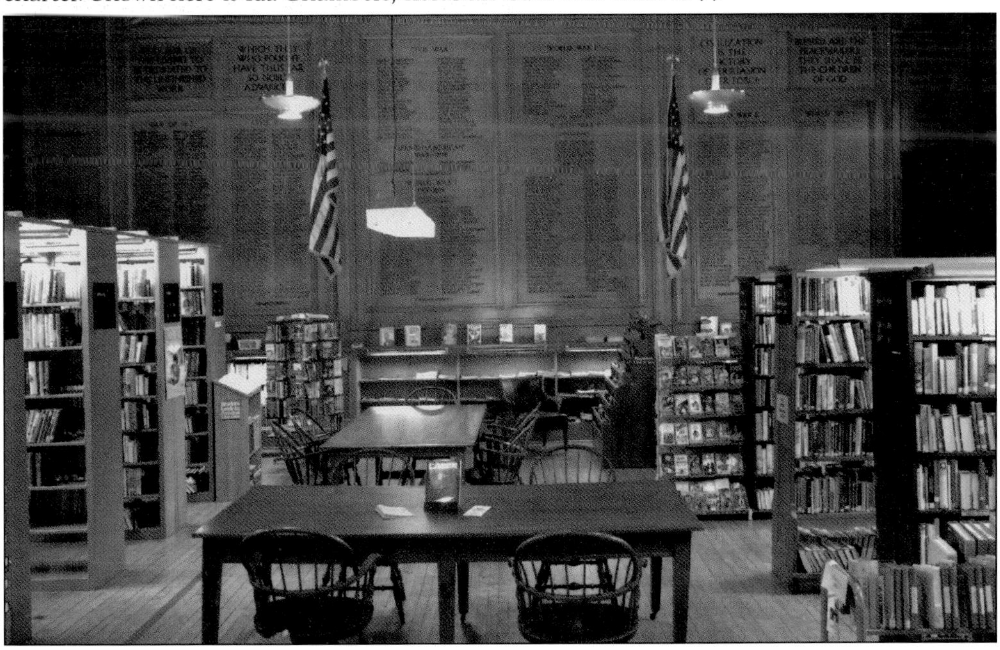

The memorial wall in the Scottsville Library was donated by R. T. Miller Jr. in memory of the area residents who had fought for their country. The gold stars next to names indicate those who died. Carl Schmidt designed the wall, and professor Dr. Alfred Jones selected the quotations. The evening chimes heard from the library were also presented as a memorial at the dedication held in 1947.

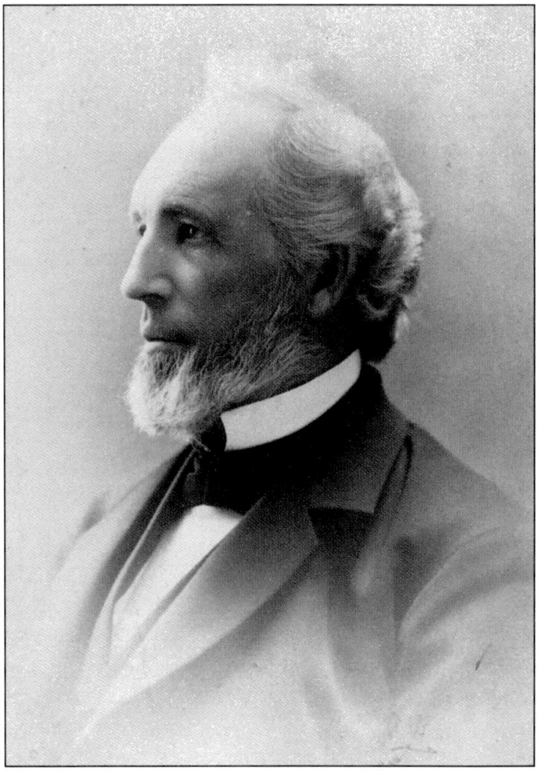

Dyer Dayton Stanley (D. D. S.) Brown, a prominent lawyer, was appointed Scottsville postmaster in 1852 and was Monroe County clerk in 1858 to 1860. He was a delegate to the Republican national convention of 1860. Brown was a paymaster of the Army of the Potomac. He owned the *Rochester Daily Democrat* newspaper from 1865 to 1870. He was a director of the Rochester and State Line Railroad. (Courtesy of Richard LeRoy.)

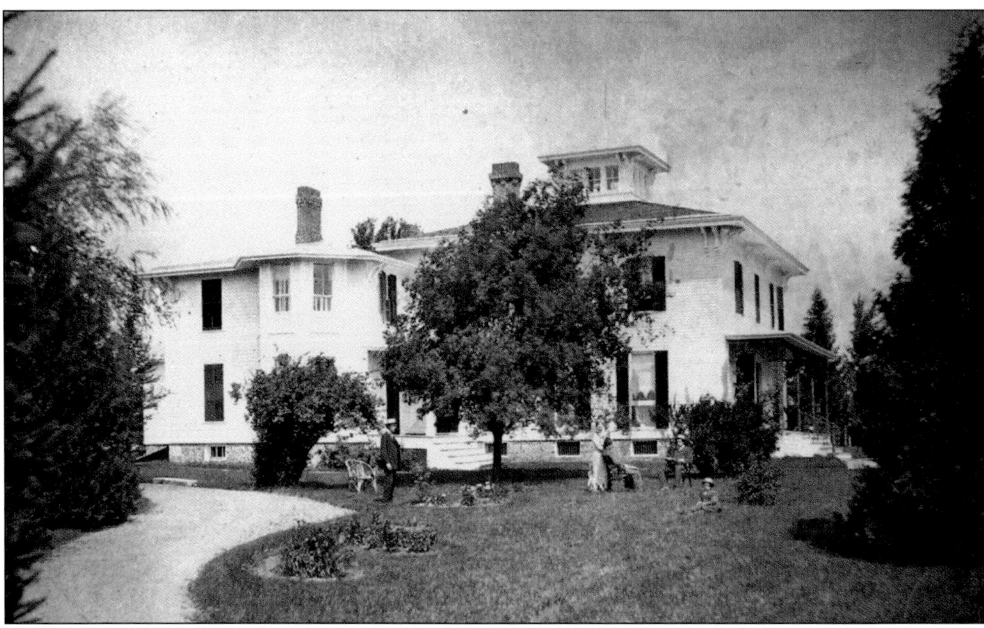

In 1856, Brown built the largest residence in the village, an Italianate-style house at 41 Brown's Avenue. He donated the land for Beckwith and Brown's Avenues for easy access to the village and his property. In 1936, his granddaughter Margaret Brown converted its 24 rooms into apartments. Great-grandson Selden Brown II, Scottsville's mayor from 1965 to 1975, lived here with his extended family until 1976. (Courtesy of Richard LeRoy.)

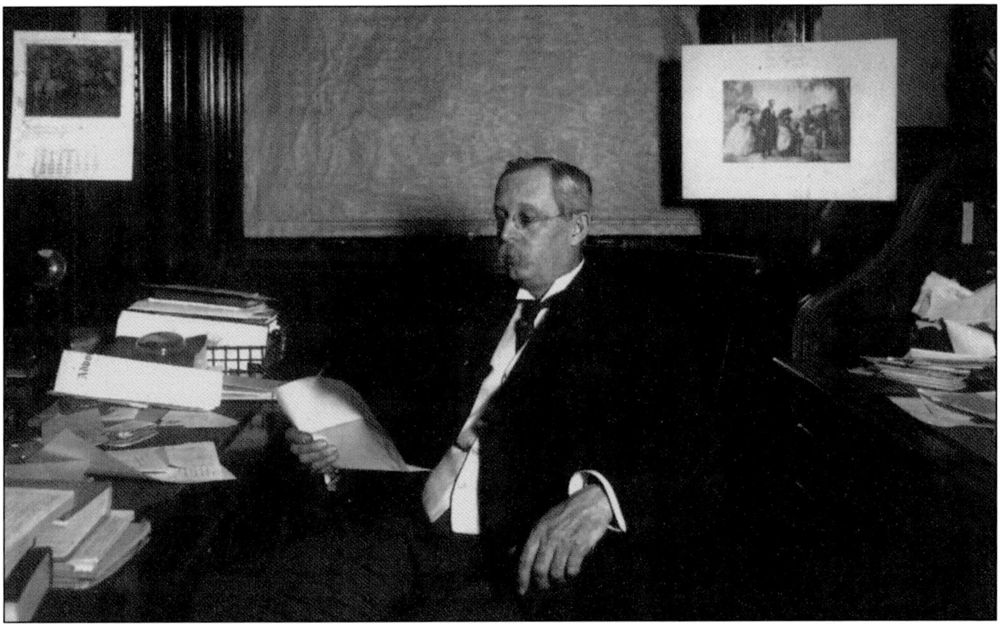

Selden Stanley Brown, son of D. D. S. and Mary Ann Ensign Brown, was a surrogate judge in Rochester from 1905 to 1925 and a prominent citizen in Scottsville. He was active in securing a new railroad station on the Baltimore and Ohio Railroad line. He was the prime organizer in 1885 to build Grace Episcopal Church, and for its first 50 years, he was senior warden. (Courtesy of Richard LeRoy.)

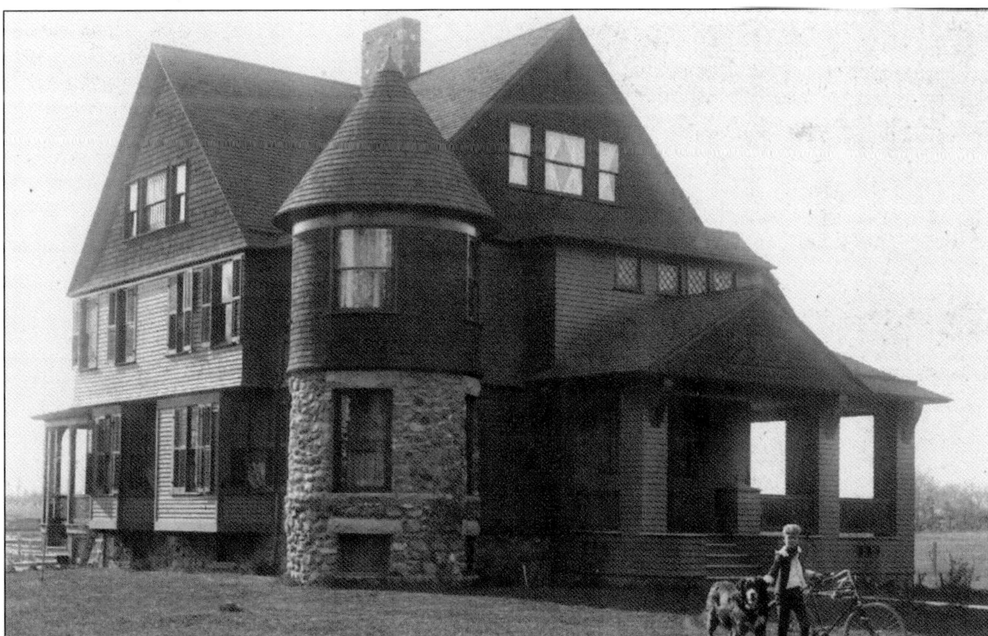

Built in 1898, the residence of Selden S. Brown at the corner of Brown's and Maple Avenues was built in the Queen Anne style. It has a distinctive two-story round tower with a conical roof on the southeast corner. S. King Brown, the son of Selden and his wife, Adele Franklin, poses in the yard with his dog Roy. (Courtesy of Richard LeRoy.)

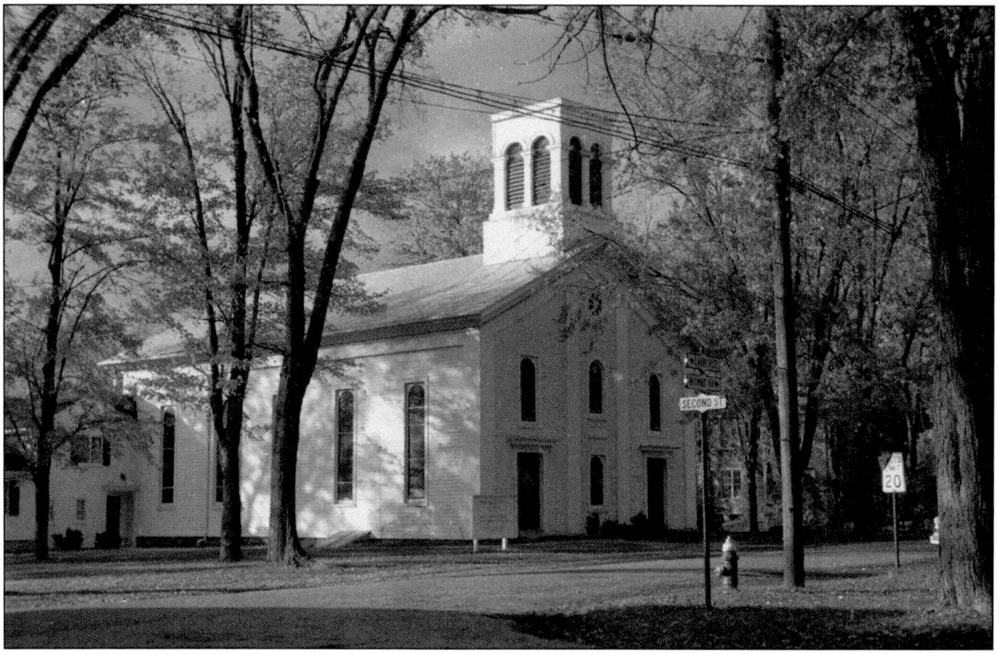

The original church of the First Presbyterian Society of Wheatland, built in 1832, faced south at the end of Chapel Street and was destroyed by fire in 1856. The church accepted D. D. S. Brown's offer of a lot on the west side of his proposed street. The new church was built by Luke Marvin for $6,000 and was completed in May 1857. Its steeple was destroyed by lightning in 1941.

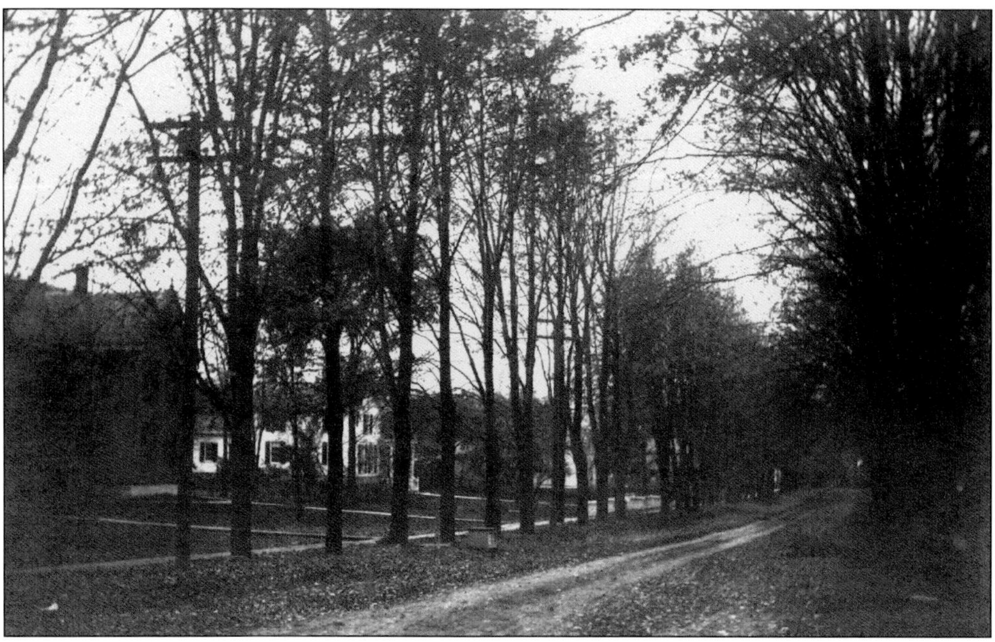

Beautiful maple trees lined Brown's Avenue looking south toward the village. After the avenue was opened in 1856, D. D. S. Brown gave land for the site of the Union School in 1870 and in 1885 for the building of Grace Episcopal Church. Residences were erected by local builders on lots sold by Brown. (Courtesy of Richard LeRoy.)

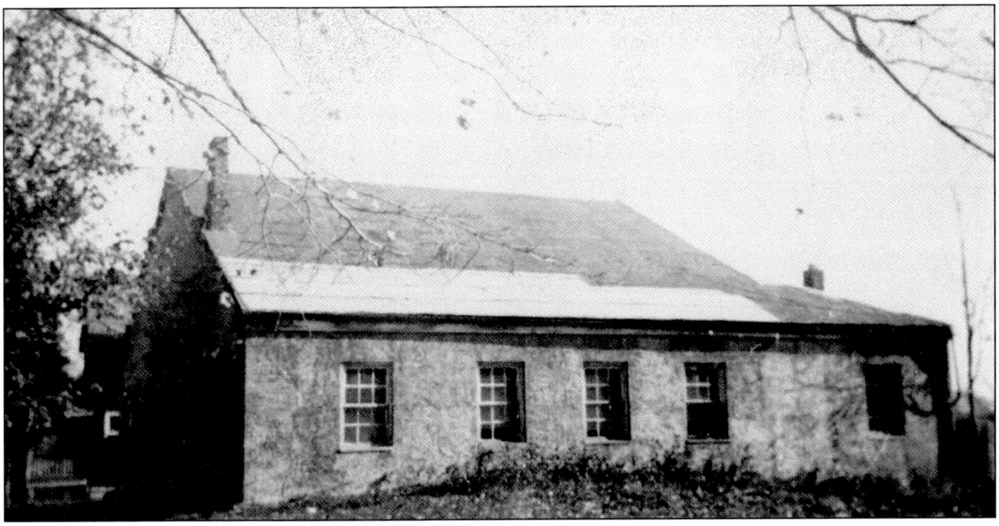

Wheatland District No. 1 schoolhouse in Scottsville was built in 1841 at 4 East Genesee Street near Rochester Street. The brick school had two rooms and an entry at the left side of the picture. In 1844, an addition was built using bricks from school No. 10 on North Road. This school was used until 1870, when the new school was opened on Brown's Avenue, and this building became a residence.

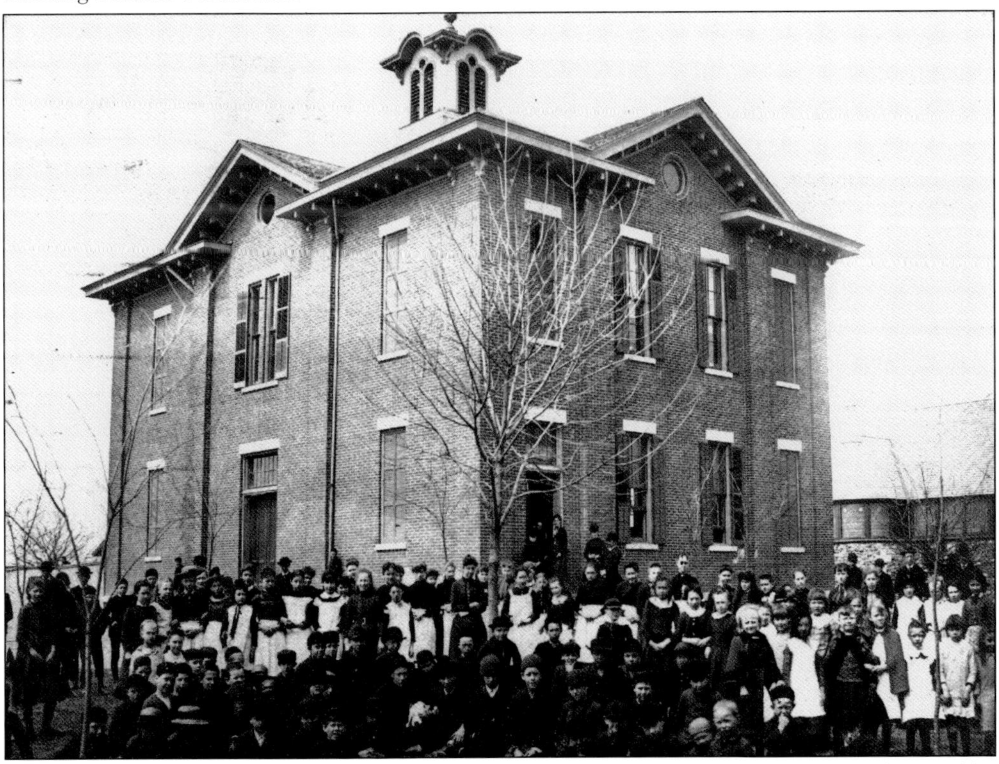

The Scottsville Union High School was built at 5 Brown's Avenue in 1870. It was designed by Charles Ellis, a leading local architect, who lived in the Shadbolt-Krenzer house at 337 Quaker Road. This Italianate brick building had the high school upstairs and the elementary classes downstairs. Prof. Frank Brown, the principal, and his five teachers offered a rigorous academic curriculum.

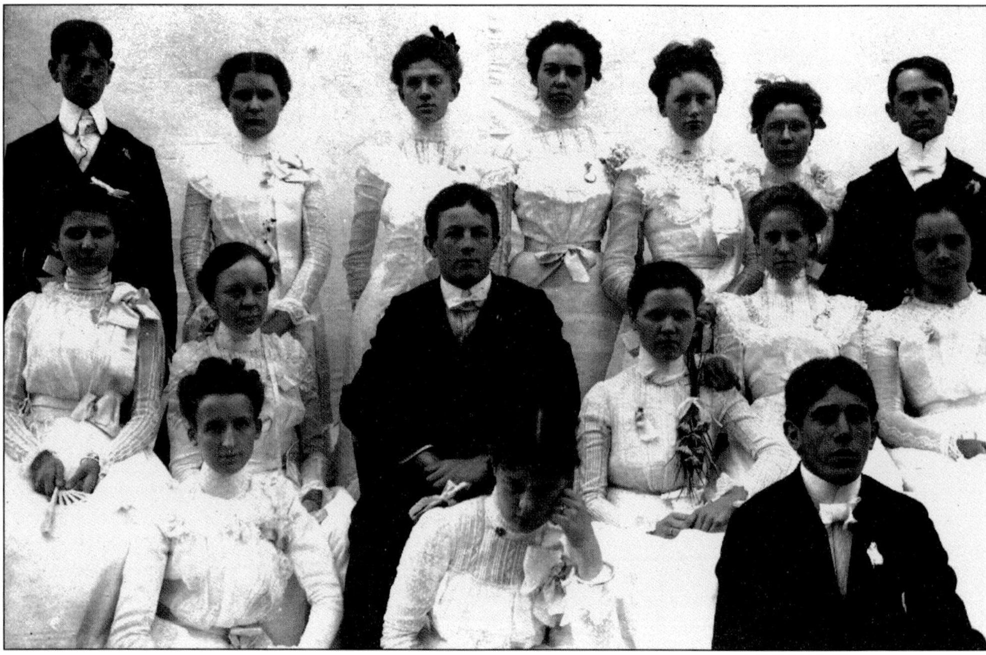

Sixteen students graduated from Scottsville Union High School in 1900. The graduation exercises were held in Windom Hall. They are, from left to right, (first row) Francis Fifield, Marjorie Mordoff, and Clarence Budlong; (second row) Mary Weingand, Grace Rogers, Harry Hart, Etta Bowerman, Irena Rogers, and Ida Salyerds; (third row) Ray Sickles, Mattie Cox, Ann Rogers, Lola Welcher, Florence Davis, Jenne Galusha, and Chester Slocum.

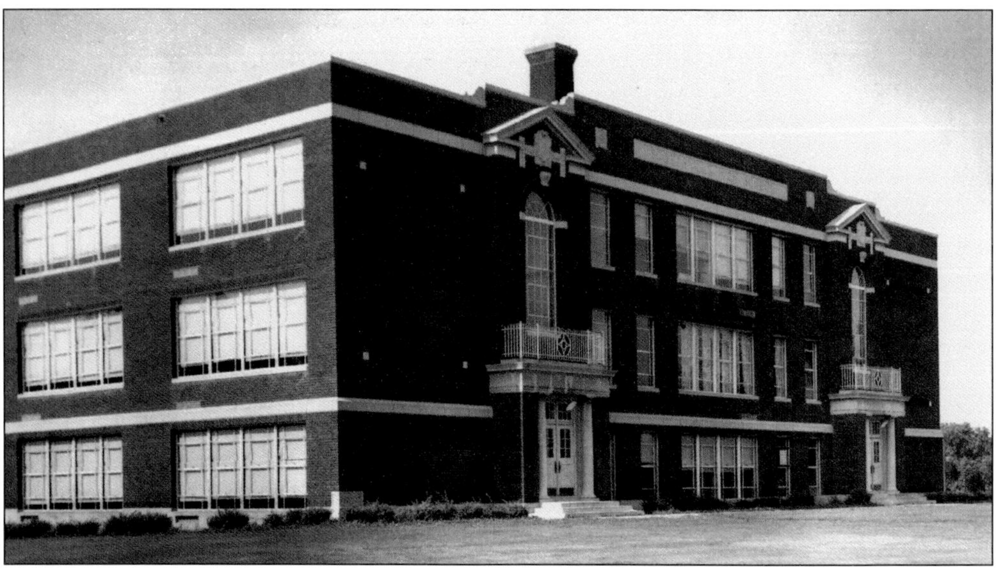

The new Scottsville High School was built on the corner of Beckwith Avenue and Rochester Street in 1927. The facility housed grades 1 to 12. The building was made of brick, had three floors, and included a combination auditorium and gymnasium. High school students came to Scottsville from all the Wheatland district schools as well as from schools in Industry, Clifton, Chili, and the Ballantyne Road area.

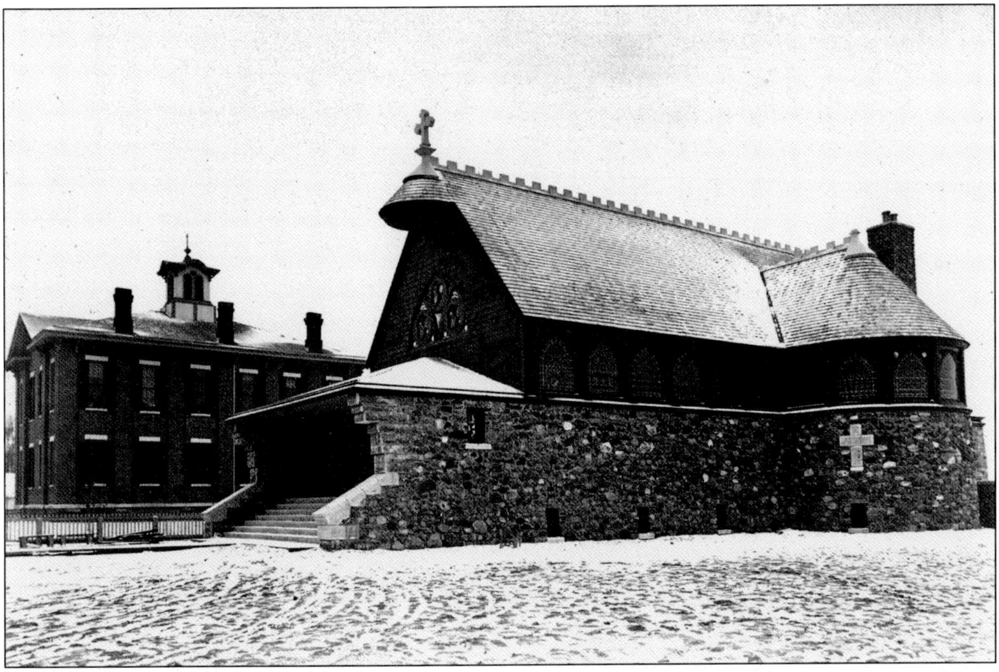

By 1884, Episcopalians were holding services in St. Joseph's Hall. Desiring a church, they hired Charles and Harvey Ellis of Rochester to develop a plan. The church, at 9 Brown's Avenue, was completed in 1885, seating 120 people and costing $3,925. The local stones for the outside walls were carefully selected, and the roof ridge featured a metal crenellation. The Richardsonian Romanesque–style church is shaped like a cross with entry doors in the east and a sloping center aisle leading to the altar in the west. The stained-glass windows show the influence of famed artist Harvey Ellis. (Courtesy of Richard LeRoy.)

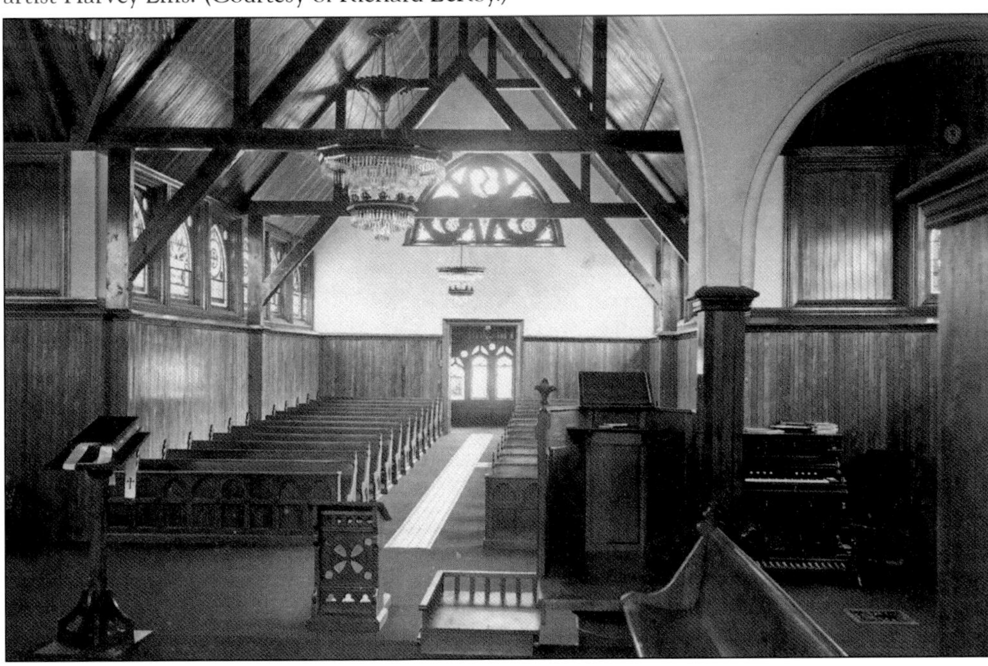

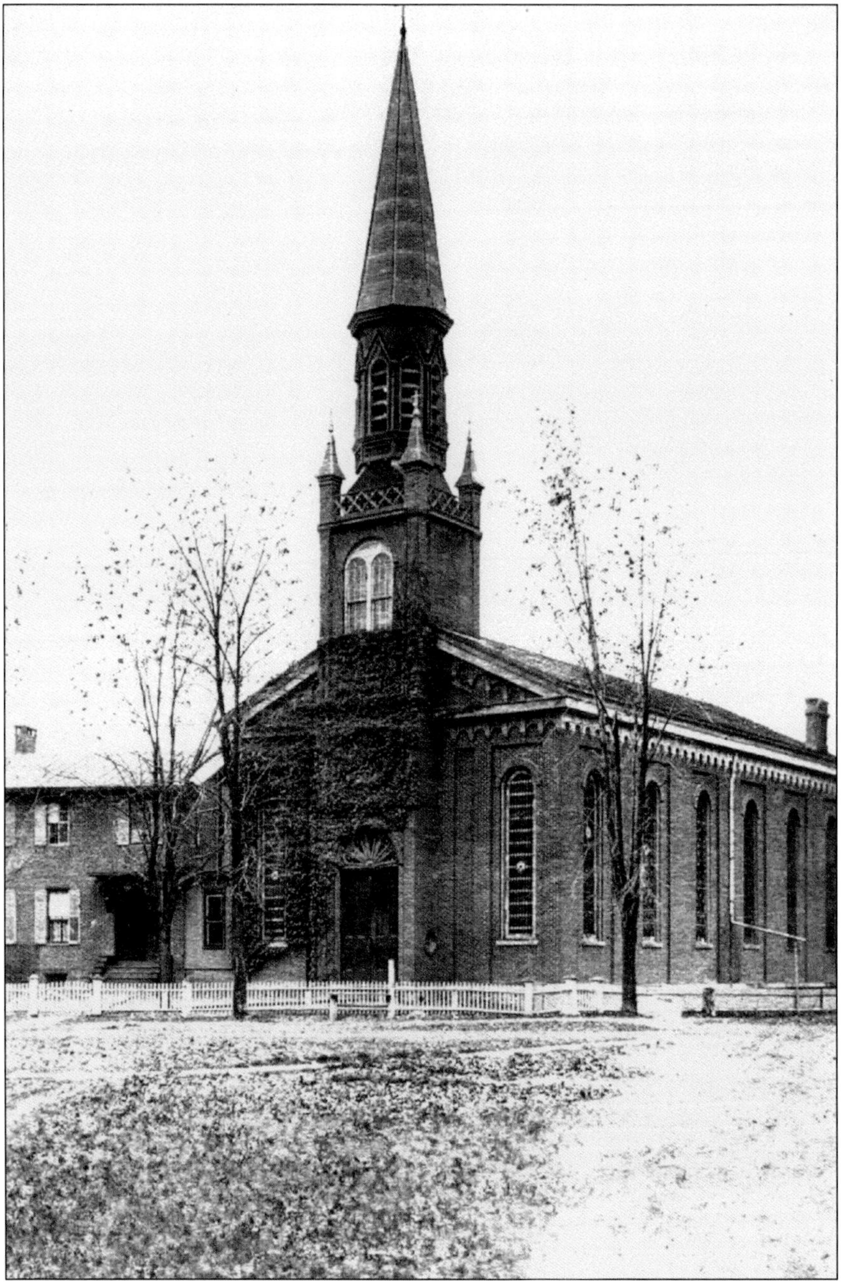

In 1841, Patrick Rafferty, a local carriage maker, provided room at his home for the first Catholic mass in Scottsville. Once a month, a visiting priest from Rochester celebrated mass. By 1843, members had purchased a site at 99 Main Street, on the corner of Caledonia Avenue. The cornerstone was laid in 1853 for St. Mary of the Assumption. Louis Charboneau of Rochester was the architect and builder. The Romanesque Revival–style building, 40 feet by 80 feet, features round-arched windows with stained glass, decorative corbelling along the cornice and in the front gable, a bell-tower, and pointed spire. Completion occurred over a period of years. At left in the photograph is the old brick rectory, which was razed in 1911, and a new rectory was built. (Courtesy of Timothy Hallock.)

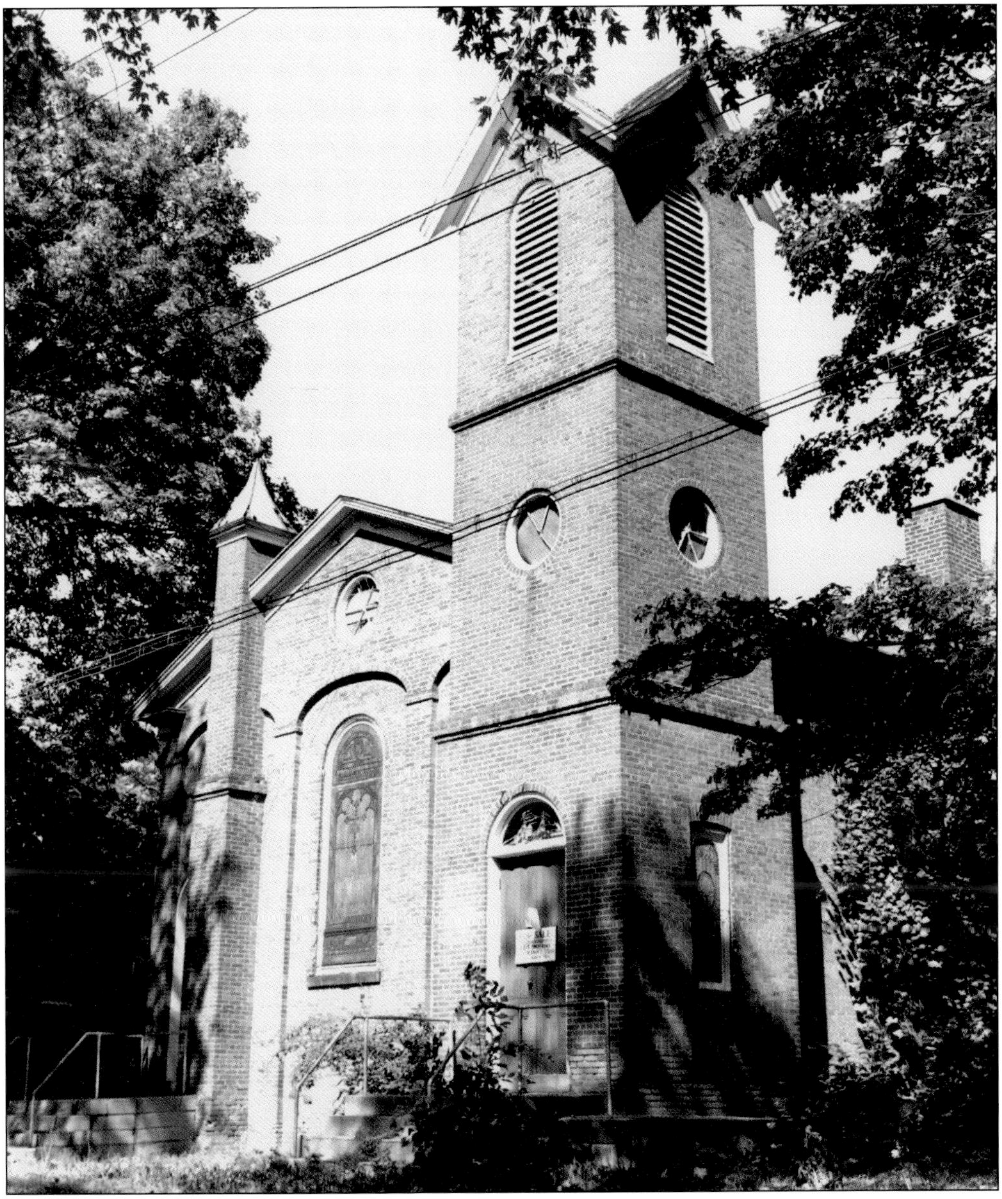

The Methodist Episcopal Church was organized in 1827 after meeting in a schoolhouse for some years with the Presbyterians. They voted to build a brick edifice measuring some 32 feet by 44 feet at 8 Church Street. Powell Carpenter, Dr. E. G. Munn, and Joseph Cox were among the liberal donors who helped raise the $2,000 required. The first service was held in the new church in 1828. In the 1870s, a complete remodeling added stained-glass windows and a Gothic Revival–style tower. The congregation disbanded in 1944, and the building was demolished in 1961. (Courtesy of the family of Fredrick W. and Mary R. Kentner.)

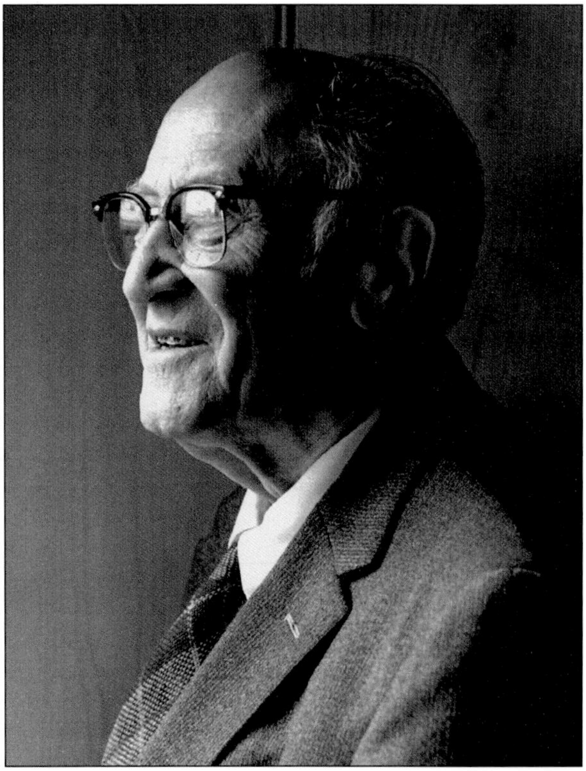

In 1944, Carl F. Schmidt, a well-known architect, artist, and historian, moved to 10 Rochester Street with his wife, Ann. He wrote and privately published 15 books, most featuring his extraordinary measured drawings. Schmidt's *Greek Revival Architecture in the Rochester Area* (1946) and *History of the Town of Wheatland* (1953) remain important references today. He documented architectural styles, fads, building materials, and garden structures. (Courtesy of Andrew Olenick.)

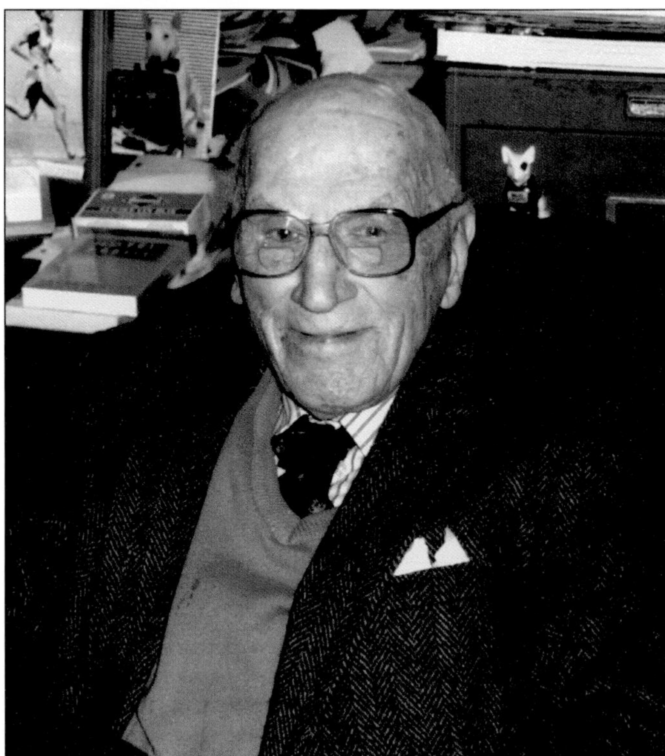

Henry W. Clune and his wife, Charlotte, built their home in 1927 at 50 Brown's Grove. He wrote the popular Seen and Heard column for the *Rochester Democrat and Chronicle* for 60 years. Many world luminaries visited Scottsville to be entertained at the Clune's. Henry wrote six novels, three memoirs, and a history of life along the Genesee River. He died at age 105 in 1995. (Courtesy of Peter Clune.)

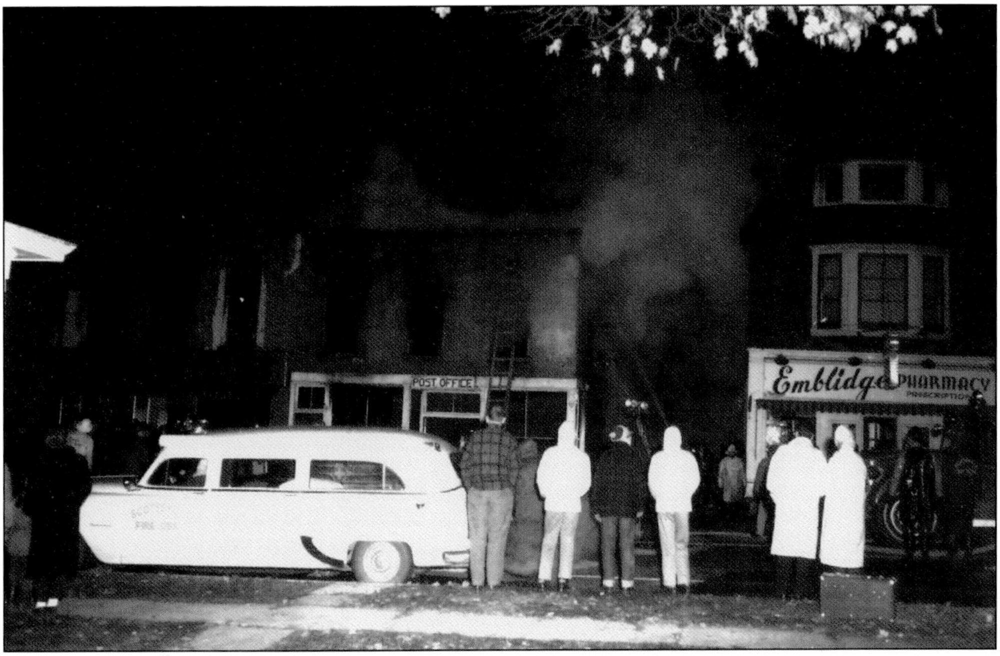

On November 8, 1959, fire destroyed the 1820s Dunn's store building at 32 Main Street, housing the post office, Harts Food Store, and second-story apartments. Two families were rescued. The neighboring 1887 Emblidge Pharmacy building sustained only minor damage. Postmaster Archibald Veghte said only a small amount of mail was lost, and they would temporarily relocate to the library. (Courtesy of the family of Fredrick W. and Mary R. Kentner.)

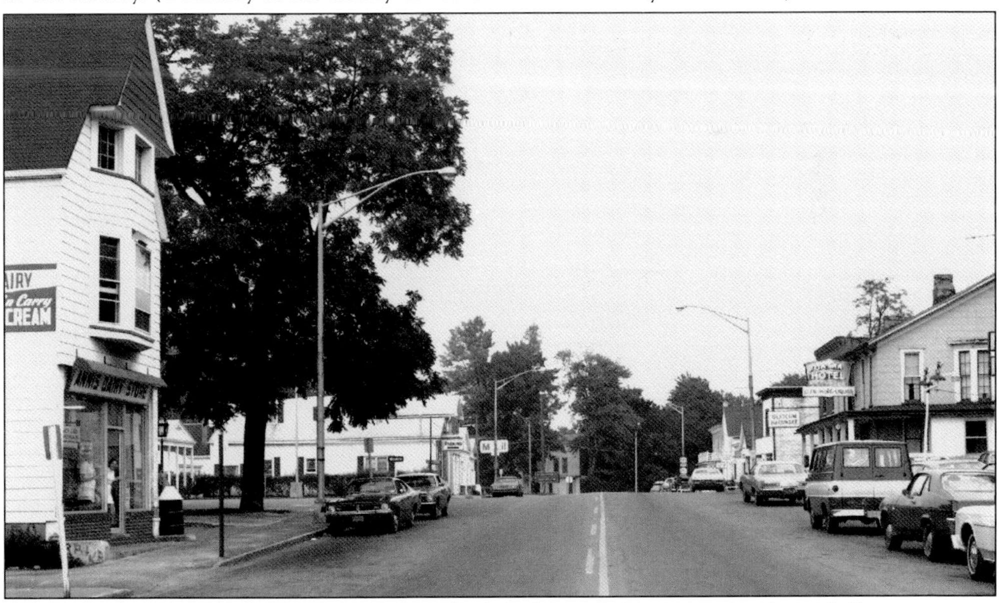

The 1887 building at 30 Main Street, on the left, housed drugstores for three different owners: Dr. L. C. Galpin, William Losee and his son Byron, and Norman Emblidge. Then it became the Annis Dairy, as seen in this 1960s photograph. Down the street, on the north side, is a sign for the new village parking lot. The Oatka Hotel and Slocum Hardware are on the south side of Main Street.

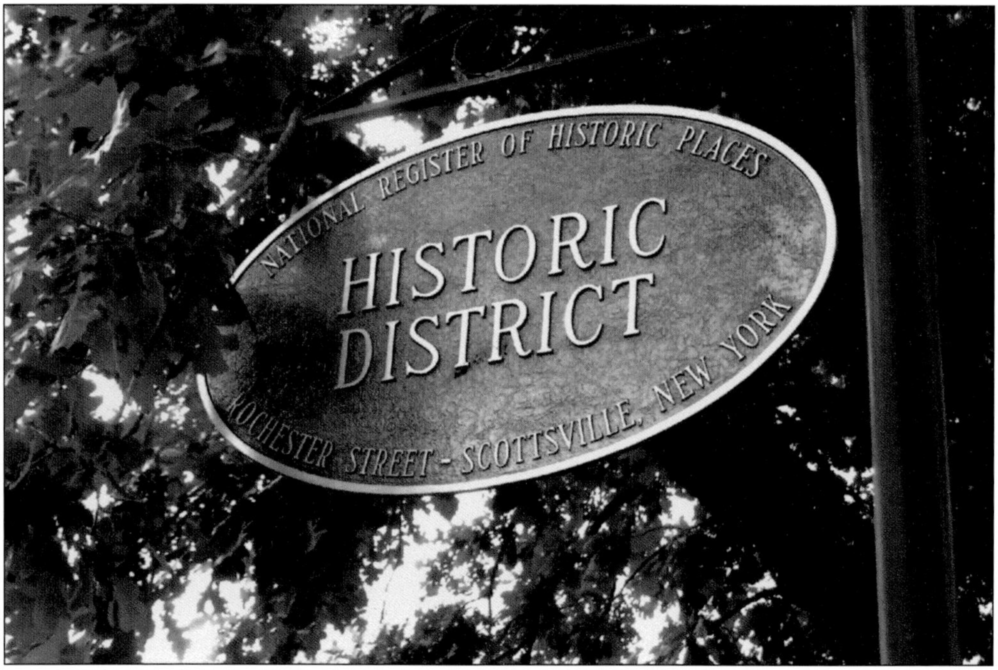

The Rochester Street Historic District was established by a village ordinance in 1971 to maintain the 19th-century character of the area. Its 40 homes include many in the beautiful Greek Revival style, built in the 1830–1850 years of growth and prosperity. After much research by the local homeowners, the district was listed on the National Register of Historic Places in 1973. (Courtesy of Elizabeth Murray.)

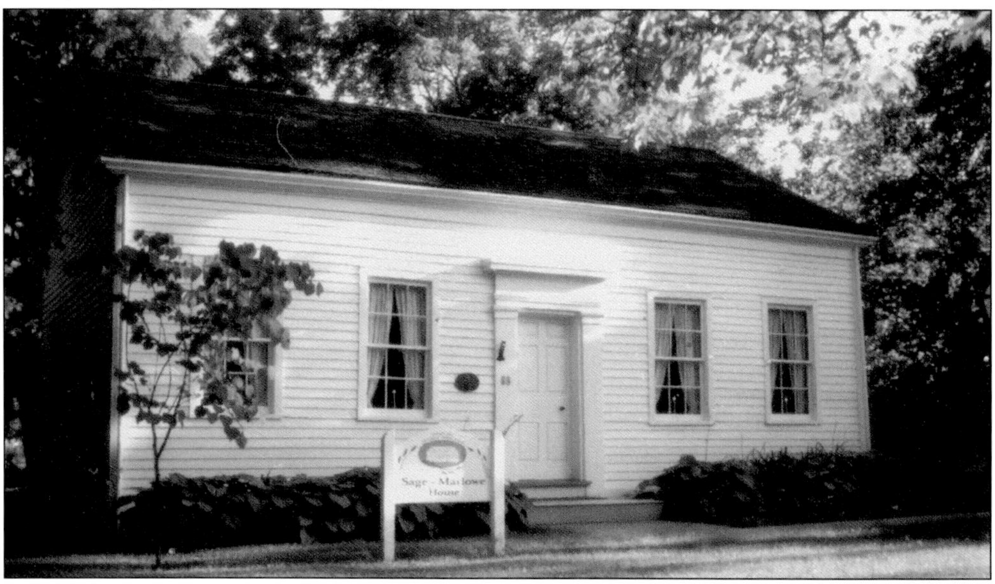

The small 1830s Sage-Marlowe House at 69 Main Street is a vernacular Federal-style cottage, although later interior trim reflects the Greek Revival style. Simeon Sage was likely the original owner, and Henry Marlowe was the last owner. The house was acquired in 1985 and then restored by the Wheatland Historical Association. Through the efforts of Shirley DiStefano a meeting room was added to the back of the house in 2000.

Seven

Roads and Railroads

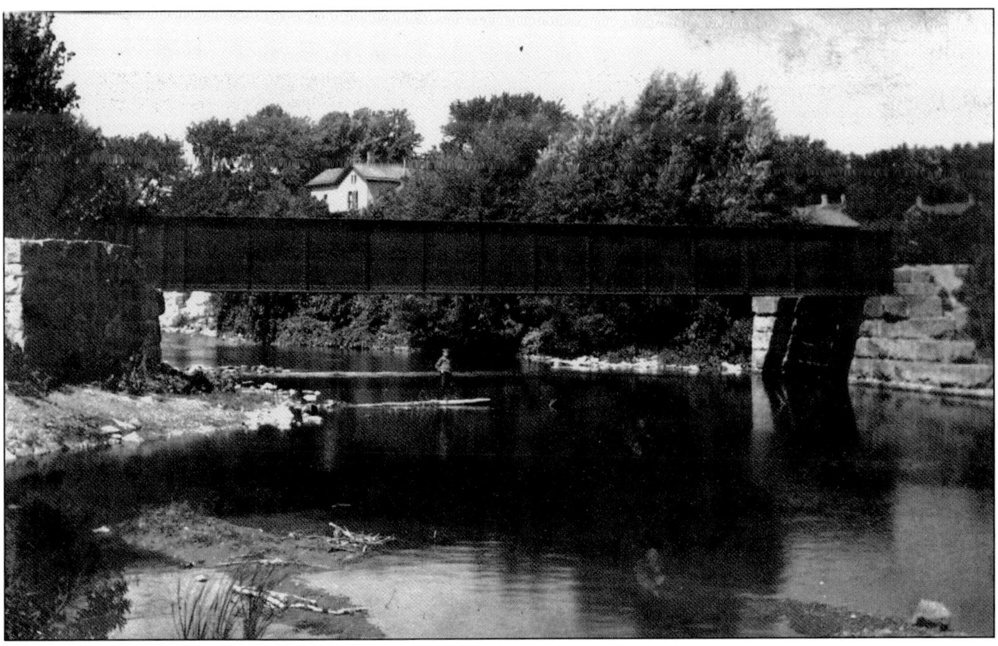

The Genesee Valley Canal right-of-way was sold in the early 1880s for railroad use. A track was laid where the towpath had been, and this steel bridge was built across Oatka Creek. Trains began to run from Rochester to Scottsville in 1883, providing Scottsville with both passenger and freight services. The New York State Greenway Trail now follows the old canal right-of-way. (Courtesy of Richard LeRoy.)

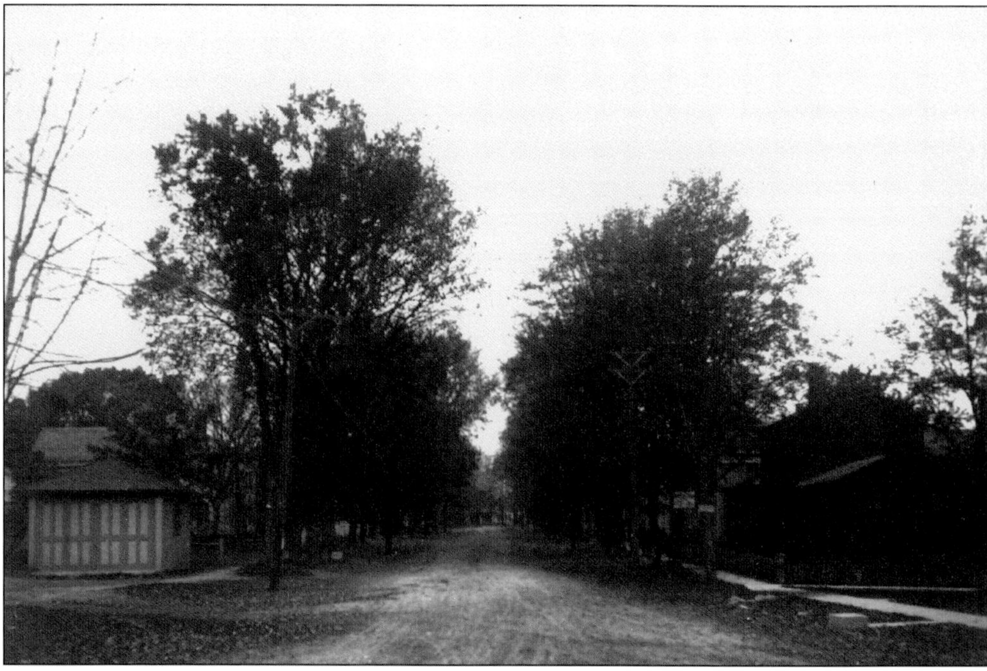

Rochester Street followed an old Native American trail north along the Genesee River. Settlers cleared trees and brush and widened the road to make way for wagons. Many beautiful homes in the Greek Revival and other early architectural styles were built here before 1900. The house at 8 Rochester Street, on the right, was built in 1831 from bricks made in Scottsville. (Courtesy of Timothy Hallock.)

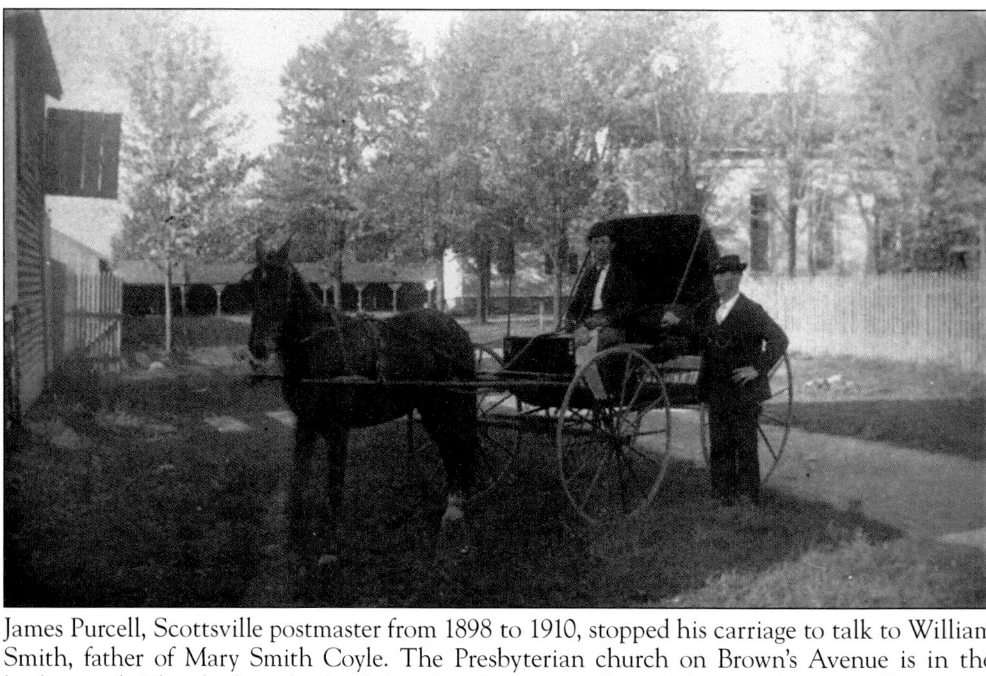

James Purcell, Scottsville postmaster from 1898 to 1910, stopped his carriage to talk to William Smith, father of Mary Smith Coyle. The Presbyterian church on Brown's Avenue is in the background. The sheds in back of the church were used to shelter the horses and carriages during services.

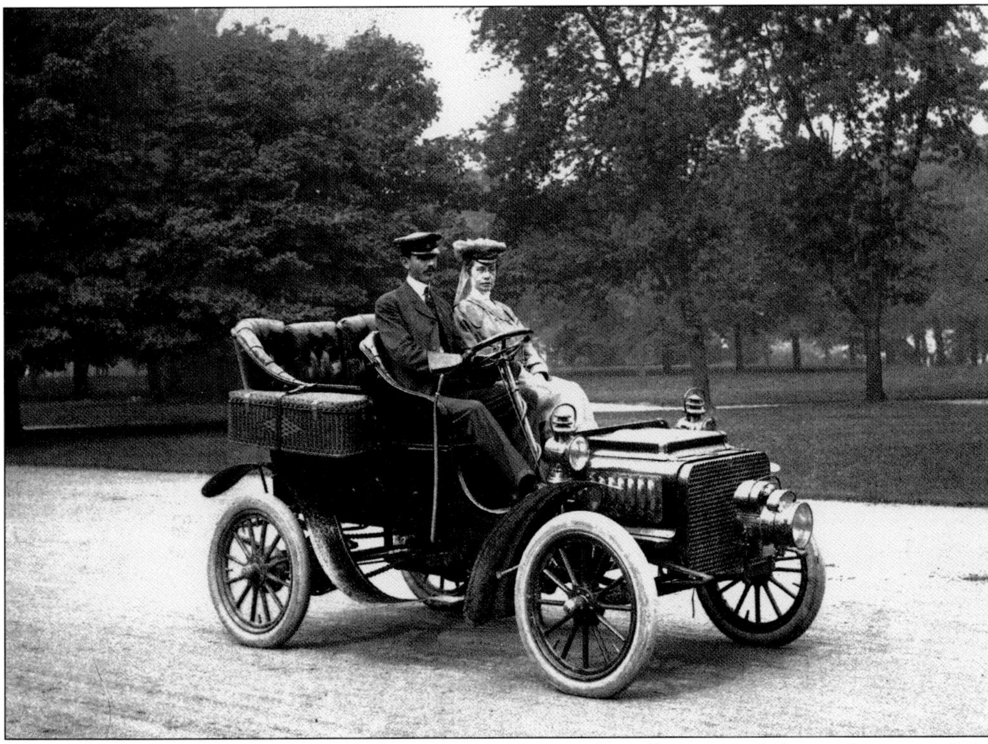

About 1910, James Miller and his wife, Alice Whitworth Miller, owned this early automobile. They were married in 1898 and were proprietors of the Miller property in Valley Rock, New Mexico. James Fraser Miller was the second son of Romanta and Etta Fraser Miller of 1089 Bowerman Road.

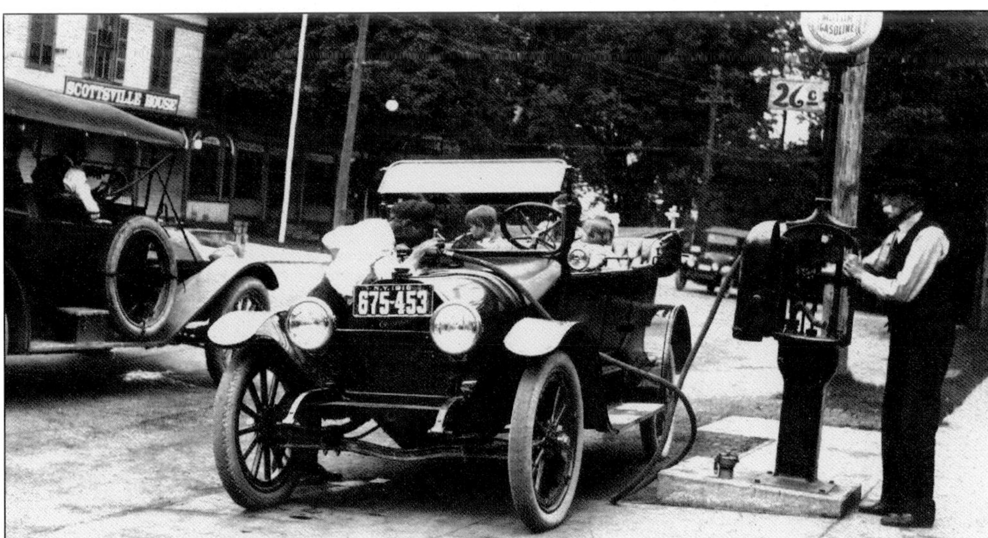

As soon as gasoline pumps were available, Isaac Van Hooser installed one in front of his store. He sold gasoline cheaper than the city dealers, so many city people would drive to Scottsville and have their tanks filled at Van Hooser's pump. In 1918, when gasoline was selling for 36¢ a gallon, he reportedly sold more than 60,000 gallons during the year.

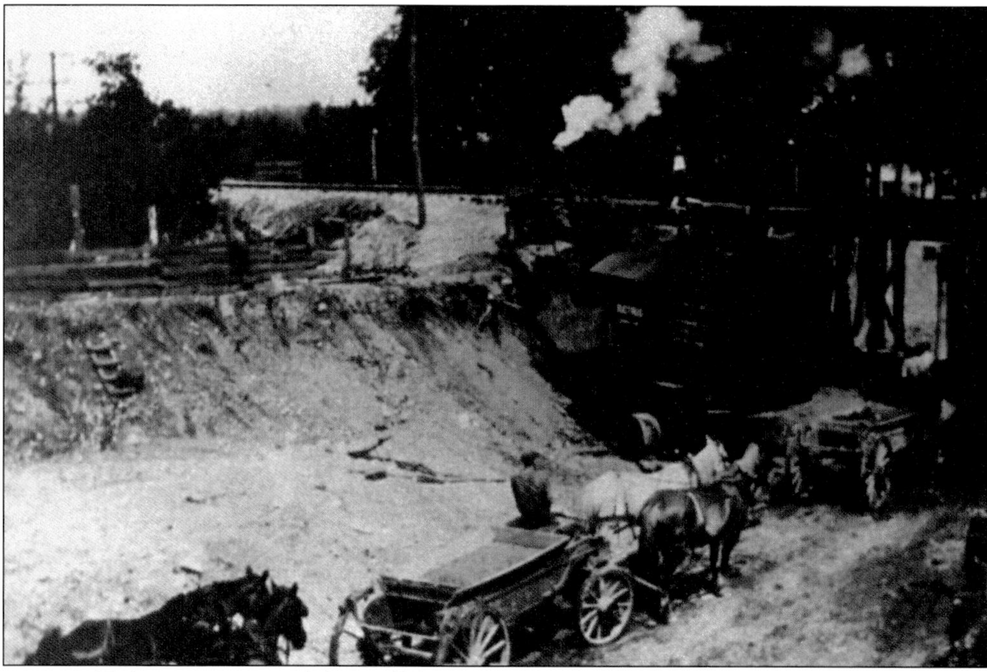

In 1914, Chili Avenue crossed the Buffalo, Rochester and Pittsburg Railroad tracks at grade just west of the intersection of Main Street with Caledonia and Chili Avenues. Because this created a hazardous situation, the railroad constructed a bridge and lowered the highway, forming an underpass. This excavation photograph, looking generally east, shows a steam shovel next to the temporary bridge. (Courtesy of Richard LeRoy.)

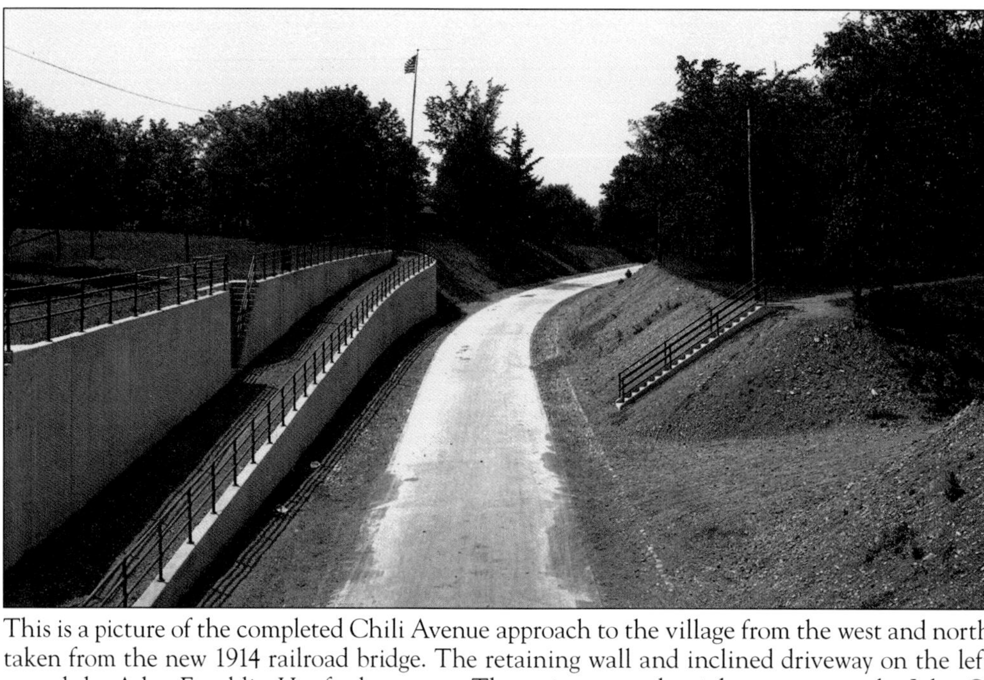

This is a picture of the completed Chili Avenue approach to the village from the west and north taken from the new 1914 railroad bridge. The retaining wall and inclined driveway on the left served the Adm. Franklin Hanford property. The stairway on the right went up to the John C. McVean home. (Courtesy of Richard LeRoy.)

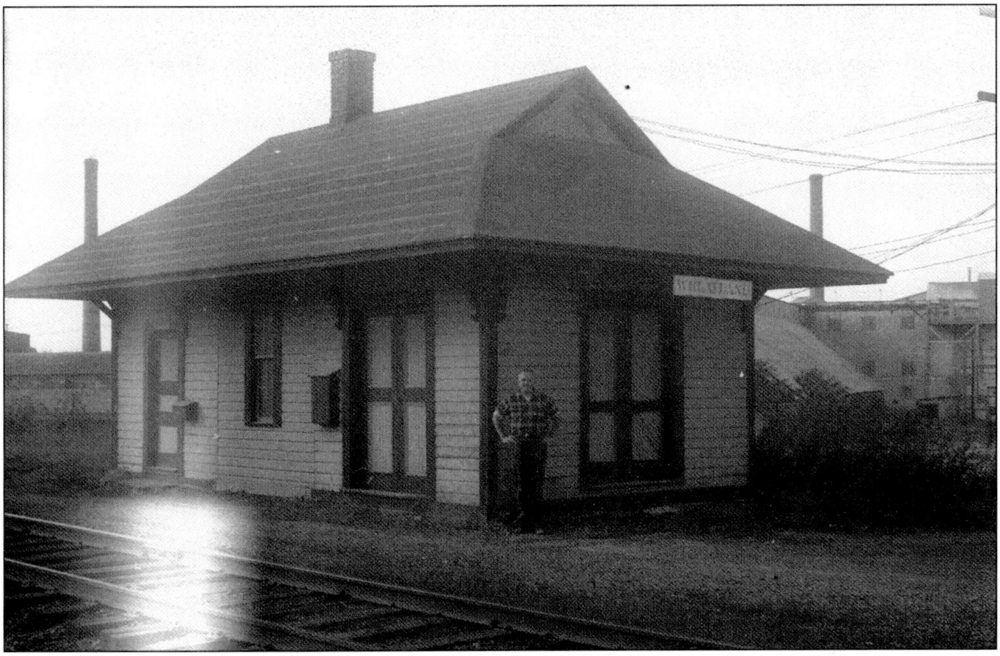

The Rochester and State Line Railroad built this station around 1874 at Garbutt, a mining center. When business there diminished, the station was moved to Wheatland Center Road in 1941, where there was freight business from the Ebsary Gypsum Company. Robert Quigley, stationmaster, is pictured here. In the 1970s, the building was closed and then demolished.

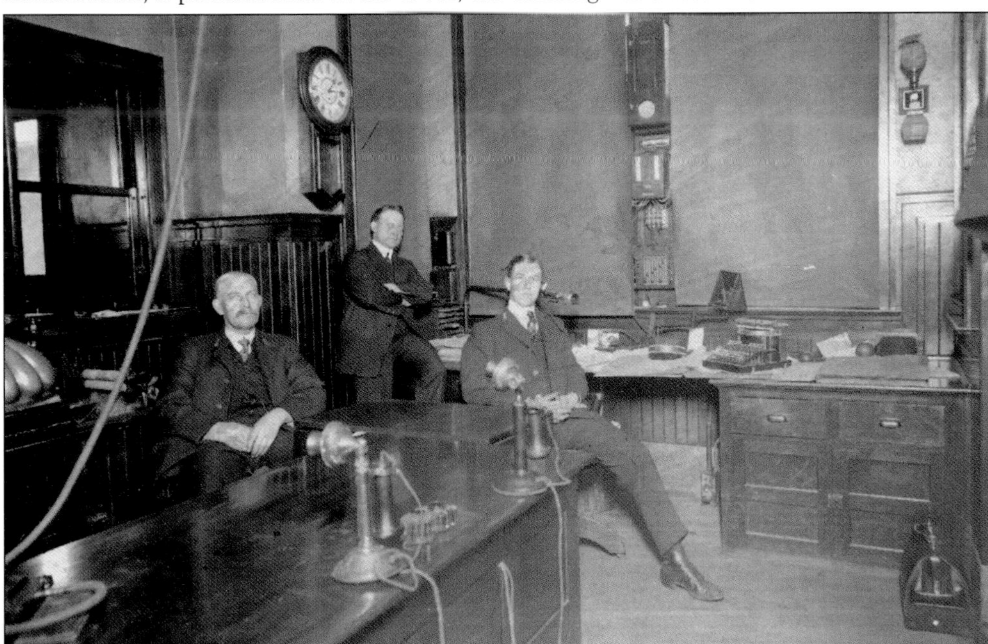

The new Mumford station, built in 1912, was located on Main Street, Route 383. The workers pictured in the office of this Baltimore and Ohio Railroad station are, from left to right, George C. Hadley, station agent; a railroad inspector; and James Baldeck, stationmaster. Notice the old-style telephone and typewriter on the desks in this 1930s view.

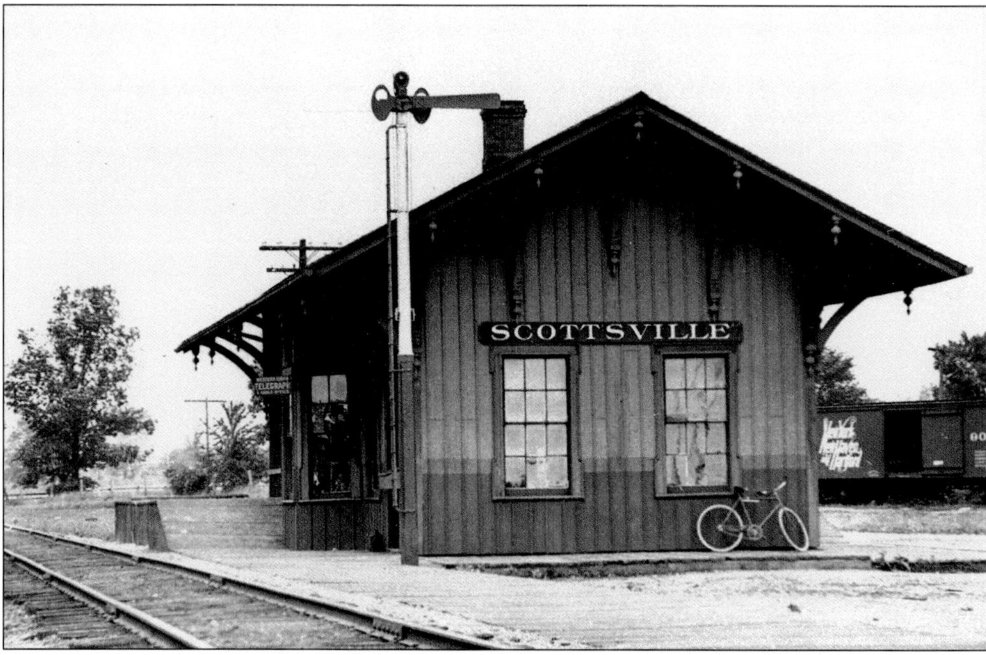

In 1874, the Rochester and State Line Railroad opened from Rochester to LeRoy with passenger and freight service. Mail was delivered to the Scottsville station by train. A siding on the other side of the station served feed mills and coal yards in the area. The only access to the station was by Maple Street going from Brown's Avenue.

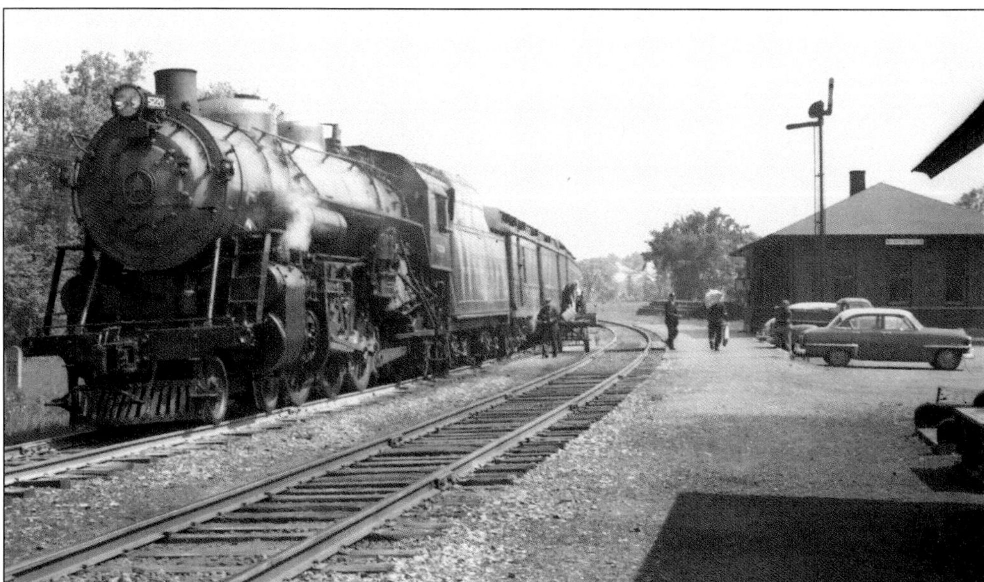

D. D. S. Brown, Oliver Allen, and Donald MacNaughton were energetic in pushing for the 1874 State Line Railroad. Wheatland issued bonds for $70,000 to aid in its construction. Its name changed to the Buffalo, Rochester, and Pittsburg Railroad, and in 1930, it became part of the Baltimore and Ohio Railroad system. Passenger service was discontinued in 1953, and railroad mail service to Scottsville ceased at that time. Robert Quigley was the last stationmaster in the Scottsville station.

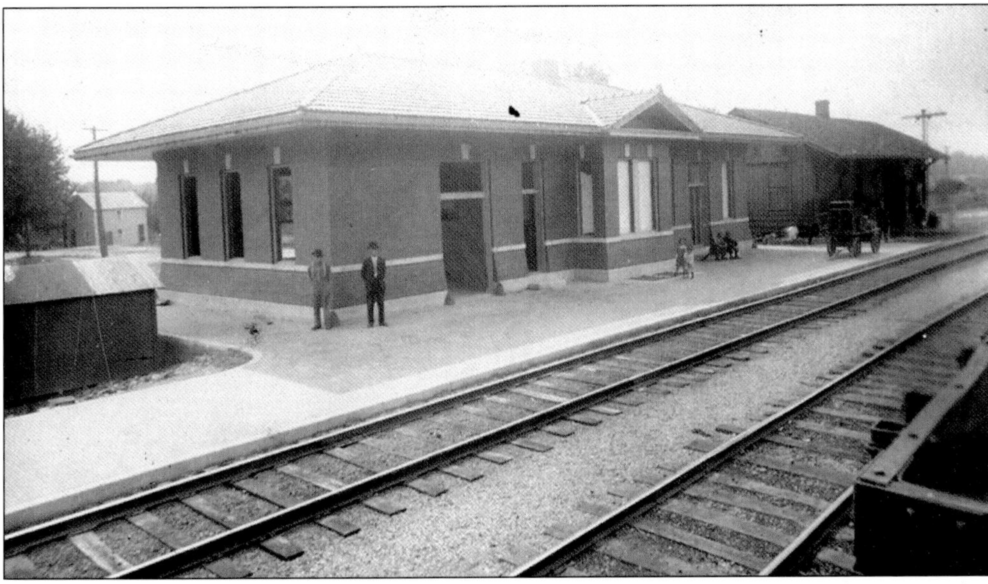

In 1911, the Buffalo, Rochester, and Pittsburg Railroad built a new station at the west end of Maple Street. This photograph (above) shows the new building under construction with the old one, on the right, still in use. Surrogate judge Selden S. Brown (below) speaks from an improvised platform. Next to him on the right, lawyer David Salyerds, son of businessman Isaac Salyerds, awaits his turn. Along with the Scottsville band, they received a delegation of railroad officials and led the dedication ceremony. (Courtesy of Richard LeRoy.)

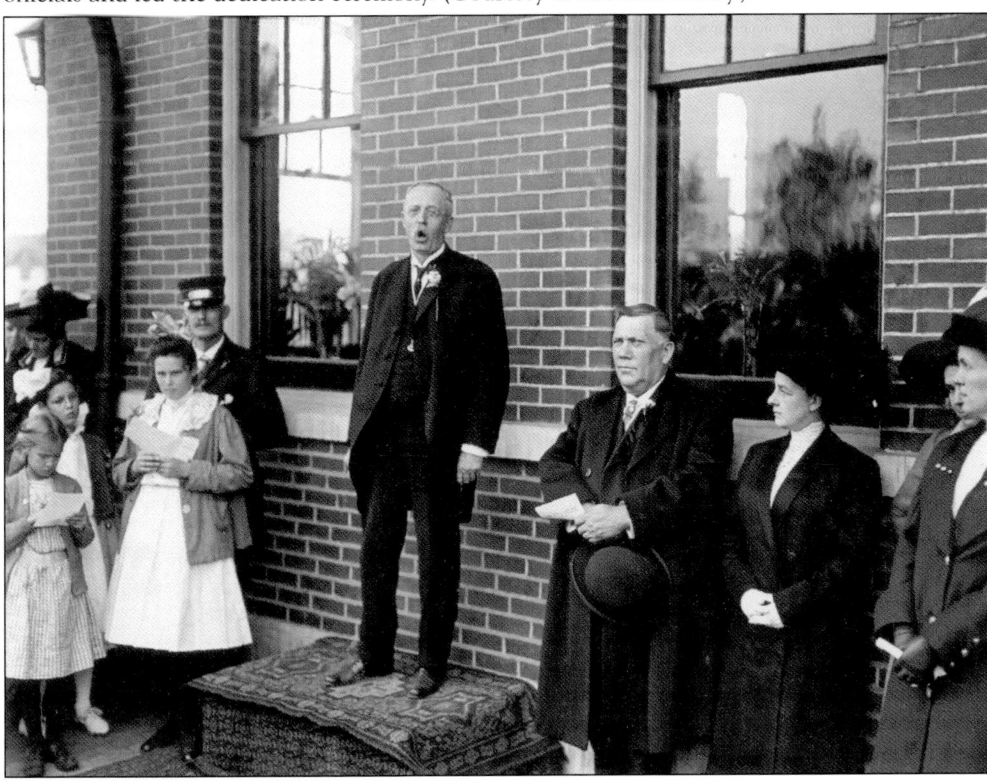

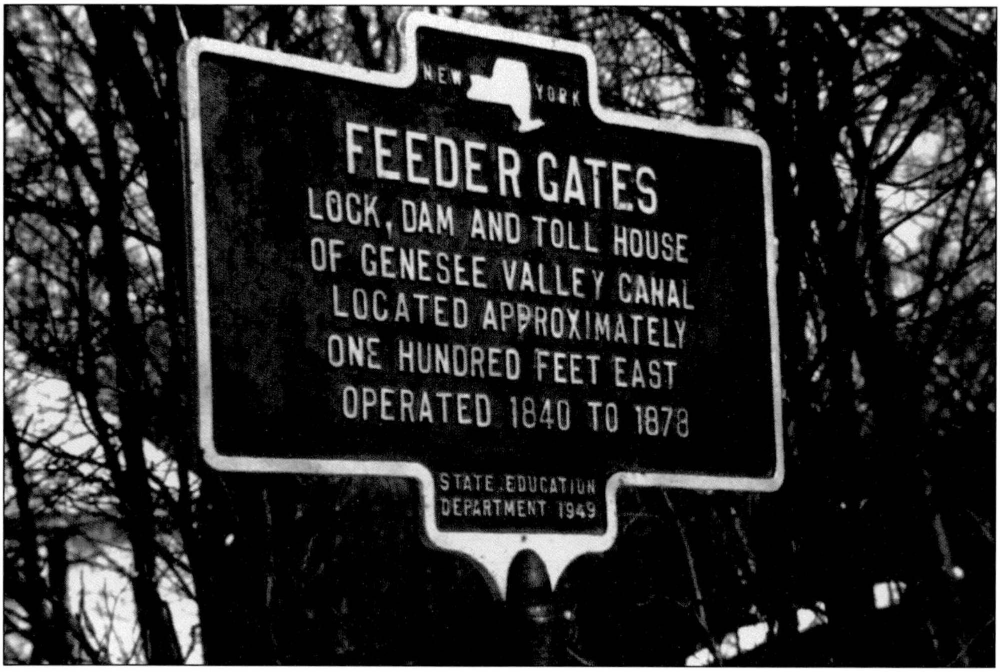

On the north bank of Oatka Creek, just east of the River Road bridge, two early canals, the Scottsville and Genesee River Canal and the Genesee Valley Canal, were constructed, using gates and a lock at this location. The Scottsville canal was financed locally by Powell Carpenter, Abraham Hanford, Dr. Freeman Edson, William Haynes Hanford, and Isaac Cox. New York State was responsible for financing the Genesee Valley Canal.

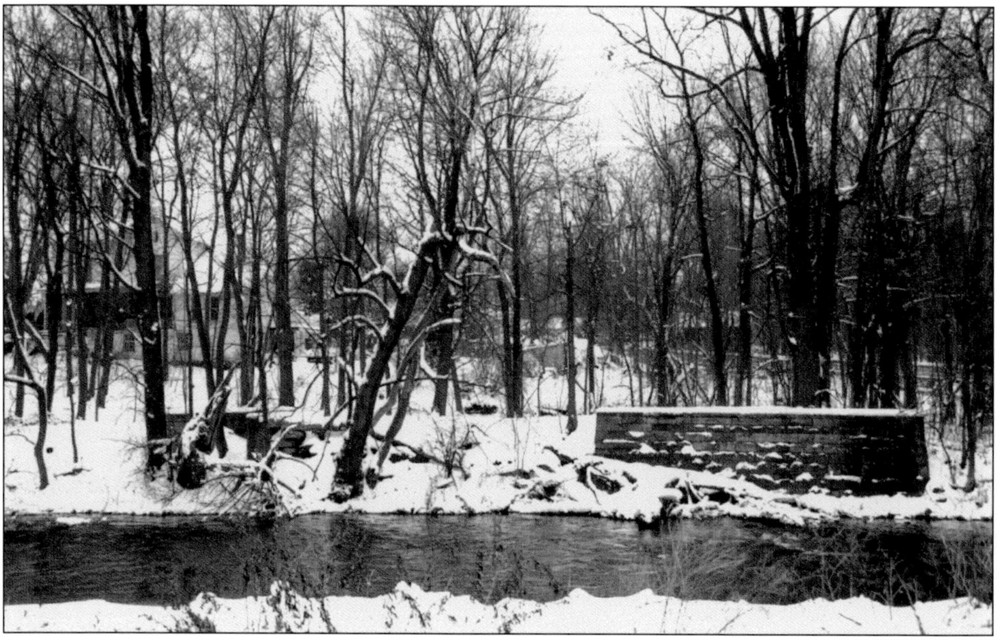

Portions of the 1830–1840s stone dam and walls of the Genesee Valley Canal are visible today in Canawaugus Park and from the New York State Greenway Trail, just north of the bridge. (Courtesy of the Landmark Society of Western New York.)

Eight

Social Gatherings and Events

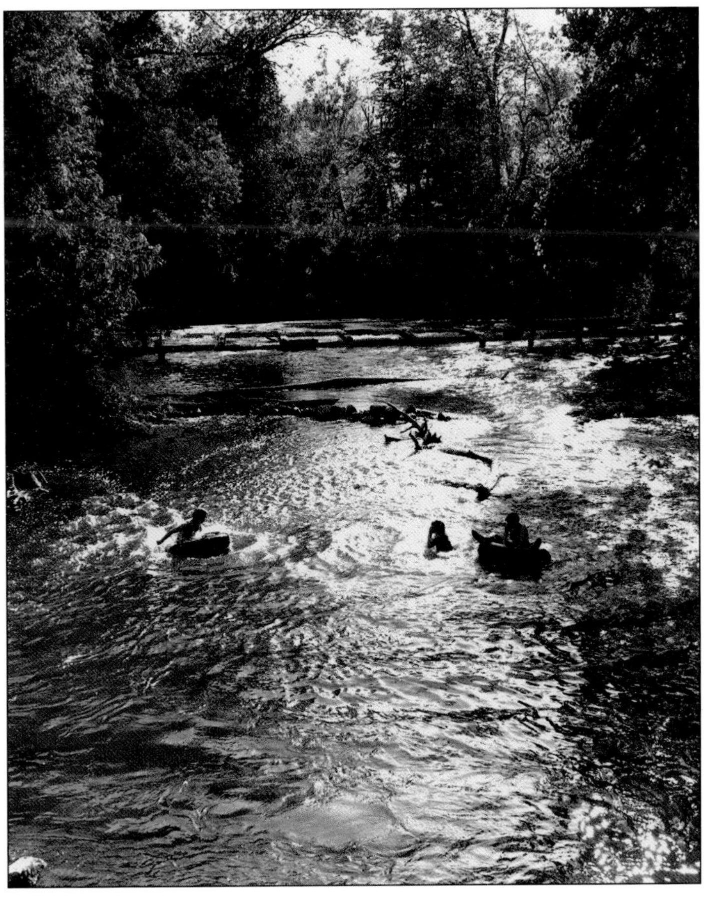

A wooden dam built in 1826 on Oatka Creek formed a swimming hole just west of the Bowerman Road bridge. The swimming spot was a popular place on a hot summer day. Many a youngster enjoyed a refreshing dip here, and others have fond memories of the great times at the creek. Anglers found their favorite fishing spots, and hikers enjoyed the scenery and the hiking trails.

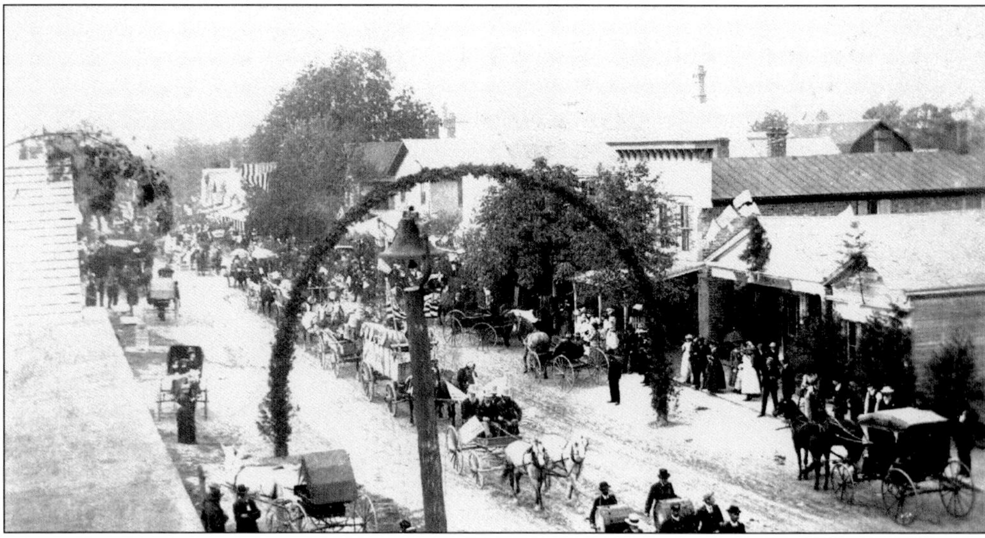

On September 13, 1889, Wheatland's centennial celebrated the arrival of the Sheffers, the first permanent settlers west of the Genesee River. Oliver Allen was president of the festivities. Parade marshal Volney Brown led the march from Caledonia Avenue to Brown's Grove in Scottsville. This view of Main Street looking west includes the decorative centennial arch and the bell in front of the Salyerds' Block fire station.

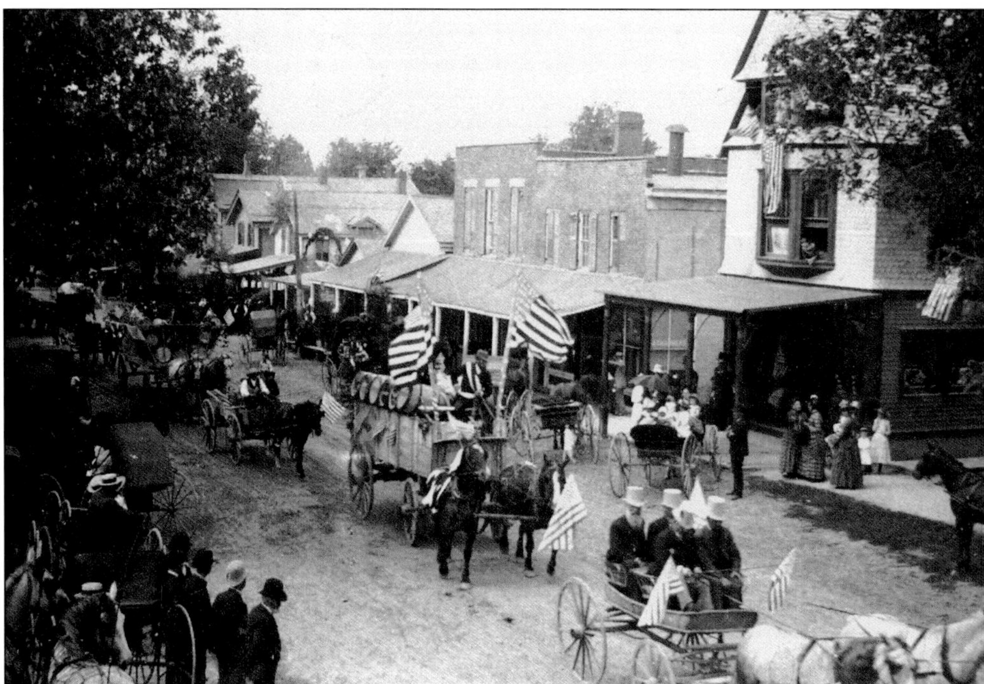

This centennial photograph shows people lining Main Street to see the floats go by. On the right, at 30 Main Street, is the large store building recently constructed in 1887 by Myron Pope with Charles Ellis as architect. Dr. L. C. Galpin had a pharmacy there. It continued as a drugstore until the popular Annis Dairy opened in the 1960s.

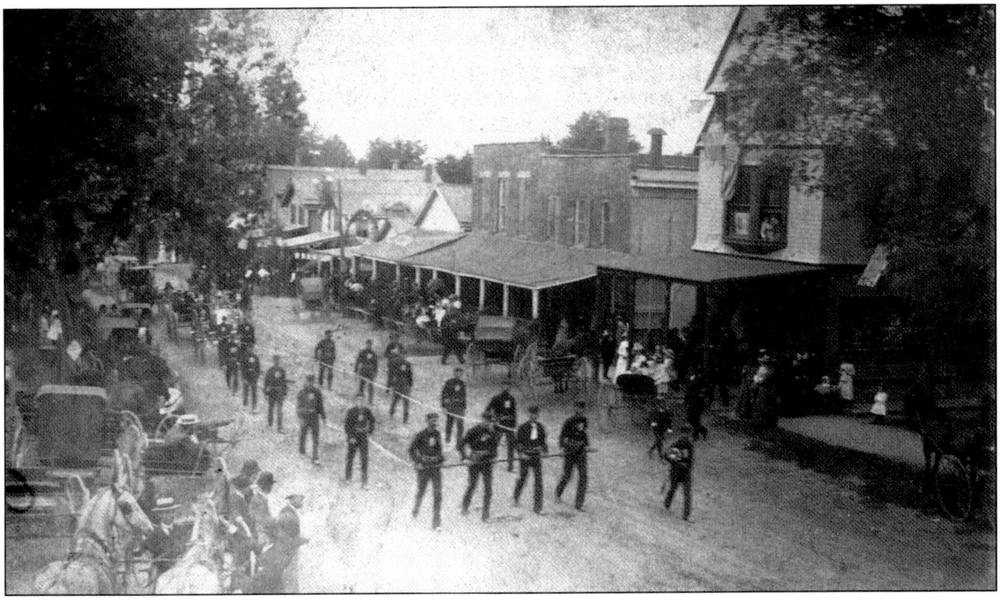

In the 1889 parade, the Scottsville Fire Company marched with some of its equipment. Many carriages line Main Street with its covered wooden sidewalks that offered protection from the elements and the dirt of unpaved streets. After the parade and dinner at Brown's Grove, George E. Slocum and state senator Donald MacNaughton spoke on local history. Music, exhibits, dancing, and fireworks completed the Wheatland Centennial Celebration enjoyed by an estimated 4,000 persons.

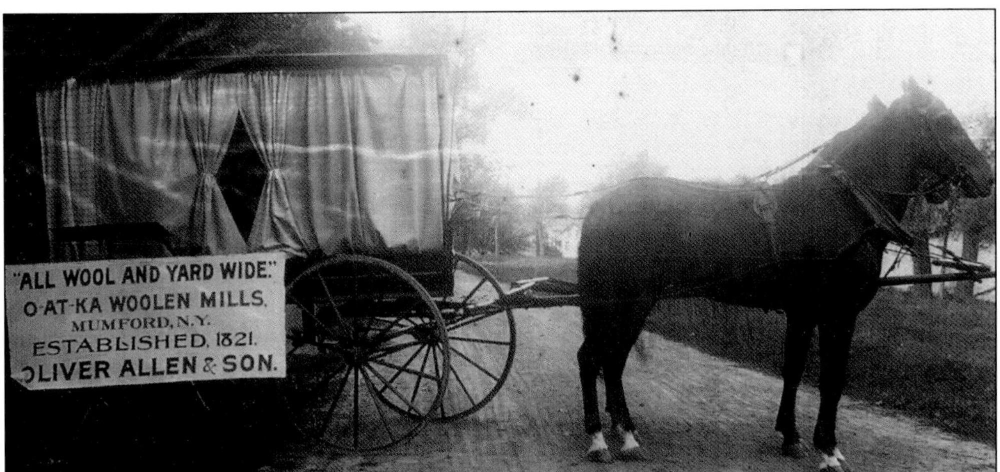

The Allen Woolen Mills on Armstrong Road in Mumford sent this float to the 1889 centennial parade. The carriage, driven by Patrick Harrigan, was decorated with samples of woolen materials produced by the mills. There was great demand for these goods in the city markets.

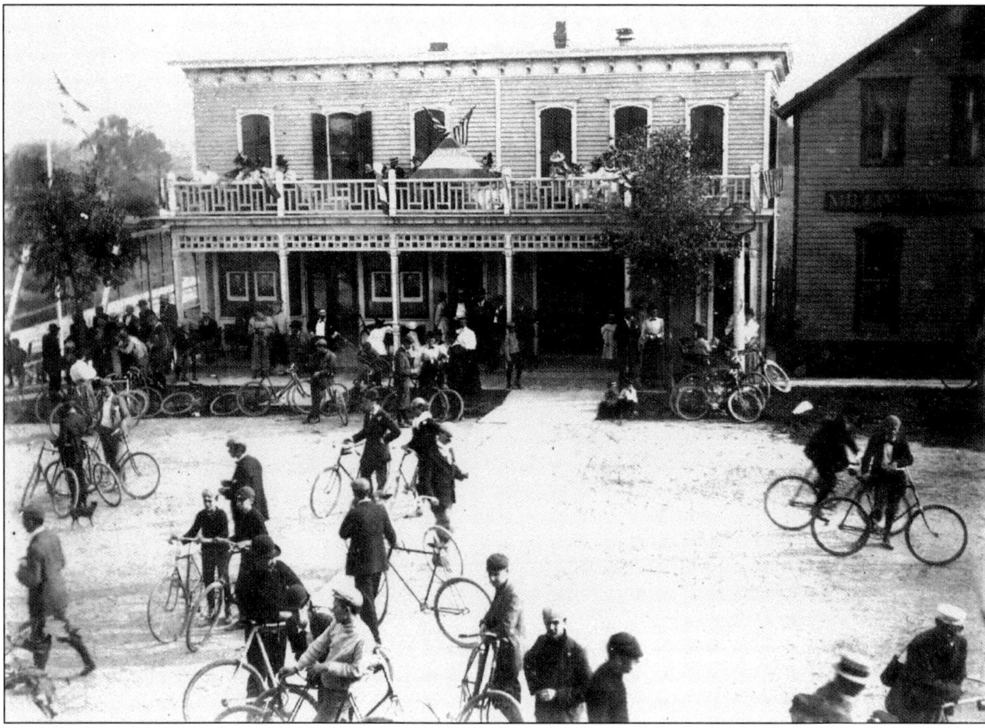

On Saturday, September 12, 1896, more than 1,500 "wheelmen and wheelwomen" arrived in the village on a cinder path. Where the cyclists entered Scottsville, John Talcott Wells had erected a large arch in the form of his patented roof truss. This night was long remembered as one of the liveliest nights in Scottsville's history.

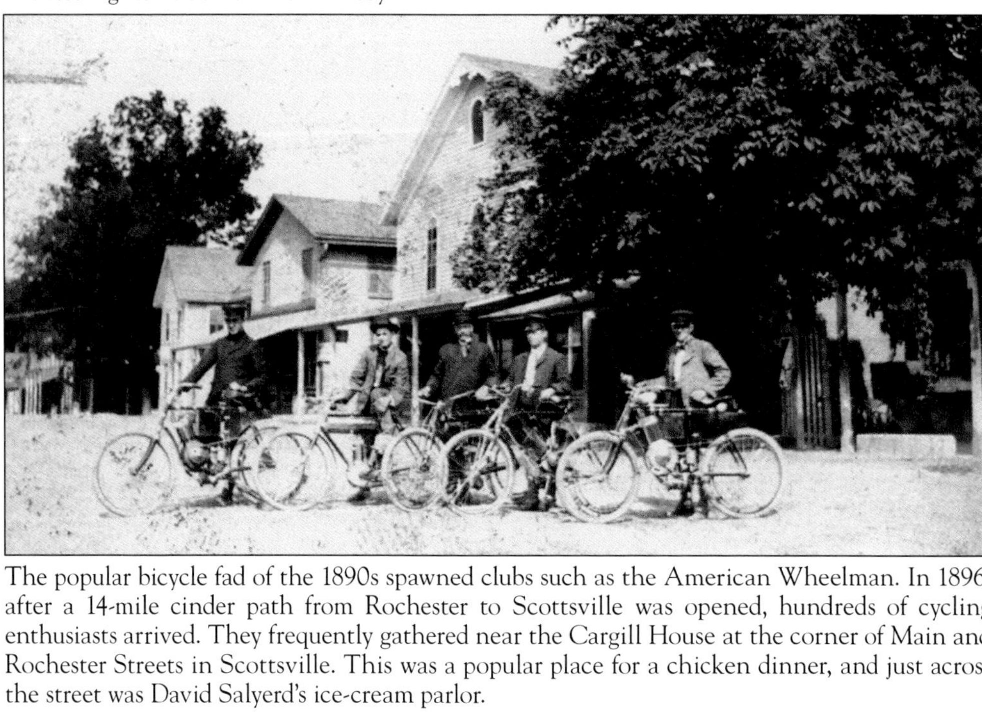

The popular bicycle fad of the 1890s spawned clubs such as the American Wheelman. In 1896, after a 14-mile cinder path from Rochester to Scottsville was opened, hundreds of cycling enthusiasts arrived. They frequently gathered near the Cargill House at the corner of Main and Rochester Streets in Scottsville. This was a popular place for a chicken dinner, and just across the street was David Salyerd's ice-cream parlor.

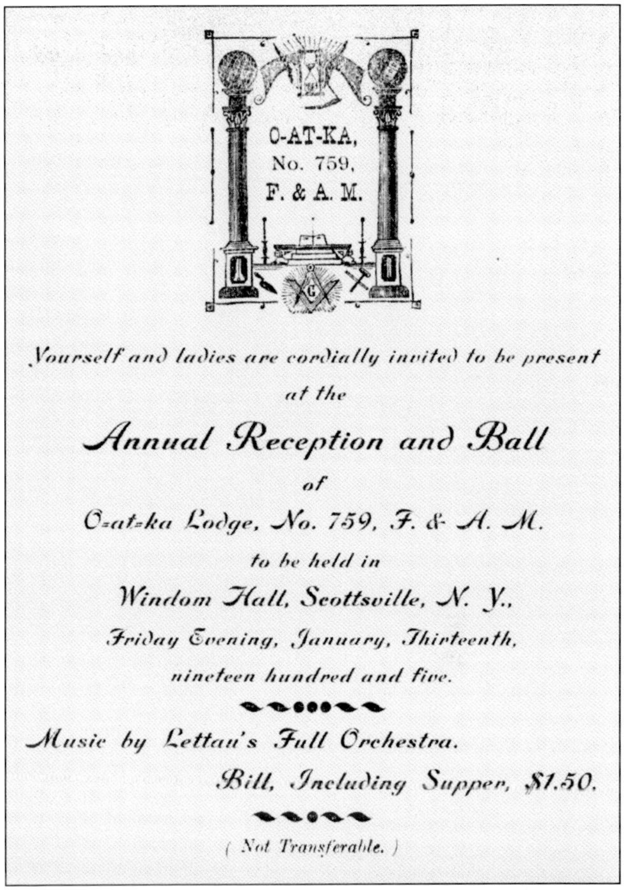

O-AT-KA,
No. 759,
F. & A. M.

Yourself and ladies are cordially invited to be present at the

Annual Reception and Ball

of

O-at-ka Lodge, No. 759, F. & A. M.

to be held in

Windom Hall, Scottsville, N. Y.,

Friday Evening, January, Thirteenth, nineteen hundred and five.

Music by Lettau's Full Orchestra.

Bill, Including Supper, $1.50.

(Not Transferable.)

With the dedication in 1892 of Windom Hall, Scottsville had a first-rate hall for theatrical and community events. It was built by Myron Pope, with Charles Ellis as architect, and sponsored by local citizens James Kelly, Selden Brown, Isaac Van Hooser, Thomas Brown, and Isaac Salyerds. The 20-by-40-foot stage was used by the Scottsville Dramatic Club. Besides plays, the building hosted commencements, church and lodge meetings, suppers, dances, and a library reading room.

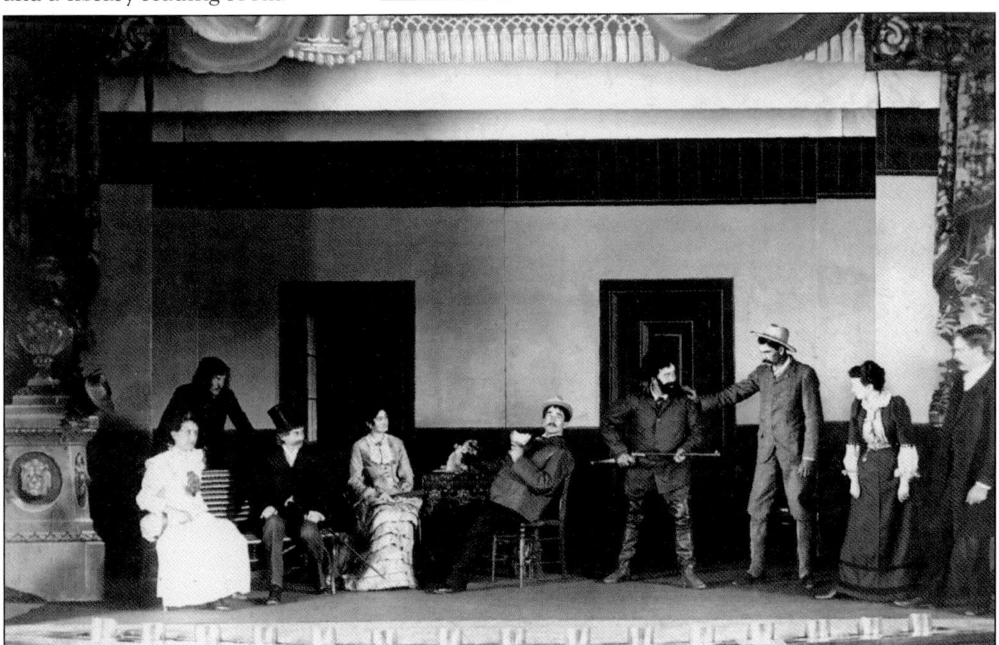

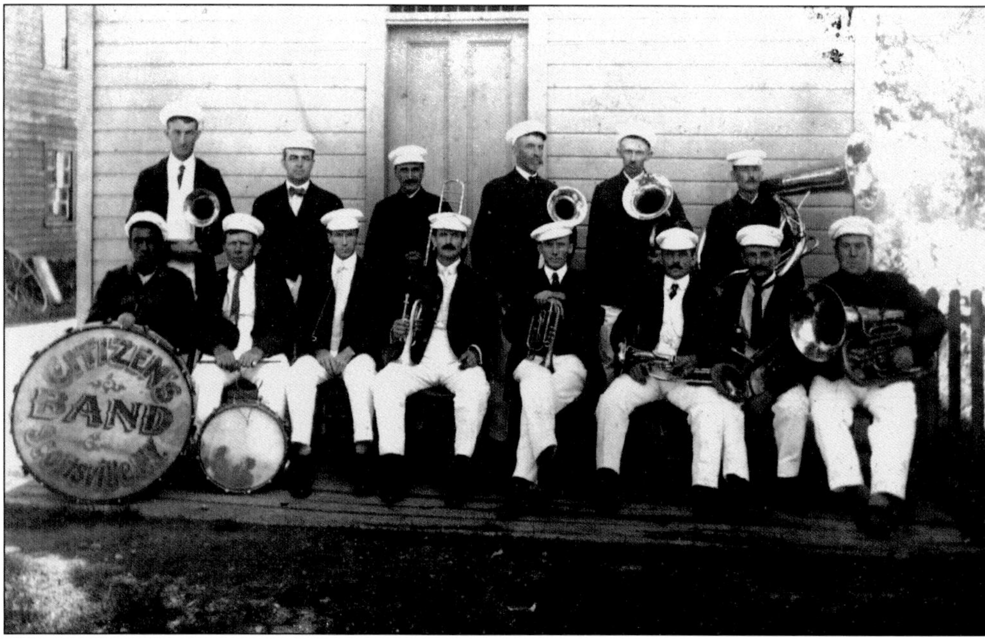

Scottsville Citizens Band members looked smart in their uniforms as they presented a concert at Windom Hall on April 5, 1904. The members of the group are, from left to right, (first row) Howard Thompson, Byron Mowson, Theron Cox, Clifford Reed, Max Estes, William Horton, James Cameron, and William Mattice; (second row) John Burrell, Edward Childs, Horton Fellows, Milton Stokoe, Thomas Stokoe, and Charles Shadbolt. They are in front of the town jail behind the old fire hall.

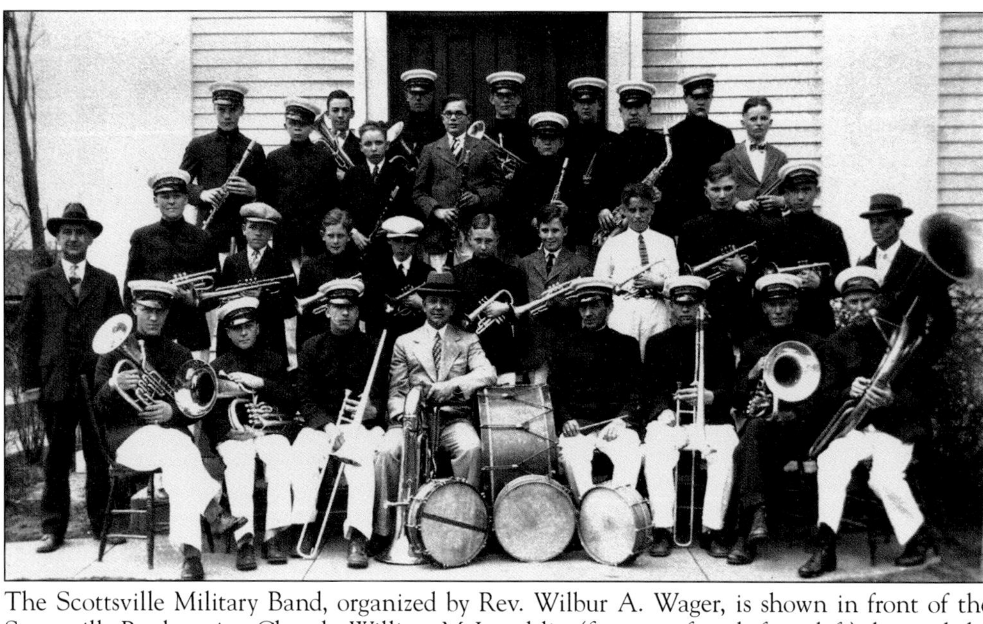

The Scottsville Military Band, organized by Rev. Wilbur A. Wager, is shown in front of the Scottsville Presbyterian Church. William McLaughlin (first row, fourth from left) directed the group that included musicians of all ages. LeRoy M. Slocum Jr. (second row, far left) acted as manager, and his sons, William and LeRoy III, played instruments in the band.

CONCERT

OF

SCOTTSVILLE CITIZENS BAND.

AT

WINDOM HALL,

TUESDAY EVENING, APRIL 5, 1904.

PROGRAM.

1. Medley Overture, " The Cavalier, " — *Prendiville.*
   BAND.

2. Solo. Spring Song, — *A. C. Mackenzie.*
   Miss Sarah L. Jones.

3. Serenade, { a. Cupids Charms, b. Loves Response, } — *Miller.*
   BAND.

4. Recitation, " Too Late for the Train." — Miss Elizabeth Stewart.

5. Duett for Violin and Piano, Serenade, — *Tit'l.*
   Mr. & Mrs. E. L. Galusha.

6. Selection by Quartette, C. V. Lodge, H. Post, Wm. Dunn, Frank Dunn.

7. March, " America Triumphant." — BAND.

INTERMISSION,

8. Waltz, " Poetica," — *Moses Tobani.*
   BAND.

9. Solo, Selection, — Miss Mary L. Salyerds.

10. Serenade, " Sweet Dreams." — *Miller.*
    BAND.

11. Cornet Solo, " New American," (Triple Tongue.) — Everett Hart.

12. Selection by Quartette, C. V. Lodge, H. Post, Wm. Dunn, Frank Dunn.

13. A few Steps, — Howard Thompson.

14. Two Step, " Southern Smiles," — BAND.

Dancing immediately after the Concert.

The popular hometown Scottsville Citizens Band concerts featured a variety of instrumental pieces. Other local performers presented readings, quartets, duets, and solos. After the concerts, the audience danced late into the evening.

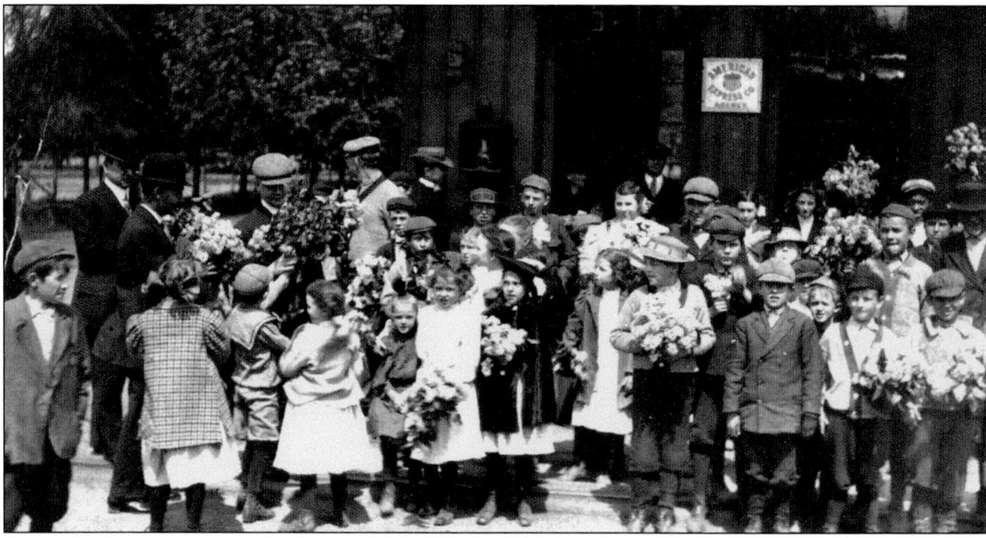

Young Mumford schoolchildren gather at the first Mumford railroad station on Depot Street. They were all eager to carry a bouquet for the Arbor Day program. Around 1900, when this photograph was taken, Mr. Hicks was the school principal.

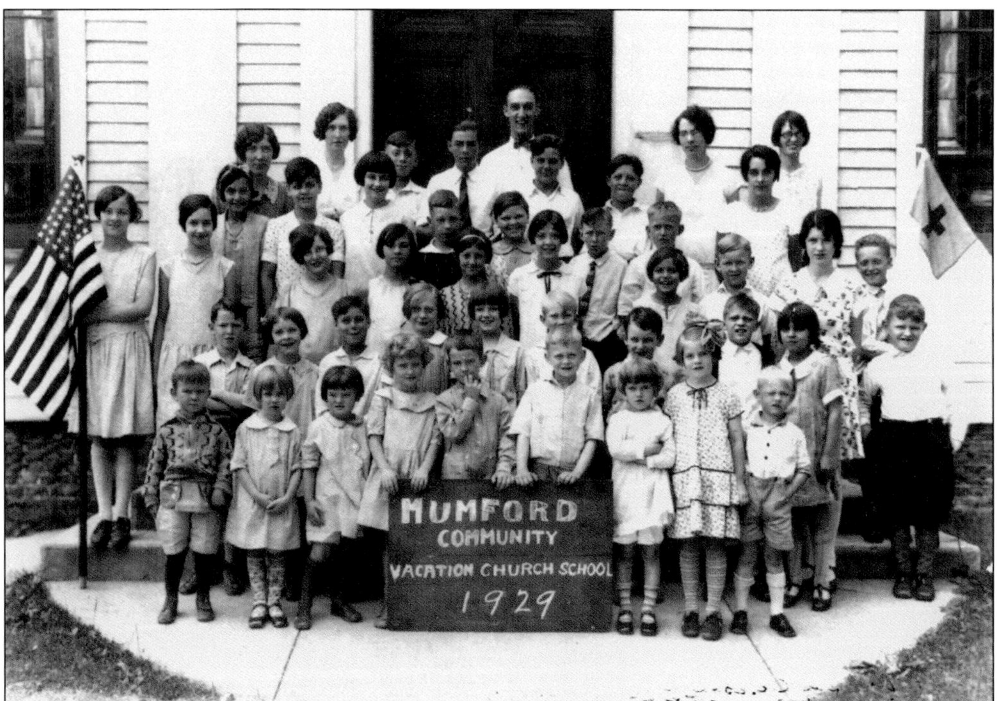

Children of all ages are gathered in front of the First Baptist Church of Mumford for the community vacation church school. The tall man in the back row, Albert Sheckalls, was the student pastor at the Mumford Baptist church from 1927 until 1930.

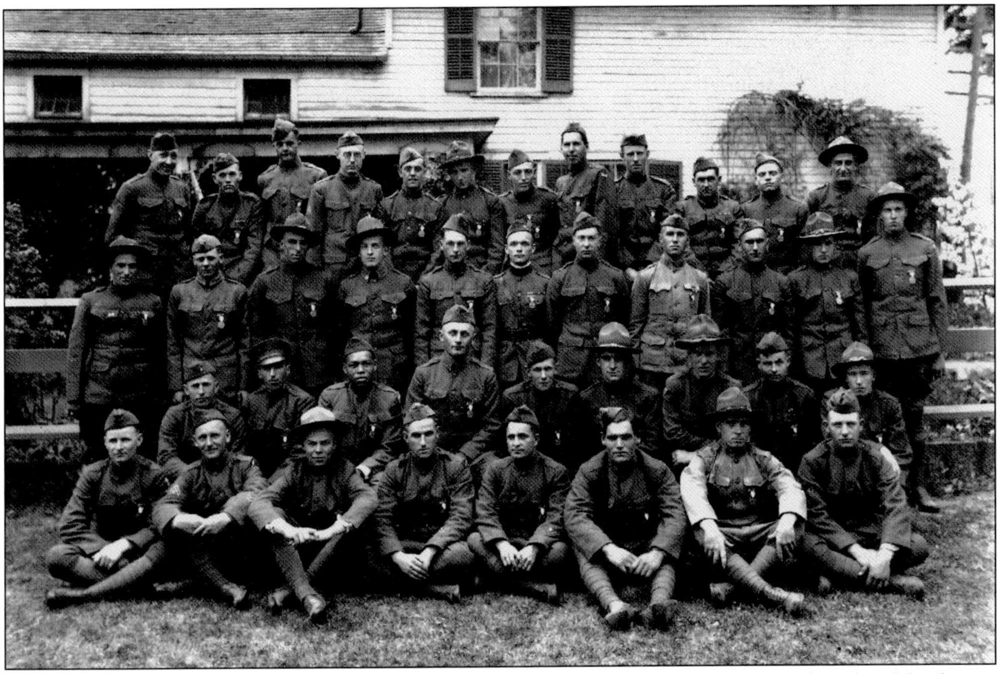

The armistice ending World War I finally came on November 11, 1918. Wheatland had sent about 100 soldiers and all but two returned. They were welcomed on July 12, 1919, with a parade through Scottsville. Crowds gathered in an open lot at 25 Main Street for speeches and prayers by local officials and clergy.

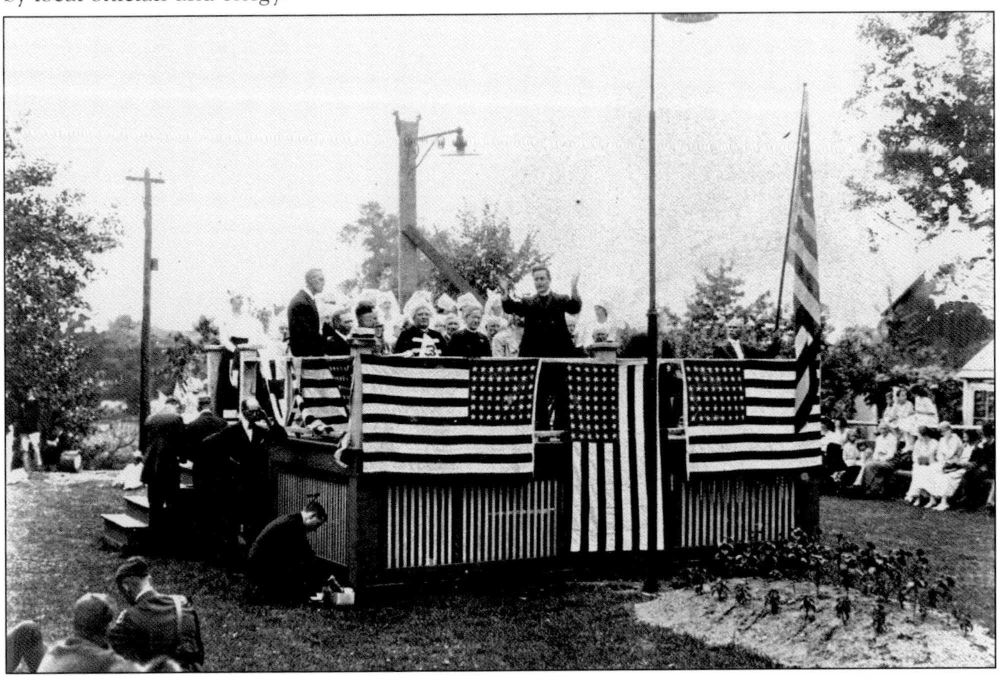

Fr. Patrick McArdle from St. Mary's Roman Catholic church leads the townspeople in a prayer of thanksgiving for the safe return of the soldiers. At the 1919 celebration, each veteran received a medal, and a dinner was held in their honor at Windom Hall.

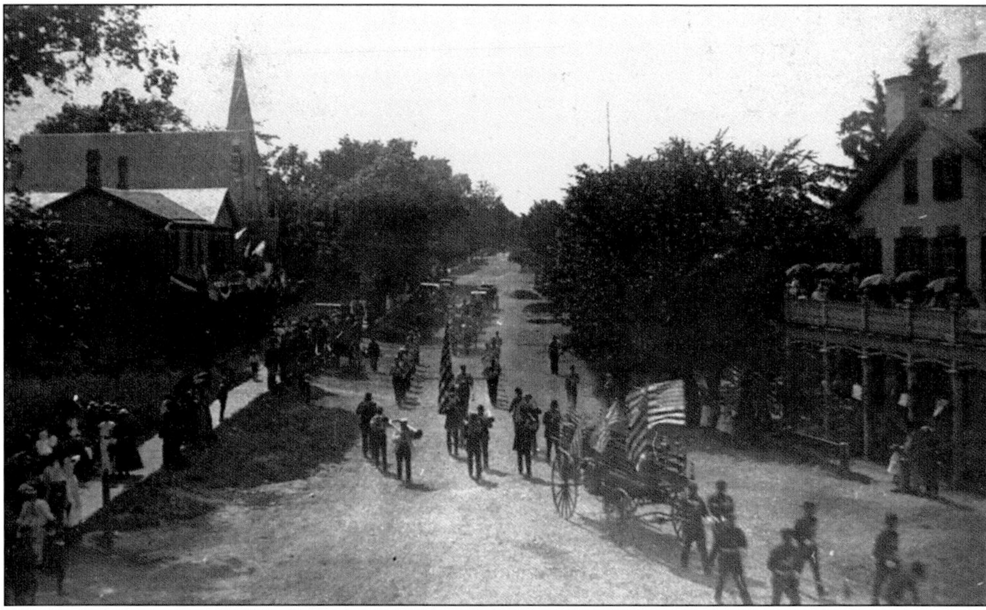

This Mumford parade formed on William Street and then marched up George Street to turn onto Main Street. Flags flew from the Donnelly House on the left, and citizens watched from the porches of the Exchange Hotel at the right. This was likely a Memorial Day celebration about 1900.

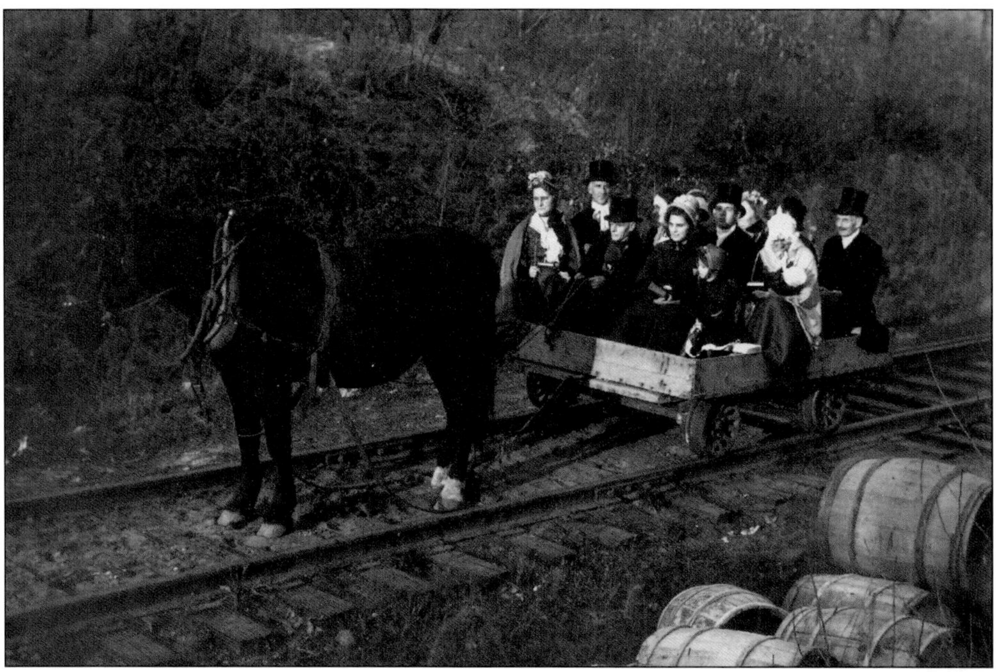

In 1836, a New York State charter was obtained to build the Scottsville and LeRoy Railroad. The leading stockholders in this venture were E. H. S. Mumford and Philip Garbutt. It was completed only as far as Caledonia, and service was discontinued after a few years. Horses pulled the cars over wooden rails. This photograph shows a float depicting the horse railroad in the 1938 centennial parade.

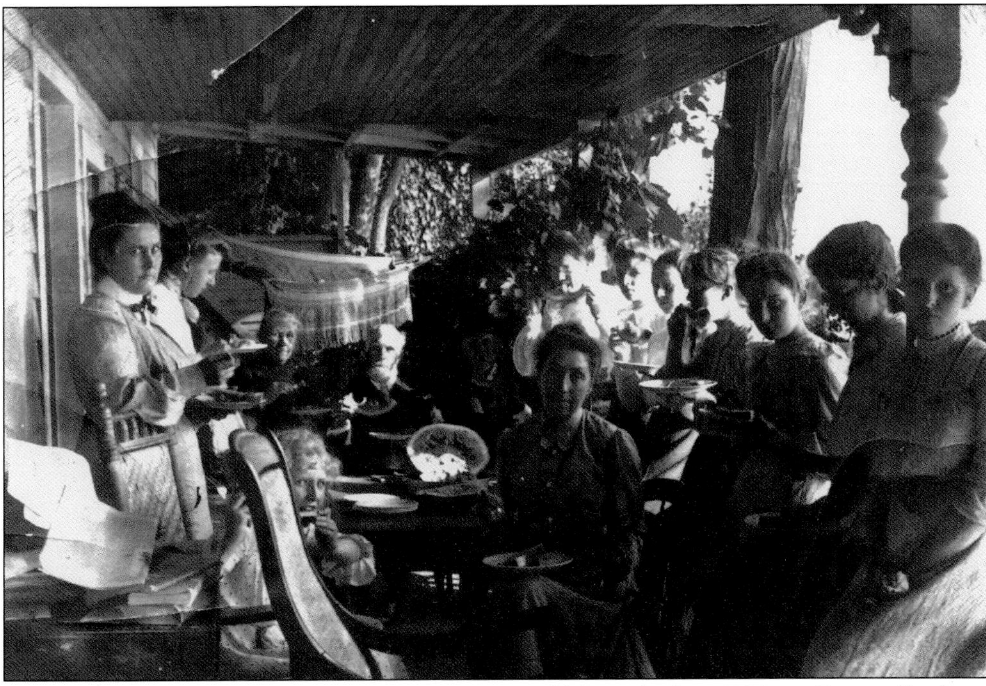

Social gatherings at home were an important part of life in the late 1800s in Scottsville. Some friends and family members gather on the porch one summer day to chat and enjoy a watermelon treat. (Courtesy of Walter Cushman.)

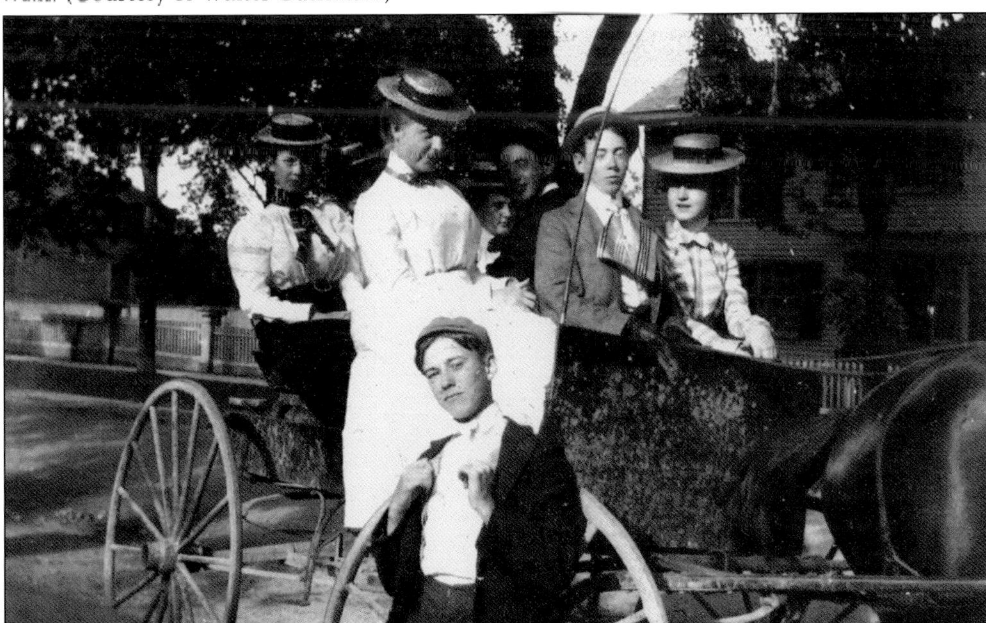

These young people are off to a party at their relatives, the Hanford Edsons at 7 Rochester Street in Scottsville. John Hanford (seated in the first row, center) is the driver of this carriage stopped in front of the house at 12 Rochester Street. John's sister, Ruth, is at the far left in the back seat. (Courtesy of Richard LeRoy.)

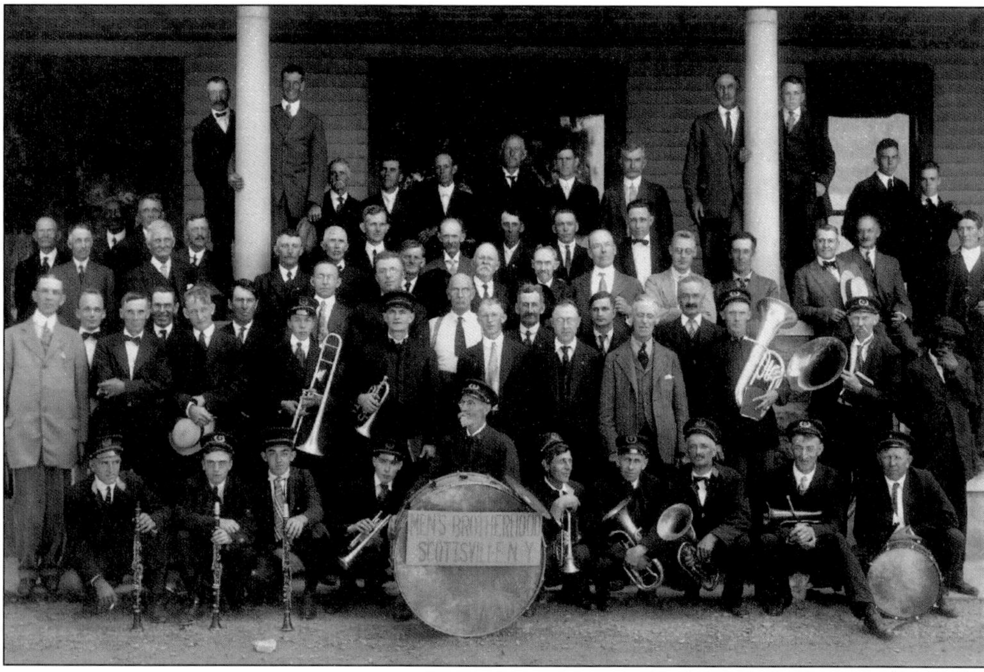

The Brotherhood began in 1917 as a men's Sunday school class at the Union Presbyterian Church in Scottsville. Its purpose was later broadened to civic improvement, and membership was opened to all men in the village. The popular annual picnic shown here was held in 1919 at Troutsburg near Hamlin Beach. The Brotherhood continued until 1949.

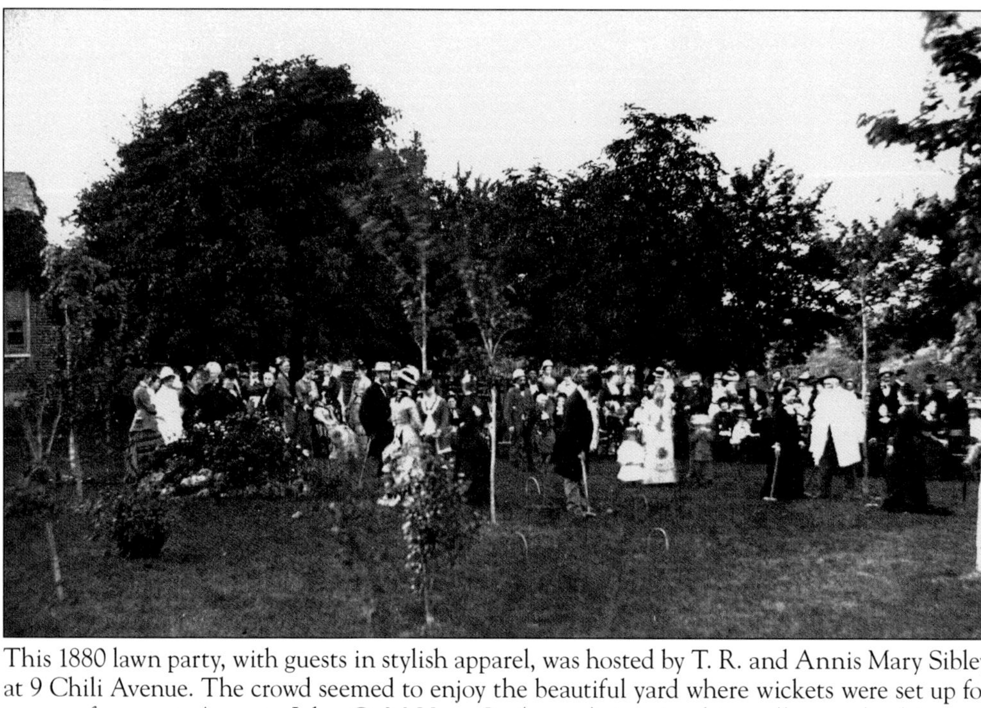

This 1880 lawn party, with guests in stylish apparel, was hosted by T. R. and Annis Mary Sibley at 9 Chili Avenue. The crowd seemed to enjoy the beautiful yard where wickets were set up for games of croquet. A guest, John C. McVean Sr. (center), is using his mallet to play his turn. (Courtesy of Richard LeRoy.)

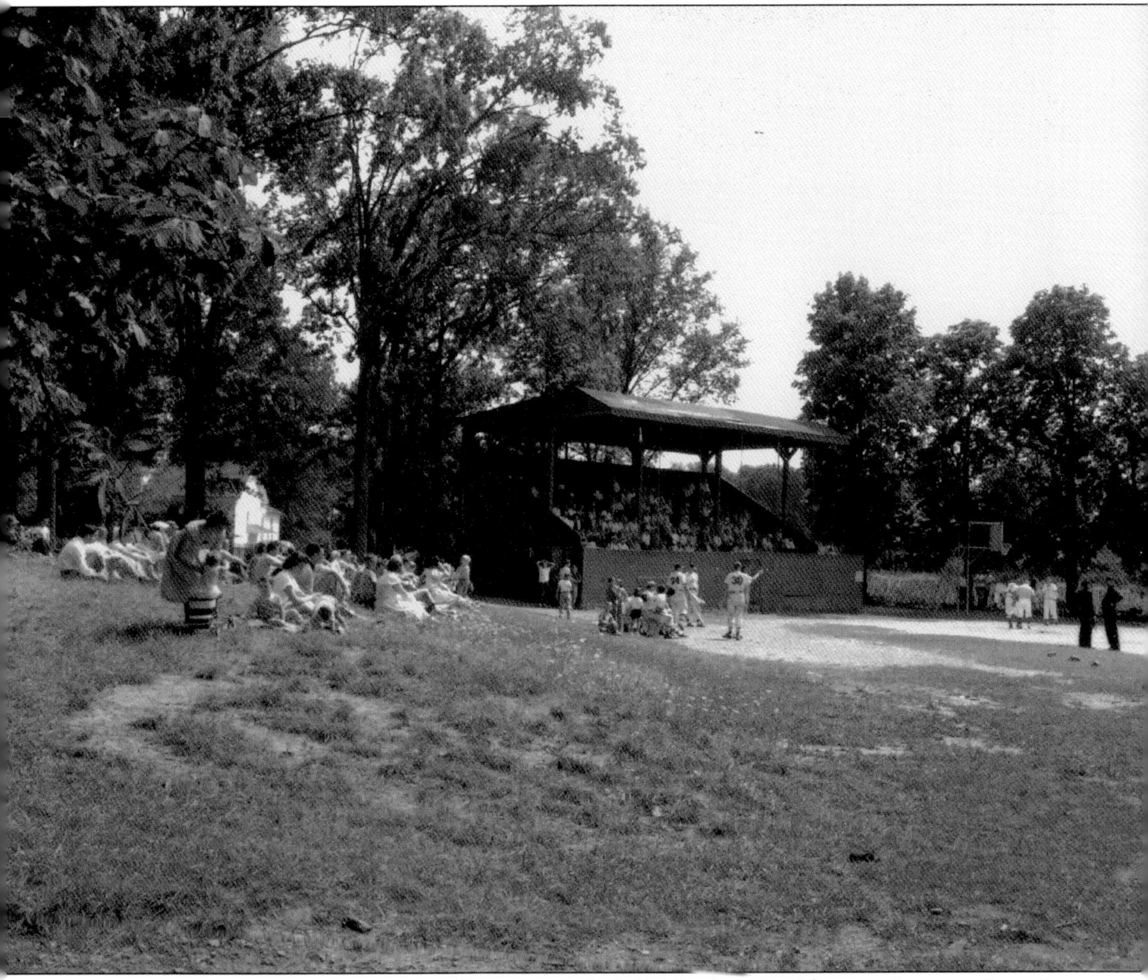

In 1921, local philanthropist R. T. Miller Jr. provided the funds to build a wooden grandstand behind the Brown's Avenue High School. The Village of Scottsville maintained the structure for spectators and as a location for the summer youth recreation program. This Sunday afternoon game features teams from Scottsville and Churchville. The grandstand deteriorated after a half century of Wheatland weather and was demolished in the 1970s. (Courtesy of the family of Fredrick W. and Mary R. Kentner.)

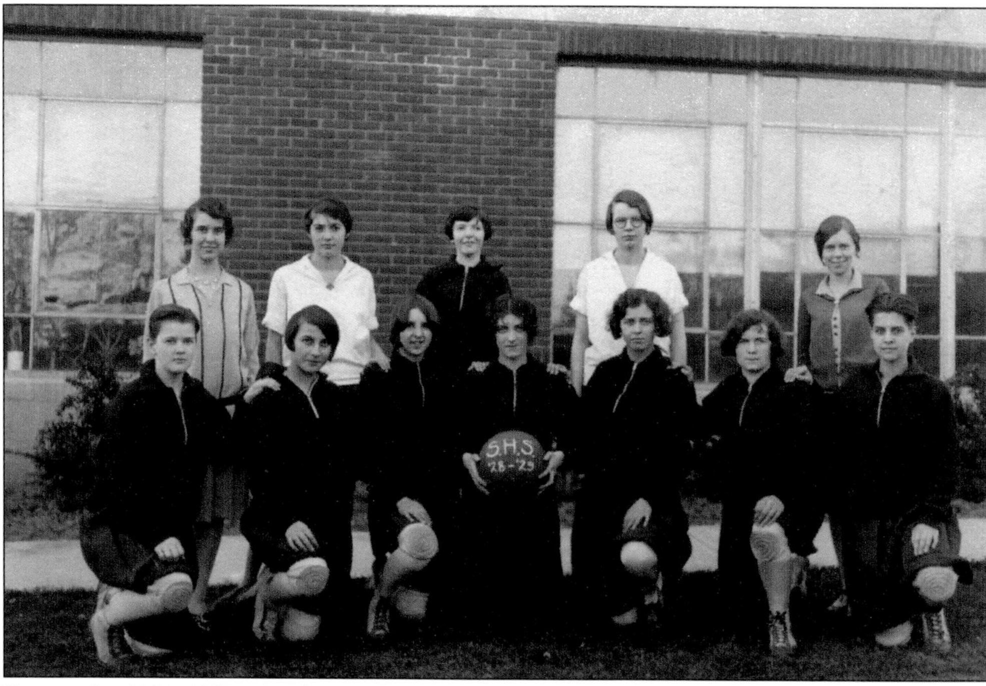

During the 1928–1929 school year, there were no physical education classes at Scottsville High School. Those wishing to play a sport signed up for a team. Teacher Helen Scott (second row, left) and, next to her, student Barbara Brown were a part of this volunteer girls' basketball team.

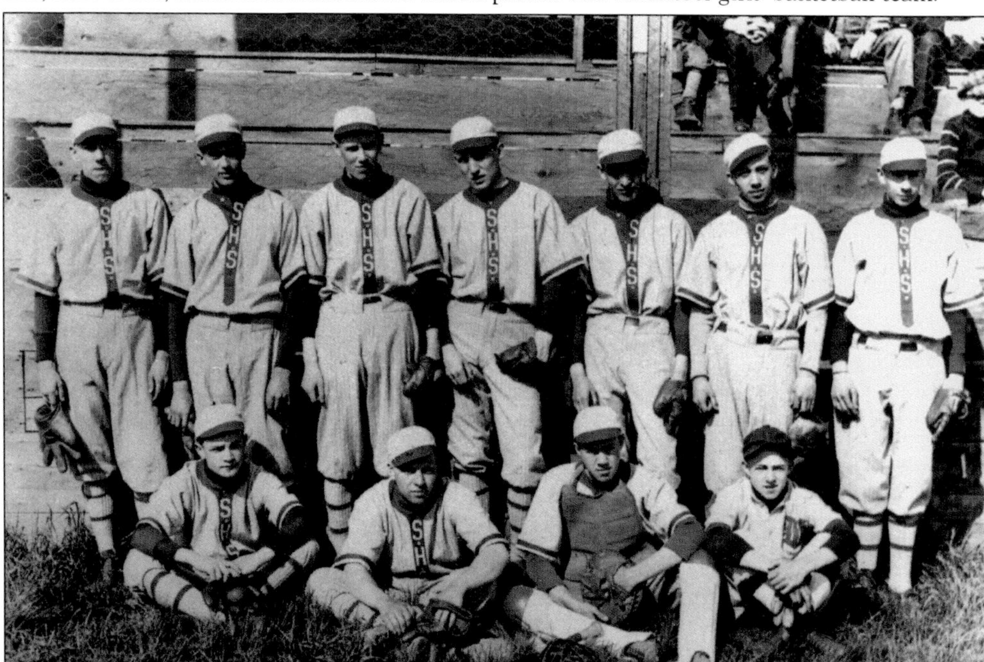

This picture shows boys on the Scottsville High School team dressed in their new baseball uniforms. They were photographed in front of the Brown's Avenue grandstand where fans were ready to watch the team play ball.

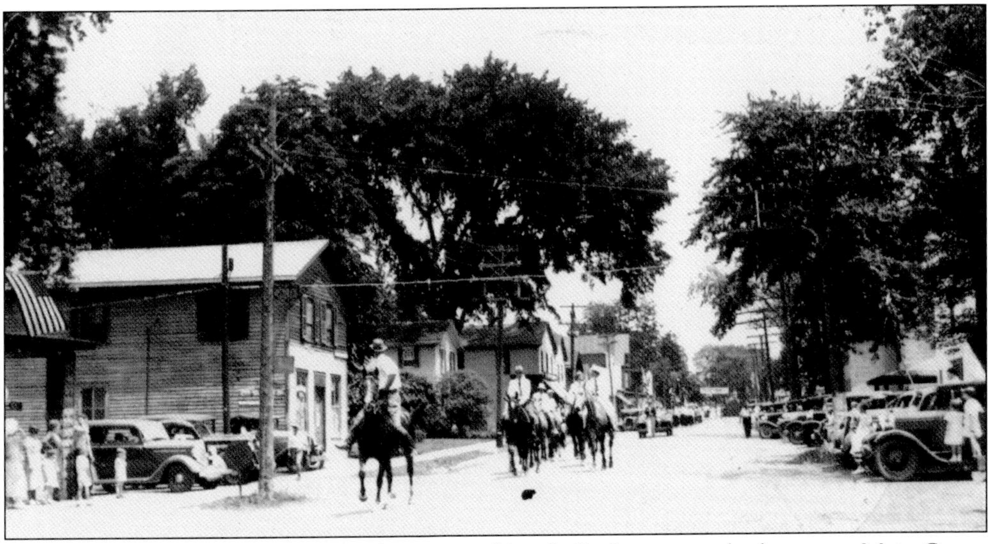

On the Fourth of July in 1935, the firemen and baseball players marched west on Main Street in Scottsville. Townspeople, with their automobiles, lined the streets to view the parade. The building on the left, at 54 Main Street, housed the pool hall and barbershop, run for many years by Bill White.

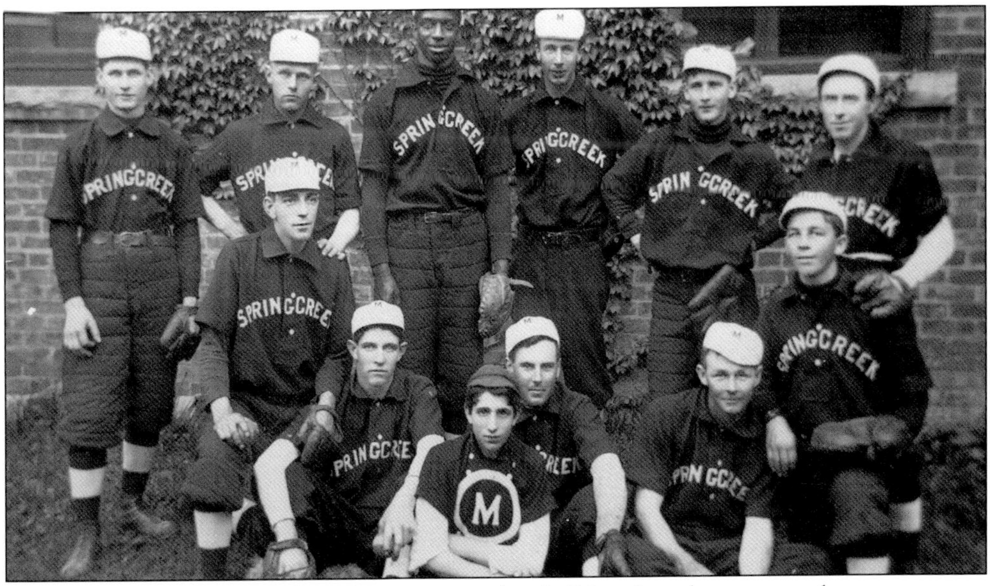

Begun in Upstate New York at Cooperstown, baseball has long been a popular sport among young men. And that has certainly been true in Wheatland. This photograph shows members of the 1907 Mumford Spring Creek team. They are, from left to right, (first row) Bill Cavanaugh, Domenic Borrela (with the M on his shirt), John Freeman, and Charles Nichols; (second row) Harry Harvey and John Kime; (third row) Joe Callan, Arnold Horning, Tom Simms, Don Campbell, Dan O'Donnell, and Harvey Freeman.

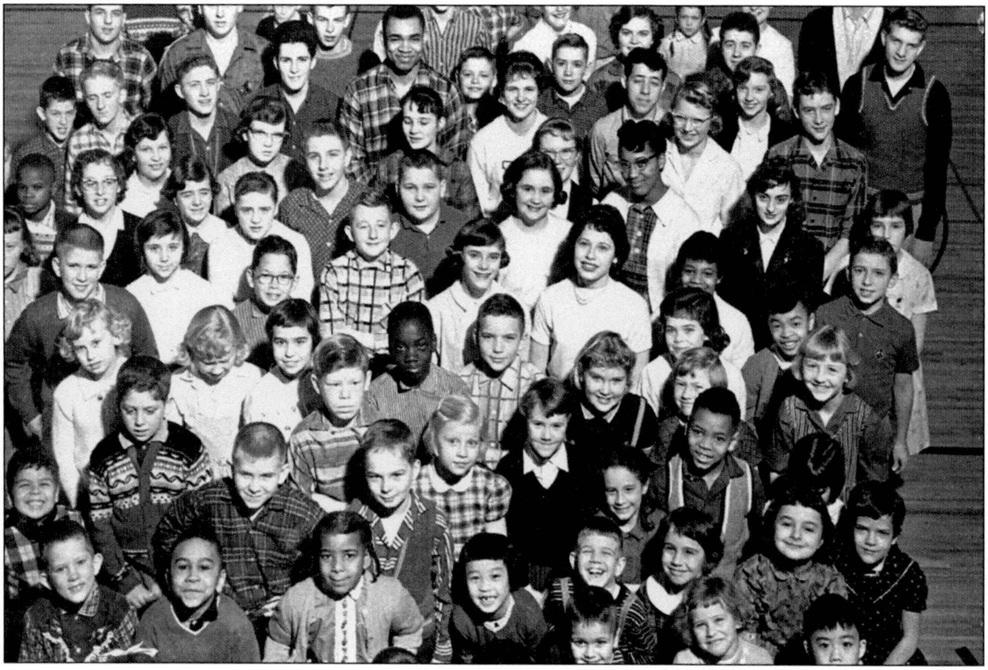

In 1959, nearly 100 students from Wheatland-Chili Central School were included in a special picture taken by Robert Phillips. It represented a cross-section of American children in recognition of the golden anniversary of the White House conference on children and youth. Eastman Kodak displayed this photograph at the White House, Grand Central Station in New York City, and the 1964 New York World's Fair.

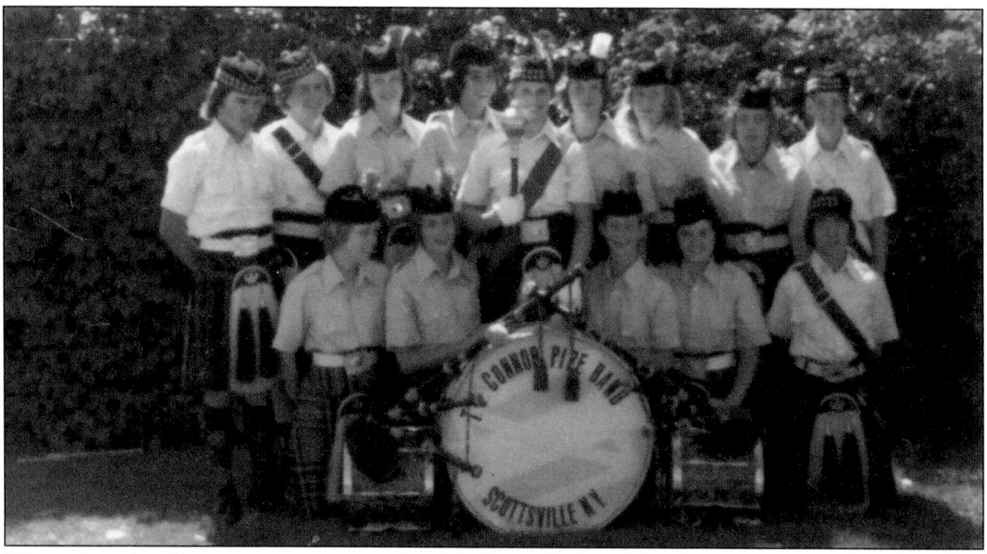

Throughout his 33 years as principal at Scottsville and Wheatland-Chili High School, Thomas J. Connor had dreamed of a Scottish bagpipe band. Successful businessman Thomas Doran, a 1933 graduate, provided the funds. Upon Connor's 1962 retirement, a band was organized by Donald and Joyce Mole. School secretary Ruth LeRoy sewed the 18 woolen plaid uniforms needed by the pipers, drummers, and drum majorette shown here. This is a photograph of the group in the mid-1970s. (Courtesy of Dennis Livingstone.)

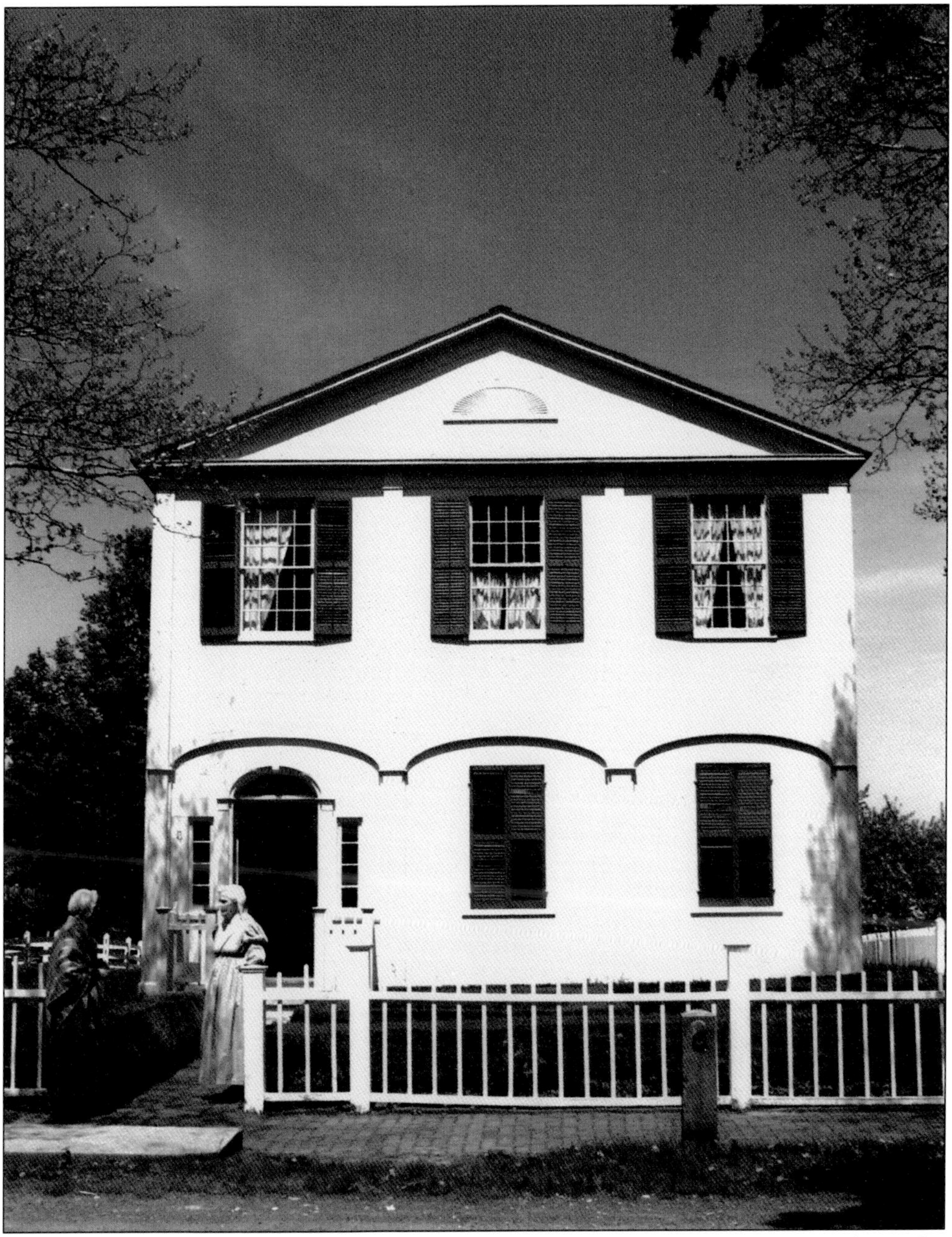

This Federal-style homestead of John McKay, constructed in 1814 in Caledonia was relocated to the Genesee Country Village and Museum. America's third-largest historic village opened in 1976 on Flint Hill Road, just outside Mumford. Rochester businessman John Wehle and architectural historian Stuart Bolger assembled all types of 19th-century buildings for the Genesee Country Village and Museum. Today interpreters explain some 68 restored, fully-functioning structures and a half-dozen heirloom gardens. The museum's 175 acres also includes the Gallery of Sporting Art, a carriage collection, a historic baseball diamond, and a nature center. Each year thousands of visitors discover the past in Wheatland. (Courtesy of Ruby Foote, Genesee Country Village and Museum.)